The Death and

Letters of

Alice

James

The
DEATH
and
LETTERS
of
ALICE JAMES

Selected Correspondence Edited, with a
Biographical Essay, by
Ruth Bernard
Yeazell

BERKELEY
UNIVERSITY OF CALIFORNIA PRESS
LOS ANGELES · LONDON

University of California Press
Berkeley and Los Angeles, California

University of California Press, Ltd.
London, England

© 1981 by The Regents of
the University of California

Library of Congress Catalog Card Number: 78-59454
First Paperback Printing 1983
ISBN 0-520-04963-2

Printed in the United States of America

1 2 3 4
5 6 7
8 9
0

CONTENTS

ACKNOWLEDGMENTS

With the exceptions noted below, all of Alice James's letters that appear here in full are in the Houghton Library, Harvard University; they are reproduced in this volume with the kind permission of Alexander R. James, the holder of the copyright, and of the Houghton Library. Alice James's letters to Annie Ashburner are in the National Library of Scotland in Edinburgh and appear here courtesy of Alexander R. James and of the trustees of the National Library. The letter to Frances Rollins Morse of October 7, 1879, can be found in the Schlesinger Library, Radcliffe College; it is published with the permission of the library and of Alexander R. James. Alice James's letter to Mary Holton James of March 12, 1888, is among the family papers belonging to Mr. and Mrs. Henry James Vaux of Berkeley, California, and appears courtesy of Mr. and Mrs. Vaux. The manuscripts of Alice James's diary and of her commonplace book are quoted with the kind permission of their owner, Alice James Vaux of Lake Oswego, Oregon. Unless otherwise noted, all other James family papers cited in the introduction or in the notes are in the Houghton Library and are quoted with the permission of the library and of Alexander R. James.

The photographs of James family members and of Katharine Loring appear courtesy of the Houghton Library and of Mr. and Mrs. Henry Vaux.

I am grateful to the staffs of the Houghton Library and of the National Library of Scotland, who were especially helpful in locating material and in answering queries, as well as to the staffs of the Schlesinger Library, the Colby College Library in Waterville, Maine, the Pierpont Morgan Library in New York, and the Library of Congress.

To Henry and Jean Vaux, who not only allowed me to quote from the family papers in their possession but generously offered me their hospitality and friendship as well, I extend my particular thanks.

For their thoughtful reading of portions of the manuscript and their invariably helpful suggestions for its improvement, I thank my colleague Walter Anderson of U C L A, Laurence B. Holland of Johns Hopkins University, and U. C. Knoepflmacher of Princeton. I am especially grateful for the editorial wisdom and superb judgment of my former colleague Robert H. Hirst, now editor of the Mark Twain Papers, Berkeley; his generous advice and assistance lightened my editorial tasks immeasurably. Responsibility for whatever errors of judgment remain is of course my own. To Stephen C. Yeazell, who read the manuscript at many stages of its history and who gave unfailingly of his advice and encouragement, my debt is incalculable.

I gratefully acknowledge the support of the trustees of Boston University and of the regents of the University of California, whose research funds helped to defray the incidental costs of this project over several years.

Finally I wish to thank my research assistants, Laura Ferguson and Carolyn H. Handa, who not only typed much of the manuscript and helped to track down obscure allusions but shared with me the frustrations of scholarly dead ends and the joys of discoveries happily made.

ABBREVIATIONS

AJ = Alice James (1848–92)

HJ sr. = Henry James, Sr. (1811–82): *father*

MWJ = Mary Walsh James (1810–82): *mother*

WJ = William James (1842–1910): *brother*

HJ = Henry James (1843–1916): *brother*

GWJ = Garth Wilkinson James (1845–83): *brother*

RJ = Robertson James (1846–1910): *brother*

CW (AK) = Catharine Walsh (Aunt Kate) (1812?–89): *aunt, sister of Mary Walsh James*

AHJ = Alice Howe Gibbens James (1849–1922): *sister-in-law, wife of William James*

INTRODUCTION
The Death and Letters of Alice James

> Oh and I thought, as I was dressing, how interesting it would be to describe the approach of age, and the gradual coming of death. As people describe love. To note every symptom of failure: but why failure? To treat age as an experience that is different from the others; and to detect every one of the gradual stages towards death which is a tremendous experience, and not as unconscious, at least in its approaches, as birth is.
> VIRGINIA WOOLF *A Writer's Diary*

> Thus man overcomes death, which in thought he has acknowledged. No greater triumph of wish-fulfillment is conceivable. Just where in reality he obeys compulsion, he exercises choice; and that which he chooses is not a thing of horror, but the fairest and most desirable thing in life.
> SIGMUND FREUD "The Three Caskets"

Medical men had been puzzling over the case of Alice James for at least a quarter of a century, but when Sir Andrew Clark arrived in the spring of 1891, the invalid presented her latest physician with a new symptom—a painful lump in her breast. Four days after the eminent doctor's visit, she recorded his verdict in her journal. "To him who waits, all things come!" the strange entry begins. "My aspirations may have been eccentric, but I cannot complain now, that they have not been brilliantly fulfilled."[1] All things may not come to those who merely wait, but

---

1 The entry is dated May 31, 1891. This and all subsequent references to the diary follow the orthography and punctuation of the original manuscript, owned by Alice James Vaux of Lake Oswego, Oregon, and now in the possession of Professor and Mrs. Henry Vaux of Berkeley, California. Entries are identified by date. Passages from the diary have been edited according to the same principles as the letters; for an account of these principles and occasional alterations in AJ's text which have seemed necessary for the sake of clarity, see Note on the Text and Alterations in the Manuscript. For the entire diary, interested readers should consult *The Diary of Alice James*, ed. Leon Edel (1934; rpt. New York: Dodd, Mead, 1964), though

one thing inevitably does: what the only sister of William and Henry James thus celebrated as a splendid triumph was her own impending death. Unlike his numerous predecessors, with their vague talk of "nervous hyperaesthesia," of "spinal neurosis," and of "suppressed gout," Sir Andrew had spoken in terms unmistakably fatal. "Ever since I have been ill," his patient wrote, "I have longed & longed for some palpable disease, no matter how conventionally dreadful a label it might have. . . ." Few diseases are so literally palpable as a cancerous breast tumor; to the eccentric aspirations of the Jameses' only daughter, Sir Andrew's diagnosis promised a brilliant fulfillment indeed. "This unholy granite substance in my breast," as Alice later called it (January 1, 1892), had become the stuff of a curious victory.

For what is striking about Alice James is not merely that she welcomed death, but the terms on which she did so. Though the journal entry calls attention to the irony of her case, the juxtaposition of a fatal tumor with the language of aspiration and fulfillment is not wholly ironic. After more than twenty years of evasive doctors and obscurely debilitating symptoms—of mysterious "heart attacks" and fainting spells, of aching head and stomach and strangely paralyzed legs—the lump in Alice's breast was a welcome sign, the solid emblem of a perverse kind of achievement. And in the James family, that most intellectually prolific of American households, achievement of some sort must have seemed imperative. "Within the last year," Alice wrote of her novelist brother some two weeks after Sir Andrew's visit, "he has published the 'Tragic Muse,' brought out 'The American' & written a play 'Mrs Vibert' (wh. Hare has accepted) & his admirable comedy; combined with William's Psychology, not a bad show for one family!" "Especially," she added, "if I get myself dead, the hardest job of all" (June 16, 1891).[2]

---

the text of Edel's edition often differs in varying degrees from that of the original manuscript.
2 Like all entries in Alice's diary beginning with that for December 31, 1890, this one was dictated; dated June 16, 1891, it is in the hand of Katharine Loring, Alice's companion and friend. But in this case Alice herself apparently returned to the text, self-consciously revising the record to insist on death as her own difficult vocation: "Not a bad show for one family! especially if I get myself dead," Katharine wrote at the invalid's dictation; and then that invalid added, in her own hand, the vehement afterthought—"the hardest job of all." William had

"A sick chamber may often furnish the worth of volumes," Jane Austen had observed in *Persuasion*,[3] but she surely intended no such literal equation as this: dying had become Alice James's chief vocation. Like the writing of William's *Psychology*, the task had taken much longer than expected, its issue repeatedly anticipated and repeatedly postponed; but in December of 1891, with "the grand mortuary moment," as she characteristically termed it, "so near at hand,"[4] the end of Alice's life work was finally in sight.

The sickroom was of course a place Alice shared intermittently with most of the Jameses: neurasthenia, like intelligence, seems to have run in the family. Medical reports and advice fill their letters to one another: insomnia, digestive disorders, backaches, and headaches came and went among them in rapid succession. William suffered from a weak back and severe eyestrain, which eventually disappeared with as little apparent cause as it had arrived; Henry complained frequently of back pains and poor digestion; of the two younger sons, one died at thirty-eight of a bad heart, and the other struggled for much of his life with anxiety and alcoholism. To both Henry Sr. and William came especially dramatic moments of emotional crisis—analogous episodes of "perfectly insane and abject terror," in the father's words and "panic fear" in the son's: alone in a dark room, each confronted an hallucinatory, demonic presence and felt himself on the edge of total psychic and spiritual col-

a more conventional reading of the achievements of this year. To William Dean Howells, he wrote: "The year which shall have witnessed the apparition of your Hazard of N. F. [*Hazard of New Fortunes*] of Harry's Tragic Muse, and of *my* Psychology, will indeed be a memorable one in American Literature!!" (August 27, 1890).

3 Jane Austen, *Persuasion*, in *The Novels of Jane Austen*, ed. R. W. Chapman, 5 vols. (Oxford: Clarendon, 1933), vol. 5, 156. The observation is Anne Elliot's; the inhabitant of the sick chamber is Mrs. Smith.

4 AJ to WJ (December 2 [1891]). Unless otherwise noted, all the James family letters are from the collection of James papers in the Houghton Library, Harvard University. When a letter itself is undated, dates which can be deduced from internal evidence are provided in brackets; when this cannot be established with reasonable certainty, such a date is followed by a question mark.

lapse. "There fell upon me without any warning," William later wrote, "just as if it came out of the darkness, a horrible fear of my own existence." [5] Indeed all save the mother seem to have endured repeated, if less acute, attacks of "nerves" and depression: it was melancholy as much as backache which drove William to Germany's mineral baths in his youth and to New England's "mind-curers" in middle age. Yet amidst all this suffering of the spirit and the flesh, only Alice retired permanently to her bed and took up the profession of invalid.

And hers was not a case with any obvious compensations: for all her nervous intelligence, the youngest James child produced no works of philosophy or psychology, no fiction or criticism or drama. Nor was she an Elizabeth Barrett Browning, that ailing heroine of Wimpole Street whose history would so readily assume the consoling shape of popular drama and romance. Alice's suffering issued neither in poetry nor an elopement; she met no Robert Browning and published nothing but a dry little anecdotal letter to *The Nation*. Like many other nineteenth-century women, the Jameses' daughter confined her literary efforts to her correspondence, a commonplace book, and, for a brief period, her journal. But in the very making of those efforts—in the simple act of recording, as well as in the language

5 See *The Literary Remains of the Late Henry James*, ed. William James (Boston: Houghton Mifflin, 1884), pp. 59–60; and William James, *The Varieties of Religious Experience* (New York: Longmans, Green, 1902), pp. 159–161. In the passages quoted, both father and son offer accounts of their own experiences fictitiously attributed to someone else. In *Society the Redeemed Form of Man* (1879) Henry James, Sr., recorded the shattering experience that he later came to call by the Swedenborgian term "vastation" as if it had occurred to one "Stephen Dewhurst"; only in his edition of his father's *Literary Remains* did William publicly identify the imaginary Dewhurst as his father. In his *Varieties of Religious Experience*, however, William in turn disguised his own "panic fear" by attributing it to an anonymous Frenchman whose account of the event William had ostensibly translated—even as he disingenuously added a footnote directing the reader to the earlier family record: "For another case of fear equally sudden, see HENRY JAMES: Society the Redeemed Form of Man, Boston, 1879, pp. 43 ff" (p. 161). True to family form, it was William's own son, yet another Henry, who eventually revealed the identity of the anonymous Frenchman.

and facts of the record—there is nonetheless something peculiarly compelling. Alice claims our attention less in spite of her
invalidism than because of it, and she claims it with a distinctively Jamesian energy.

I

Alice kept her journal only during the last three of her forty-four
years (1848–92), and she kept it a sort of secret: neither Henry
nor William knew of its existence until after her death. Indeed,
she had been dead two years before her novelist brother read it
for the first time and discovered with uneasy surprise how all
his own anecdotes and gossip—some of it "'coloured,'" as he
said, to enliven the sickroom—had been silently committed to
paper.[6] Henry was not then reading the original manuscript of
his sister's diary, yet it is one of the more striking facts about
those ostensibly private pages that many of them had first been
recorded by the hands of others—dictated by the invalid to her
nurse or to her companion and close friend Katharine Loring on
the numerous days when Alice herself felt too ill to write. To
subject one's private journal to all this stenographic activity tes-
tifies, at the very least, to a certain ambivalence about its privacy. And that ambivalence is wholly characteristic: despite her
apparent wish for secrecy, Alice had asked that the manuscript
be typewritten before her death, and "though she never said so,"
Katharine Loring reported, "I understood that she would like to
have it published."[7] In 1894 Katharine responded, with an appropriately ambiguous gesture, by having four copies of the journal privately printed, one for herself and one for each of the surviving brothers. But in the following century, Alice's journal
would twice receive less equivocal forms of publication—first
in a 1934 volume, *Alice James: Her Brothers, Her Journal*, produced with Katharine's encouragement and intended to cele-

6 HJ to WJ & AHJ (May 28, 1894).
7 Katharine Peabody Loring to Margaret James Porter (June 6,
   1934). Margaret James Porter (1887–1947) was the only daughter of William James. She objected strenuously to Katharine
   Loring's decision to publish the diary, in part because she
   feared lest "unsympathetic readers . . . read her confidences
   out of curiosity and judge her by the Diary as a neurasthenic
   and unadmirable character!" (Margaret James Porter to Mary
   Vaux [May 1934?]).

brate several of the little-known members of the family; and
again thirty years later in an edition by Leon Edel simply titled
The Diary of Alice James. Born of the need to memorialize the
self as much as to commune with it, Alice's journal is now an
unmistakably public record—and one of the principal documents in the case.

The rest of the story is told in letters—Alice's own and those
of her lavishly epistolary relations. Though the journal directly
records only the last three years of her life, she had been corre-
sponding with family and friends for more than thirty: the earliest letter that has been preserved is a note from the twelve-
year-old girl to her "dear old good-for-nothing home-sick papa,"
begging that briefly absent gentleman to "make haste home."[8]
Yet this short note is a relative anomaly; most of the letters that
survive date from the last eight years of her life, years which she
spent as a confirmed invalid, her confinement to the sickroom
varied only by occasional airings in a bath chair. Whether such
"padded seclusion"—her own impatient phrase[9]—drove her to
ever more abundant correspondence or whether mere chance
has selected the letters which remain, it is impossible to say.
From 1884 until her death, Alice lived in England and wrote
chiefly to William James and his wife; for most of that time her
lodgings were close enough to Henry's to make regular letters
between them unnecessary. In the previous decade, the situation had been reversed—William and his sister lived near each
other in the United States, and Henry was in Europe—but that
disproportionately few of Alice's letters from these years survive may well owe something to her fraternal correspondents'
feelings toward posterity: dreading violation by future biographers, Henry burned most of the letters he had received,[10] while
William apparently did not. Alice herself may have further
blurred the record by destroying her own letters to her parents
after their death. Though she often apologizes to her correspondents for not writing because she has been ill and implies
thereby that words come more readily to her with the return of
health, the fact remains that the younger and presumably less
bedridden Alice is a vague and relatively undocumented figure.

8 AJ to HJ Sr. (March 11, 1860).
9 AJ to Fanny Rollins Morse (October 7, 1879) (Schlesinger).
10 See Leon Edel, *Henry James: The Untried Years, 1843–1870*
    (Philadelphia: Lippincott, 1953), p. 17.

Coincidence may have helped to edit the record for us, but it is nonetheless the case that the Alice we know best is Alice sick and Alice dying.

Indeed what is most interesting about the few adolescent letters that have survived is how blandly unself-conscious they are, how little they seem to tell us of their author or to hint at the terrible breakdowns soon to come. These are the casually gossiping letters of the young New England female to her friends, letters that briefly allude to ladies' social clubs and sewing bees, tell of visits paid and received, engagements, marriages, and the weather. Occasionally arch ("I suppose you have heard of Jenny Watson's engagement to Ned Perkins. Is it not funny, he is more than five years younger; can you possibly imagine marrying a boy so much younger than yourself? It would not be so strange if Ned Perkins was not so very immature, but he always seemed to me to be a perfect infant"),[11] sometimes cloyingly sweet ("You are the best & dearest little girl in the world to write to me so often when you have so many other people who are so much more deserving of your goodness"),[12] they are most often simply girlish and naive, conventionally mild in their sentiments and liberally sprinkled with the likes of "little," "delightful," and "dear." Scarcely arresting in themselves, these letters claim our attention chiefly for what they leave unsaid—though they perhaps help to make imaginable the woman who for the rest of her life would be capable of fainting at a word.

If the accounts of others add some color to this sweetly neutral and unrevealing self-portrait, they generally do little to sharpen its blurred lines or to add depth to its flatly conventional surface. To Emerson's son Edward, affectionately describing the fierce yet good-humored verbal battles that enlivened meals at the James family table, Alice is a figure at the edge of the frame—"the quiet little sister" who "ate her dinner, smiling, close to the combatants"—while the father and sons shouted, teased one another, and gesticulated with the dinner knives.[13] In one of William's early letters home she puts in a rather charming and certainly more concrete appearance as the

11 AJ to Fanny Morse (July 22 [1866?]).
12 AJ to Fanny Morse (April 3 [1866?]).
13 Edward Waldo Emerson, *The Early Years of the Saturday Club, 1855–1870* (Boston: Houghton Mifflin, 1918), p. 328.

"cherry-lipped, apricot-nosed, double-chinned little Sister," the
"beloved Sisterkin" whose own letters could "inflame the
hearts of her lonely brothers with an intense longing to smack
her celestial cheeks."[14] But more typical of this fraternal correspondence is a vague and extravagantly idealized image, the half-
mocking invocation of a young woman all sisterly tenderness
and consolation:

> Thou seemest to me so beautiful from here, so intelligent,
> so affectionate, so in all respects *the thing* that a bro. shd.
> most desire that I don't see how when I get home I can do
> any thing else than sit with my arm round thy waist appeal-
> ing to thee for confirmation of every thing I say, for approba-
> tion of every thing I do, and admiration for every thing I am,
> and never, never for a moment being disappointed. (Rome,
> 1873)

Rather ironically, in the light of Alice's own future career, it is
William's frequent illnesses that most prompt these teasing visions of her as angelic nurse and comforter:

> I am quite sick and feverish to night and sit under my lamp
> wrapped up in my overcoat writing à la seule que j'aime and
> wishing for nothing so much as an hour or two of her volu-
> ble & senseless though soothing & pleasing talk. Her trans-
> parent eyes soft step, and gentle hands, her genial voice and
> mood never seemed to me more desirable or more lovable
> than now. (Cambridge, 1862)

> A fortnight ago I caught the "influenza" in Teplitz and
> was sick for a week, 36 hours with raging fever and me cryin
> all the time for to have you sitting by me stroking my brow,
> and asking me if there was nothing, *nothing* you could do to
> alleviate my sufferings. And me casting my eyes up to
> heaven & solemnly shaking my head, like Harry, to com-
> mand sympathy, and saying in a feeble voice, "no! dear,
> nothing" and then you saying how beautiful & patient I
> was. Whole dialogues did I frame of how I wd. work on your
> feelings if you were there and longed to cleave the Ocean
> once more to press you in my arms. (Dresden, 1868)[15]

14 Henry James, *Notes of a Son and Brother* (New York: Scrib-
   ner's, 1914), Chap. 2.
15 WJ to AJ (December 24, 1873); WJ to AJ (October 19, 1862);
   WJ to AJ (March 16, 1868).

How he "wd. work on" her feelings—indeed how he *did*, we cannot finally know. His biographer has speculated on the coincidental timing of Alice's severe breakdown in 1878 and William's decision to take a wife[16]—also, ironically, named Alice; but whatever responses this epistolary flirtation may have evoked in his correspondent, William's amorous rhetoric hardly renders Alice herself a less elusive figure. With her "transparent eyes soft step, and gentle hands," the woman whom William imagines at his bedside is less Alice herself than a faintly erotic Angel in the House. And though another of his letters home sports a playful sketch of her with wings sprouting from her head, accompanied by an allusion to the "heavenly tone" of the "lovely babe's temper," the evidence suggests, in fact, that the youngest of the Jameses often bore little resemblance to that soothing figure of Victorian fantasy.[17]

But if it is also clear that Alice was not always the "quiet little sister" of Edward Emerson's family scene—"O my beloved child," William wrote from Berlin in 1868, "how much I wd. like to be with you and have you 'sass' me as of yore"[18]—the very delight in "sassing" that all the Jameses shared and that characterized William in particular makes it difficult to distinguish Alice as she really was from the affectionate teasing with which he surrounded her. As early as 1860 he was addressing his twelve-year-old sister in verses replete with "mildly beaming" moon, "yellow sand," and a lovelorn speaker who bemoans her proud refusal of his hand by threatening to drown himself in despair:

> Adieu to love! adieu to life!
> Since I may not have thee,
> My Alice sweet, to be my wife,
> I'll drown me in the Sea!
> I'll drown me in the sea, my love,
> I'll drown—me in—the Sea![19]

16 Gay Wilson Allen, *William James: A Biography* (New York: Viking, 1967), p. 221.
17 WJ to family (November 1861). William's sketch is reproduced in Allen, *William James*, p. 82. On the Victorian fantasy of an Angel in the House, see Alexander Welsh, *The City of Dickens* (London: Oxford University Press, 1971), pp. 167–195.
18 WJ to AJ (January 9, 1868).
19 WJ to HJ Sr. (Sunday morning, 1860).

Yet with her "childlike form" and "golden hair" the heroine of
William's poem is not so much Alice as a sort of Bostonian An-
nabel Lee. Amusing and suggestive as it is, all this ironic hyperbole finally tells us more about its author than its object—more
about the imagination of the brother and even of the age than
about the sister invoked as "so in all respects *the thing* that a
brother should most desire."

2

And even while William's imaginary angel was stroking the fraternal and feverish brow, his actual sister was enduring grave
crises of her own. By the time of her nineteenth birthday, at
least, Alice's health seems to have seriously broken down. Family letters casually allude to her illness throughout her adoles-
cence, but in the years between 1866 and 1869 scarcely a note
passes from one James to another without some reference to
Alice's medical history; indeed, for them to write of Alice now
is almost automatically to note the current state of her health.
Elliptical as these notations often are, they sketch what was to
become in ensuing years a familiar tale—a wearyingly repetitive
story of attempted cure, fragile recovery, and recurrent collapse.
In the winter of 1866–67 Henry Sr. reports that his ailing daughter is in New York, "undergoing *Motorpathy*" with a certain Dr.
Taylor;[20] in January a maternal letter refers hopefully to accounts of her "blooming appearance" and trusts that "the good
work of restoration is almost completed," but two months later
we learn from William that the invalid herself "judges it best to
stay at Dr. Taylor's till the first of May to 'clinch' her cure, as
she says." Finally back home in June, Alice is visiting a friend in
Brookline when she is suddenly taken sick once again, and her
mother must be summoned to fetch her. "She is all right now,"
Mary James announces to her two youngest sons on June 5; but
five days later she is writing to William that "Alice . . . from a

20 Alice's Dr. Taylor was Charles Fayette Taylor (1827–1899), a
    successful orthopedic surgeon and inventor and also some-
    thing of a practical psychotherapist, who included among his
    patients a number of neurasthenic women. The author of *The
    Theory and Practice of the Movement Cure* (1861), he treated
    nervous invalids with a set of exercises known as the "Swed-
    ish movements"—presumably what Henry Sr. here alludes to
    as "Motorpathy."

little overexertion, has had one of her old attacks; and a very bad one. She will have dear child to live with the extremest care." And so it goes: in March of the next year Alice is reported improving, being "manipulated daily on the Monroe system,"[21] but by April the Monroe treatment has been abandoned (the doctor in question has for some reason refused to come), and the Jameses have now resorted to "electricity" and "Sulphuric ether"[22]—thus far to little effect. "All our time and thoughts are given now to dear Alice who is no better," Mrs. James writes; "her nervous turns are very frequent and brought on by the slightest exertion." Even the resolutely optimistic mother must confess her helplessness and frustration: "It is a case of genuine hysteria for which no cause as yet can be discovered. It is a most distressing form of illness, and the most difficult to reach, because so little is known about it."[23]

"Genuine hysteria" verges on an oxymoron, but there seems no reason to doubt the rough accuracy of the diagnosis: all the evidence suggests that Mary James confronted in her daughter as typical a case of that baffling condition as any that were to present themselves to Freud and Breuer some twenty years later

21 By the "Monroe system," Mrs. James seems to refer to a systematic form of muscular manipulation or massage ("rubbing," as she elsewhere calls it); Dr. Monroe was a local doctor who appears to have treated several of the Jameses for a somewhat miscellaneous list of ailments.

22 The local application of mild electric currents to various parts of the body was fairly common in the nineteenth century as a method of treating nervous and muscular disorders; the theory of "galvanism," as it was called, rested on an analogy between electrical and nervous "energies." "Sulphuric ether"—technically a misnomer for $(C_2H_5)_2O$ or ethyl ether, which is produced by the action of sulphuric acid on ethyl alcohol—is a colorless, volatile liquid widely used in the second half of the century as an anaesthetic. The record does not reveal whether Alice was experimenting with it simply to deaden pain or to produce complete insensibility.

23 HJ to RJ ([winter 1866–1867?]) (Vaux collection of James family papers); MWJ to AJ ([January 1867?]); WJ to GWJ & RJ (March 13, 1867); MWJ to RJ & GWJ (June 5 [1867]) (typescript: Vaux); MWJ to WJ (June 10 [1867]); MWJ to RJ (March 29 [1868?]) (typescript: Vaux); MWJ to RJ (April [1868]) (typescript: Vaux); MWJ to GWJ (April 5 [1868?]) (typescript: Vaux).

in Vienna. From the facial neuralgias and stomach pains to the fainting spells, the mysterious "attacks" and the partially paralyzed legs, every one of Alice's symptoms was to prove the familiar currency of the *Studies on Hysteria*; like the women whose curious histories would fill that volume, Alice's was a case of physical effects out of all proportion to their apparent causes. From time to time her doctors would talk vaguely of rheumatism and gout (conditions Freud would attribute to several of his patients as well), but it was always to Alice's "nerves" that observer and patient alike were compelled to return. Indeed, whatever part the merely organic may have played in her troubles, there was "no organic disease ever so painful," her mother reported, that "she would not willingly except [*sic*] in place of her nervous suffering."[24]

Whether such nervous suffering would have yielded to Freud's talking cure, it is of course impossible to say. That sexual anxiety and repression were in part the cause of her prolonged collapse is very likely; all her life she would remain, so far as one can tell, a virgin, and it is not hard to find in her own strained allusions to sex the signs of an intense, if suppressed, disquiet. As one young Cambridge couple after another was to announce its engagement or marriage in the course of the next ten years, the casual irony of Alice's gossip could give way to sudden and disturbing vehemence: "Sargy always had the capacities of a cormorant" is the particularly acid verdict on one recent bridegroom; "so he is able to swallow her [his new wife] whole, not having to think about her as she is going down must make it much easier."[25] If this bitterly grotesque image of marital union is, at the very least, disconcerting, so too are the repeated, almost obsessive references she would make in later years to the vast number of babies habitually produced by the English poor—a political concern that Alice uneasily sensed had for her its private sources as well: "I wonder if it is indelicate in a flaccid virgin to be so preoccupied with the multiplication of the species, but it fairly haunts one, something irresistible & overwhelming like the tides of the sea or the Connemaugh flood, a mighty horde to sweep over the face of the earth" (June 18, 1889). To a post-Freudian reader, such preoccupations in "flaccid virgins" are likely to seem not so much indelicate as inevitable—

24 MWJ to Mary Holton James (February 23 [1879?]) (Vaux).
25 AJ to Sara Darwin (March 23 [1874?]).

the surfacing in a displaced and characteristically impersonal form of forces long suppressed, of tides "irresistible and over-whelming" indeed.

But if it is easy enough to imagine Alice's condition become the raw stuff of another case history, to be appended to those of Anna O. and Elisabeth von R., it is virtually impossible to trace the emotional shape such a history would have actually assumed. In the 1860s Charcot was just beginning neurological work at his clinic in France; the publication of his pupil's *Studies on Hysteria* was more than two decades away. Observant and acutely intelligent as they could be, the James family were hardly given to the sort of painstaking detective work in which Freud would later engage; when it comes to suggesting the direct causes of Alice's breakdowns, the particular links of emotion and event to which her flesh had thus given expression, the record is generally blank. To guess at the unconscious meanings of Alice's recurrent crises is to beg nearly as many questions as one answers; the private images, the immediate associations of Freud's *Studies* elude us. And as that collection of mystery tales repeatedly demonstrates, it is just such private and seemingly arbitrary connections that always supply the clue.

3

"Owing to muscular circumstances my youth was not of the most ardent," Alice was to recall years later in her journal; "but I had to peg away pretty hard between twelve & twenty-four 'killing myself,' as some one calls it—absorbing into the bone that the better part is to clothe oneself in neutral tints, walk by still waters & possess one's soul in silence" (February 21, 1890). It is a striking statement, this brief reminiscence from the woman of forty-two—a memory of her youth as an exercise in self-destruction. Recalling her efforts at colorlessness and silence, she nonetheless sees in her struggle a kind of grim energy—writes of "pegging away pretty hard," in her perversely active verb, at the strenuous task of "killing" herself. Of course it is merely a metaphorical dying to which Alice's journal here alludes, not to the sort attended by physicians. But the terms of this casual autobiography are nonetheless oddly resonant: by speaking of self-containment as if it were a kind of suicide, the bedridden invalid establishes a sinister continuity with her younger self, suggests that even as a quiet New England girl she had already been engaged in the work of "getting herself dead." And though the link between restraint and illness may be in part simply rhetorical, it is not wholly so: one kind of deadness, "absorbed into the bone," may well have prompted the other. As autobiography, the passage is doubtless something of a distortion: the human need to see one's past as continuous with one's present is, after all, very strong, and memory selects its facts accordingly. Not all Alice's young womanhood was neutral colors and silence, nor even the struggle to achieve them. "Alice had yesterday some unusual experiences," her mother reported cheerfully from Maine in the summer of 1870: "She began the day with a sea-bath, and ended it with a ride on top of the hay cart into the barn——She was the leader in the frolic, which will give you an idea of her improving condition."²⁶ Two years later she would give further evidence of improvement by joining Henry and their Aunt Kate on a five-month tour of Europe; if she was not the leader in this more extended frolic (Henry taking it upon himself to act as cicerone for the two women), her brother could still announce to those at home that Alice "simply does every thing, & does much of it on foot."²⁷ In the spring of 1873 she traveled by herself from Cambridge to New York, evidently delighting in what her mother called this "wonderful assertion of her freedom";²⁸ a few months later she and Aunt Kate set out for Quebec—the "advance guard" for the family's summer expedition to Canada.²⁹ The following spring orders were placed for an equestrian habit and trousers, and Alice spent that summer at Breadloaf, Vermont, engaged in an invigorating course of horseback riding and mountain air. Indeed, to those who chronicled her progress, it sometimes seemed as if motion alone could eventually make her well: "*Change* as we have sought it, seems to me to have been the great agent in her marvellous improvement during the last two months," Henry concluded in the midst of the European experiment of 1872; "she is like a person coming at last into the faculty & pleasure of movement & it is the most *active* part of her life here which does her the most good & leaves the most substantial effects behind it."³⁰

26 MWJ to HJ & RJ (July 10, 1870).
27 HJ to HJ Sr. & MWJ (June 11 [1872?]).
28 MWJ to HJ (April 1 [1873]).
29 AJ to Annie Ashburner (September 26, 1873) (National).
30 HJ to HJ Sr. & MWJ (July 21 [1872?]).

But mere activity and change of scene were never to prove quite enough. Even the Alps had not entirely prevented an attack, though Henry had tried to make light of the episode in letters home. Within two months of her return came word from Cambridge that "the delicious breakfast of chocolate & roll in the morning does not agree with her as it did abroad";[31] more sobering news quickly followed. "Poor child!" Mrs. James was soon lamenting, "*why* is it that she has gone back so?"[32] Alice would of course recover yet again, and reports on her condition resume their guardedly cheerful tone. But through all their professions of optimism, the disheartening litany of symptoms never really ceases. For the Jameses' only daughter, even the mildest of activities—her walks, her letter writing, her visits— would continue to be shadowed by the threat of collapse.

And then in the "hideous summer of '78"—some ten years after her first prolonged breakdown—she suffered one of her most severe attacks. "Alice is half the time, indeed much more than half, on the verge of insanity and suicide," her father wrote to his youngest son, Robertson. The latter was himself battling with depression and alcohol, but Henry Sr. pleaded his entire preoccupation with Alice's case: "Any other care upon our hands, while this absorbing state of things endures, would be intolerable, especially to me whose own nerves would bear no stouter tension than they now have." The strain on the father's nerves must indeed have been great:

> One day a long time ago . . . [she] asked me whether I thought that suicide, to which at times she felt very strongly tempted, was a sin. I told her that I thought it was not a sin except where it was wanton, as when a person from a mere love of pleasurable excitement indulged in drink or opium to the utter degradation of his faculties and often to the ruin of the human form in him; but that it was absurd to think it sinful when one was driven to it in order to escape bitter suffering, from spiritual influx, as in her case, or from some loathsome form of disease, as in others. I told her that so far as I was concerned she had my full permission to end her life whenever she pleased; only I hoped that if ever she felt like doing that sort of justice to her cir-

31 MWJ to HJ (December 15 [1872]).
32 MWJ to HJ (March 21 [1873]).

cumstances, she would do it in a perfectly gentle way in order not to distress her friends. She then remarked that she was very thankful to me, but she felt that now she could perceive it to be her *right* to dispose of her own body when life had become intolerable, she could never do it: that when she had felt tempted to it, it was with a view to break bonds, or assert her freedom, but that now I had given her freedom to do in the premises what she pleased, she was more than content to stay by my side, and battle in concert with me against the evil that is in the world. I dont fear suicide much since this conversation, though she often tells me that she is strongly tempted still.[33]

Alice's need to "kill herself" had, apparently, taken more than metaphoric form. Yet for all the talk of possible violence and death, there is a spirit of gentle rationality, an air of tender Jamesian abstraction to this remembered scene. Henry Sr. approaches his child's threatened suicide as if it were a matter for moral philosophy and speculation: the author of *The Secret of Swedenborg* talks of "spiritual influx" and the battle against evil, offers a brief anatomy of suicide, and calmly grants his daughter the right to kill herself whenever she pleases. And it is just this fatherly detachment, of course, which proves so intuitively appropriate and so disarming. Though Alice's question has posed an obscure challenge, Henry Sr. implicitly refuses to be drawn into battle. The daughter speaks of killing herself to assert her freedom, but suicide is a breaking of bonds only if there are felt bonds to break: the lack of paternal resistance wholly alters the terms of her emotional equation, drains the threatened gesture of its most potent meaning. By readily acknowledging Alice's right to destroy herself, her father had rendered her powerless to do so.

He was right not to fear suicide after this conversation; despite her "mortuary inclinations," as she would later call them (February 2, 1892), Alice was never to take her own life. Even in the last stages of her cancer, some fourteen years later, she would hesitate and hold back, reluctant to hasten the unmistakable course of her dying. She had been taking morphia to ease the terrible pain, but she could not bring herself to consume an amount sufficient to kill: "on two nights [I] had almost

33 HJ Sr. to RJ (September 14 [1878?]) (Vaux).

asked for K's lethal dose," she dictated in her journal, "but one steps hesitantly along such unaccustomed ways & endures from second to second . . ." (March 4, 1892). Two days after this last entry she was dead—finally dispatched not by her own hand but by mere weakness and the complications of a common cold.

Yet if the encounter with her father thus marked a critical turning in Alice's history—a deflecting of those "mortuary inclinations," it was a turning which was to point only ambiguously in the direction of life. Alice was thirty in that hideous summer of 1878; a full decade had passed since her mother's despairing diagnosis of hysteria. But the years which the youngest of the Jameses now concluded with a sort of awful monotony had proved a time of dramatic change for the others. Even for the two younger sons, whose uncertain and troubled careers would in some ways resemble Alice's own, it had been a decade of significant achievement. Abandoning their abortive attempt to run a plantation worked by freed blacks in the South, they had each moved permanently to the Midwest, gone to work for the railroad, and found themselves wives; in 1873 Robertson had also produced a son, the first grandchild for the elder Jameses. Closer to home—and to Alice—was William, who had begun the decade in a suicidal depression much like his sister's but who now ended it, as he himself said, "in a permanent path."[34] After years of unstable health, restless wandering between Europe and America, and anxious vacillating over the choice of vocation, the Jameses' oldest son at last gave his career clear and significant shape in the summer of 1878. His first temporary appointment at Harvard—undertaken when he himself had just turned thirty—had become, effectively, a permanent one; he was now engaged in the teaching and writing which would absorb his energies for several decades. In May of 1878 his future wife put an end to an uneasy courtship of several years by accepting his proposal of marriage. A month before the wedding (which took place in July), he committed himself to posterity in another sense as well, by signing a contract with Holt and Company for the work which would emerge twelve years later as *The Principles of Psychology*.

And even as William was twice pledging himself to the future came the first public appearance of Henry's "Daisy Miller," a

34 WJ to HJ (April 18, 1874).

tale which was to prove something of a literary cause célèbre, and which would firmly establish its author's reputation on both sides of the Atlantic. In the decade just past, Henry had published his first novel and followed it with a second, a third, and a fourth; his first exercises in fiction and criticism had been succeeded by innumerable stories, sketches, and reviews. Ten years earlier he had been still at home in Quincy Street, receiving with mixed emotion William's accounts of his adventures abroad; by this crucial summer of 1878 he had himself crossed the ocean five times and taken up permanent residence in Europe. He had left the New World behind in 1875, but it is from 1878 that Leon Edel dates the real beginning of his life in the Old—Henry's social and literary conquest of London. Alice's terrible year was, in Edel's terms, the novelist's "annus mirabilis."[35]

For both William and Henry, their biographers agree, the close of the decade saw a tremendous release of energy—an abundant outpouring of written work, accomplished in a remarkable state of well-being and good health. "I never was better, more at leisure, more workable, or less likely to trifle in any manner with my vitality, physical or intellectual," Henry reported to those at home in 1880.[36] Though several years earlier Alice had also begun to teach and to write, she had never been able to adopt so exuberantly complacent a tone. Late in 1875 the youngest of the Jameses had announced her decision to join Miss Anna Ticknor's Society to Encourage Studies at Home—a voluntary organization of Boston area women who met in Miss Ticknor's Park Street house and ran a sort of correspondence course for less educationally privileged women all over the country. Alice was to instruct her correspondents in history. "You can laugh and think me as much of a humbug as you choose, you can't do so more than I have myself," she had written to a friend in describing her new role.[37] "I do not see that there can possibly be any harm in it, if we are willing to take the trouble, & it is a good deal," she had continued uneasily to defend herself a year later; "I have to

35 Leon Edel, *Henry James: The Conquest of London, 1870–1881* (Philadelphia: Lippincott, 1962), p. 341.

36 See Allen, *William James*, pp. 223–228; and Edel, *Henry James: The Conquest of London*, pp. 341–345. Henry's letter, addressed to his "beloved mammy," is dated September 11 [1880].

37 AJ to Annie Ashburner (December 26, 1875) (National).

write between thirty & forty letters every month, but I have nought else of importance to do."[38] With its simultaneous emphasis both on self-improvement and on staying at home, it was a peculiarly female and Bostonian version of the fraternal careers. But "matrimony still seems the only successful occupation that a woman can undertake," Alice had noted in the midst of it,[39] and by the end of the decade "the foolish virgins in Park Street" seem to have been abandoned.[40] In the summer of 1878 Alice James had begun neither marriage nor a genuine vocation: her only tentative engagement for the future was with suicide. That she flirted with killing herself as the final act of decision and release, her father's account suggests; certainly she was the only one of his children who had not yet managed to "break bonds or assert her freedom" in less desperate ways. Suicide clearly tempted her as an absolute act of will: for the thirty-year-old woman, it would also have proved the ultimate means of leaving home, the decisive step in what she would casually term her "mortal career."[41]

But of course she was never to take that step. With devastating gentleness, Henry Sr. had helped to save his daughter's life by depriving her of the power to end it: he had benevolently rendered her helpless. And both the benevolence of the father and the helplessness it induced in the child were characteristic of the Jameses. If several of the sons had great trouble in choosing a vocation, if William was well over thirty before he finally broke from home, such incapacities were in part the paradoxical consequence of extreme parental love. The very tenderness of the family atmosphere produced a sort of impotence in the children, made resistance and definition difficult. "Such an atmosphere was . . . doubtless delightful," the novelist would later recall,

> yet if it was friendly to the suggested or imagined thing it promoted among us much less directly . . . the act of choice—choice as to the "career" for example. . . . I marvel at the manner in which the door appears to have been held or at least left open to us for experiment, though with a tendency to close, the oddest yet most inveterately perceptible

38 AJ to Annie Ashburner (February 28, 1877) (National).
39 AJ to Annie Ashburner (April 12, 1876) (National).
40 AJ to Sara Darwin (April 8 [1880?]).
41 AJ to WJ (December 23, 1884).

movement in that sense, before any very earnest proposition in particular.

To commit oneself to some "earnest proposition in particular"
is inevitably narrowing, and Henry Sr. feared above all lest his
children be narrow; "what we were to do instead was just to *be*
something, something unconnected with specific doing, something free and uncommitted, something finer in short, than
being *that*, whatever it was, might consist of."[42] It is a splen-
didly liberating ambition, yet there is a terrible sense in which
the invalid daughter—unconnected and uncommitted with a
vengeance—most closely fulfilled its terms.

For nineteenth-century America, after all, expected rather
more from its young men than mere being; however strongly
Henry Sr. might urge his sons to remain "unconnected with specific doing," each of them eventually felt some sort of work imperative. Indeed the very anxiety which the vocational question
could arouse in them suggests how deeply the choice of career
mattered, how intense was the combined force of private need
and social pressure. Only daughters could afford with relative
ease "just to *be* something." And in a family which made of neurotic illness a common condition, almost a resource on which
all could draw, it is oddly fitting that the something Alice
should be was an invalid. To be ill in Alice's case was to put
"specific doing" out of the question—was to make eventless-
ness, in fact, the very ground of existence: "she only gets on,"
the novelist was to observe of his ailing sister, "so long as
nothing happens."[43]

When William had begun to exchange his own morbid condition for the specific doing of teaching and writing, he had celebrated the transformation in typically extravagant terms: "Dear
me!" his father reported his exclaiming one spring afternoon
during the first months of his appointment to Harvard, "what a
difference there is between me now & me last spring this time:
then so hypochondriacal . . . and now feeling my mind so

42 Henry James, *Notes of a Son and Brother*, Chaps. 5, 3; Allen
    observes that "Henry James, Sr., perhaps unintentionally, re-
    strained his children by indulgence" (*William James*, p. 64).
    See also Millicent Bell's illuminating essay, "Jamesian Being,"
    in the *Virginia Quarterly Review*, 52 (1976), 115–132.
43 HJ to WJ (May 25 [1889]).

cleared up and restored to sanity. It is the difference between death and life."[44] Though the hypochondria of his little sister was a close relative of his own (William "considers her weak nervous condition very like his own present one," the mother once wrote),[45] the younger sufferer was to experience no equivalent release. In abandoning her threat of suicide, Alice had literally made the difference between death and life; yet the moment does not so much mark the rejection of her will to die as the beginning of a curious equivocation: death would remain an intensely desired end, a goal as well as a conclusion, but she herself would not consciously determine the moment of its coming. She would resign her body to its fate, surrender herself to slower and more impersonal rhythms. She still wished to die, but her own will was now to merge with the will of Providence and the physicians. "I shall let you know if he tells me anything interesting," she wrote to William in the winter of 1884 while awaiting the verdict of her latest doctor; "I am much afraid that it wont be immediate dissolution, but on the contrary a long drawn out process."[46] Nothing interesting, in her sense, would take place for more than six years. But all the waiting was itself an act of dying, and in the last months she would write of being dead as of a wearily familiar state: "The fact is, I have been dead so long & it has been simply such a grim shoving of the hours behind me as I faced a ceaseless possible horror, since that hideous summer of '78, when I went down to the deep sea, its dark waters closed over me & I knew neither hope nor peace; that now it's only the shrivelling of an empty pea pod that has to be completed" (February 2, 1892). Though Alice had chosen not to kill herself in that hideous summer, there is thus a sense in which she was to turn the rest of her "mortal career" into a covert career in mortality.

As the family's chief invalid, then, Alice settled into a role which always seems to have had its strange attractions for the Jameses, a role with which most of the others continued to flirt at crucial moments in their lives. But before she took permanently to her bed, circumstances would briefly offer her one other part to play. In late January of 1882, the seventy-one-year-

44 HJ Sr. to HJ (March 18 [1873?]).
45 MWJ to HJ (July 1 [1873]).
46 AJ to WJ (December 23, 1884).

old mother—hitherto the single unequivocally healthy member of the family—contracted bronchial asthma; within a few days she was dead. For the greater part of the following year Alice would live alone with her father, and for most of that time she was, by all accounts, remarkably well. "Alice, I am happy to say, after many years of ill health has been better for the last few months than for a long time," the younger Henry reported; "she is able to look after my father and take care of his house—and as she is a person of great ability it is an extreme good fortune that she is now able to exert herself."⁴⁷ Aunt Kate waxed even more enthusiastic. "Mr. James and Alice are a ceaseless wonder to me," she wrote to a friend in March:

> they bear so cheerfully this heart-rending void.——Alice is a daily, hourly miracle! Her mother's death seems to have given her new life, those poor nerves having apparently found their long needed stimulus in the tremendous sense of responsibility which has fallen upon her. From the moment her mother left us, she *at once* took up the duties she laid down, and she has proved herself most thoroughly capable and efficient in the discharge of them. I feared, *all* feared, that there would come a re-action, but two months have now passed, and she seems to grow stronger, more equal to the work she has marked out for herself. If her dear mother can look down, and why may we not take the comfort of thinking that she can? how must she rejoice that to the dear child to whom she gave material existence, she has by her death given spiritual life. It has been a rare triumph of mind over matter,—but such cases are not unknown. Thanks to the Giver of all Good, that this blessing has come to us.⁴⁸

Such cases are not unknown, indeed, though to a post-Freudian reader, Aunt Kate's pious talk of "spiritual life" is likely to seem rather beside the point. In fact, it is hard not to sense in this brief interlude in Alice's history the classic shape of a small Oedipal drama—hard not to find another of Kate's ingenuous observations, "Alice said from the moment her dear mother left us, 'I would not have it otherwise,'"⁴⁹ distracting evidence of the daughter's unconsciously murderous wishes.

47 HJ to Mrs. Francis Mathews (February 13 [1882]).
48 CW to Mrs. C. P. Cranch (March 22 [1882]).
49 CW to Mary Holton James (February 9, 1882) (Vaux). Later that

Alice James in Paris as a young girl

William James as a young man in Geneva, 1859–60

Mary Walsh James

Alice James in 1862

Henry James, Sr., about fifty years old

Robertson James

Garth Wilkinson James

Henry James, Jr., as a young man

Alice James as a young woman in Boston

Katharine Peabody Loring

Sample of Alice James's handwriting, from a letter
of March 1888 to Mary Holton James

Catharine Walsh (Aunt Kate)

William James and his daughter Margaret (Peggy) in March 1892

Henry James in March 1890

Alice James and Katharine Loring in Leamington, 1889–90

Alice James in the year before her death

Whatever the deepest sources of the energies she now tapped, there is no question that by taking her mother's place, Alice had temporarily found something to *do* with herself, a motive for health and strength. But if her mother's death seems to have granted Alice new life, it appears only to have hastened the dying of her father; the very event that had called forth Alice's energies was ironically quick to render them useless. Before the year was out, Henry Sr. too was dead, having virtually willed himself to follow his wife to the grave:

he simply one day consciously ceased, quietly declined to continue, as an offered measure of his loss of interest. Nothing—he had enabled himself to make perfectly sure— was in the least worth while without her; this attested, he passed away or went out, with entire simplicity, promptness and ease, for the definite reason that his support had failed.[50]

"He had no visible malady . . . ," Henry Jr. reported to William, then abroad; "The 'softening' of the brain' was simply a gradual refusal of food, because he *wished* to die." For the elder James, apparently, no daughter could take the place of the dead. And as he "ebbed and faded away,"[51] it was not his daughter but Aunt Kate and a hired nurse who watched over him; with her father unmistakably dying, Alice once more retreated to a sickroom of her own.

Declining to eat, calmly issuing instructions for his funeral, Henry Sr. quietly ended his life. If he did not precisely commit suicide, he nonetheless made death seem a deliberate act, a conscious exercise of will. Ten years later his daughter would ambiguously repeat the performance. But like several of Freud's hysterical subjects, Alice's more immediate response to nursing another was to turn patient again herself;[52] carried off by Katharine Loring the morning after the funeral, Alice was to spend

---

spring Alice herself wrote to Robertson's wife: "Father & I are alone, & very much alone we feel, but we would not either of us have it otherwise"—AJ to Mary Holton James (May 22 [1882?]) (Vaux).

50 Henry James, *Notes of a Son and Brother*, Chap. 6.

51 HJ to WJ (December 26 [1882]).

52 Josef Breuer and Sigmund Freud, *Studies on Hysteria* (1893–1895), in *The Standard Edition of the Complete Psychological Works of Sigmund Freud*, trans. and ed. James Strachey et al. (London: Hogarth Press, 1953–1954), II, 161–162.

much of the next year under that loyal companion's care—leaving the Loring house for a few months in the spring and summer only to rest rather more formally at a place given over to retreat and collapse, an institution known as the Adams Nervine Asylum in Jamaica Plain.⁵³ In the spring of 1884 she ventured alone to New York for galvanic treatments; in the fall Katharine returned from a trip to Europe in order to help Alice in turn across the ocean, to see once more what change of place might do. "She ought," Henry wrote in anticipation, "to be prepared to spend *three* years,"⁵⁴ but she would in fact spend eight—the remainder, as it would prove, of her life. Like her novelist brother, she arrived in England and permanently assumed her vocation.

4

"For you, my dear Sister, this is the most important change in all your life," William wrote to her as soon as he learned of their father's death: "In some ways it will be a great nakedness, in others a great freedom."⁵⁵ While William sympathetically balanced emotional gains against losses, it was the nakedness *of* her freedom that Alice seems most to have felt, a terror of the physical and psychic space that had opened up around her. "In those ghastly days, when I was by myself in the little house in Mt. Vernon St.," she recalled in her diary, "how I longed to flee in to the firemen next door & escape from the 'Alone! Alone!' that echoed thro' the house, rustled down the stairs, whispered from the walls & confronted me, like a material presence, as I sat waiting, counting the moments as they turned themselves from today into tomorrow. . . ." Evoking her remembered loneliness as if it had been a ghost pursuing her through the empty house, Alice's brief narrative belongs to the same imaginative family as Henry's haunted "Jolly Corner" of almost twenty years later; in its hallucinatory terror, it resembles even more closely those thinly fictionalized accounts of their "panic fear" left us

53 A majority of his patients were unmarried, the resident physician reported in 1886, and many of these were "daughters upon whom has devolved the cares of the house and the nursing of invalid parents or relatives." S. G. Webber, *Annual Report of the Adams Nervine Asylum* (Boston: Alfred Mudge & Son, 1886), p. 11.

54 HJ to WJ (October 5 [1884]).

55 WJ to AJ (December 20, 1882).

by the father and the eldest son. "Father & Wm." indeed figure
significantly in this journal entry, but it is not of their bent for
spiritual crisis that Alice appears to have been thinking. What
she records instead is a wistful tribute to Jamesian laughter and
teasing:

> Shall I ever have any convulsive laughs again!——Ah, me! I
> fear me not. I had such a feast for 34 yrs. that I can't com-
> plain. But a curious extreme to be meted out to a creature,
> to have grown up between Father & Wm. & then to be re-
> duced to Nurse & Miss C.[56] for humourous daily fodder.
> Could you but hear the three-lettered chaff wh. I fabricate
> for 'em! for chaff of some sort I *must* have. (July 7, 1889)

The very next sentence begins the recollection of those "ghastly
days" in Mt. Vernon Street; from the loss of "convulsive laughs,"
her mind moves directly to the threat of psychic collapse. For
Alice, the record suggests, no other transition was necessary.
"Chaff of some sort"—"humourous daily fodder"—had long
since become the stuff of her survival.

The same journal entry begins by reporting the visit of a certain Miss Leppington, an Englishwoman "as delicate & spiritual
minded as if she had bloomed upon our rock-bound puritan
coast"—and a lady, one imagines, who might well call forth in
Alice thoughts of her own liability to the delicate and the spir-
itual-minded. "How fatally the entire want of humour cripples
the mind," is the invalid's emphatic verdict on her visitor (July
7, 1889). Just a few days earlier she had rendered a similar judgment on another Englishwoman:

> Read the 3rd Vol. of Geo. Eliot's Letters & Journals at last.
> I'm glad I made my self do so for there is a faint spark of life
> & an occasional, remotely humourous touch in the last
> half. But what a monument of ponderous dreariness is the
> book! What a lifeless, diseased, self-conscious being she
> must have been! not one burst of joy, not one ray of humour,
> not one living breath in one of her letters or journals. . . .
> What an abject coward she seems to have been about physi-
> cal pain, as if it weren't degrading eno' to have head-aches
> without jotting them down in a row to stare at one for all
> time, thereby defeating the beneficent law wh. provides
> that physical pain is forgotten. If she related her diseases &

56 Miss Clarke, AJ's current landlady.

her "depressions" & told for the good of others what armour she had forged against them, it wd. be conceivable but they seem simply cherished as the vehicule for a moan. Where was the creature's Vanity! & when you think of what she had in life to lift her out of futile whining! But the possession of what genius & what knowledge could reconcile one to the supreme boredom of having to take oneself with that superlative solemnity! (June 28, 1889)

Gravely chronicling each headache, the private George Eliot leaves Alice with the "impression, morally, & physically of mildew, or some morbid growth—a fungus of a pendulous shape, or as of something damp to the touch" (June 28, 1889). If the image is cruel, the vehemence of Alice's revulsion disquieting, it remains true that there is little of "superlative solemnity" in her own record of her troublesome flesh. William arrives from America to pay an unexpected visit, and she reports triumphantly that "with the assistance of 200 grains of Bromide I think I behaved with extreme propriety"—despite Henry's "anxiety as to wh. 'going off' in my large repertory wd. 'come on'" (August 4, 1889); the election of a Liberal proponent of Irish Home Rule—a fiercely cherished cause—makes itself immediately felt in the pit of her stomach, and she cheerfully exclaims against "the dominion of that mighty organ": "No fiat of the fateful three was ever more irresistible than the decrees sent forth by that pivot of my being!" (March 9, 1890). Reading her account of herself, one is struck again and again by the sheer dailiness of it all, the apparent ease with which her spirit accommodated itself to the terms of its own confinement. Writers on the James family are given to calling her stoic, and there is certainly something of brave resolution in the simple matter-of-factness of her record, her refusal, even in the privacy of her diary, to moan and complain. Not "futile whining," but comic detachment is the rule; she may speak of her stomach as the pivot of her being, but the voice which jocularly grants it dominion seems far removed from that difficult organ. Indeed, to talk thus of her body as her fate is paradoxically to emphasize the distinction between that body and herself, to treat her own flesh as an alien, if inescapable, force. The very abjectness of her surrender leaves her curiously free. For all her chronic invalidism, she remains the dryly detached observer, comically distant from her own suffering and pain.

Though she was apparently given to fainting at the slightest provocation—the mere secondhand report of an expression used by one of the local poor was enough to send her "toppling over," as she characteristically put it (June 18, 1889)—it is difficult to believe in the reality of this delicate creature, even more difficult to accept her identity with the author of the journal and the letters. Such heightened sensibilities and so casual a tone fail to square: women who write thus nonchalantly of "toppling over" do not, one assumes, actually do so. Of course the ladylike faint has gone out of fashion, and the contemporary reader may well find something almost exotic in the gesture, but what is striking is how remote Alice herself seems from the swooning woman of whom she writes: "Katharine is a most sustaining optimist, she proposed writing for me this morning, I said 'Why, you won't have time,' 'Oh yes, I'm not going until twelve, & by that time you are always back again in bed, fainted'" (January 12, 1891). This brief allusion to collapse as a sort of daily habit is sandwiched casually between one of Henry's theatrical anecdotes and Katharine's ironic comment on reported plans to institute telephone service between England and France. The fainting lady becomes simply another of the journal's passing caricatures, a figure hardly more immediate than those Alice collected from newspaper columns or transcribed into the diary from Henry's bedside gossip. Even in direct speech Alice could remain the cool historian of her dying self: the cancer in her breast had been diagnosed; the doctor came to visit; and "Alice discussed her case & her demise with him," Katharine reported to William, "as if she were talking about Queen Elizabeth."[57]

"I don't know how to approach your various calamities in the way of fires," Alice wrote from England to a Boston friend. "If one says what one feels it seems hysterical, & fond relatives invite one not to 'take on', and after all the writing out of a succession of adjectives doesn't seem to be an intelligent contribution to the occasion. . . ."[58] The conjunction of true feeling with hysteria is characteristic—and so too is the dismissal of those superfluous adjectives, the willingness to deny herself any verbal relief. "Making an intelligent contribution" depends, apparently, on self-discipline and constraint, whether in the after-

57 Katharine Loring to WJ (July 30 [1891]).
58 AJ to Fanny Morse (December 7 [1889?]).

math of a fire three thousand miles away or at the outbreak of
what William called Alice's own "bottled lightning":[59]

altho' I have never, unfortunately, been able to abandon my
consciousness & get five minutes rest, I have passed thro'
an infinite succession of conscious abandonments and in
looking back now I see how it began in my childhood, altho'
I wasn't conscious of the necessity until '67 or '68 when I
broke down first, acutely, & had violent turns of hysteria.
As I lay prostrate after the storm with my mind luminous &
active & susceptible of the clearest, strongest impressions, I
saw so distinctly that it was a fight simply between my
body & my will, a battle in wh. the former was to be triumphant to the end. Owing to some physical weakness, ex-
cess of nervous susceptibility the moral power *pauses*, as it
were for a moment & refuses to maintain muscular sanity
worn out with the strain of its constabulary functions. As I
used to sit immovable reading in the library with waves of
violent inclination suddenly invading my muscles taking
some one of their myriad forms such as throwing myself
out of the window or knocking off the head of the benignant
pater as he sat with his silver locks, writing at his table, it
used to seem to me that the only difference between me &
the insane was that I had not only all the horror & suffering
of insanity but the duties of doctor nurse & strait-jacket imposed upon me too. Conceive of never being without the
sense that if you let yr. self go for a moment your mechanism will fall into pie & that at some given moment you
must abandon it all, let the dykes break & the flood sweep

59 "*Your* letters show no effect from the fluffiness and wooliness
of your environment, and your character seems to grow more
and more like that of the young girl-heroine of whom I read
many years ago in a Boston story-paper, and whose charms
were summed up in the phrase, 'she was like 'bottled lightning.'——I suppose that when you have a catastrophe like that
recent one of which you write, you feel as if you were altogether too much like bottled lightning"—WJ to AJ (June 3,
1888). William's borrowed phrase clearly had resonance for
Alice; almost a year and a half later, she recalled it in her journal: "I shall learn to cork my self up again before long & return to my state of 'bottled lightning' as Wm. calls it an expression wh. he culled from a story he read once in a Boston
newspaper where the heroine was thus described" (December
1, 1889).

in acknowledging yourself abjectly impotent before the immutable laws. When all one's moral & natural stock in trade is a temperament forbidding the abandonment of an inch or the relaxation of a muscle 'tis a never ending fight. When the fancy took me of a morning at school to *study* my lessons by way of variety instead of shirking or wiggling thro' the most impossible sensations of upheaval violent revolt in my head overtook me so that I had to "abandon" my brain as it were. So it has always been, anything that sticks of itself is free to do so, but conscious & continuous cerebration is an impossible exercise & from just behind the eyes my head feels like a dense jungle into wh. no ray of light has ever penetrated. So with the rest, you abandon the pit of yr. stomach the palms of yr. hands the soles of yr. feet & refuse to keep them sane when you find in turn one moral impression after another producing despair in the one, terror in the other anxiety in the third & so on until life becomes one long flight from remote suggestion & complicated eluding of the multifold traps set for your undoing. (October 26, 1890)

She is recording here a crisis more than twenty years gone, but what she remembers is an affair of violent and conflicting energies, the drama of a fiercely divided self. In this allegory of inner division, Alice's body endlessly battles her will, her flesh violently rebels against her "moral power," and madness threatens on the instant that imaginary constable relaxes his vigilant control. Her very body in turn is radically split: not only parts, but abstractions of parts—the pit of her stomach, the palms of her hands, the soles of her feet—assume a dangerous and independent life, act as detached pieces of flesh with troublesome minds of their own. Indeed the whole account is strangely independent of the woman it describes, a psychic morality play in which violent inclinations toward suicide and murder "invade" her muscles as if from some foreign power, and even her will willfully "refuses" to maintain control. She imagines herself now as a battleground, now as a landscape with dense jungles and imperiled dikes, now as an entire insane asylum—doctor, patient, and straitjacket alike; though the metaphors freely mingle and mix, what remains constant is the peculiar detachment of the recording voice, the elusiveness of Alice James herself. The tone is disconcertingly offhand, even jocular, as she alludes casually to the

wish to throw herself out of the window or to "knock off," as
she airily puts it, the head of her beloved father. We have no reason to doubt the truth of her report, but the source of all this
potential violence remains obscure, the center of feeling eludes
us. "Multifold traps" are set to undo her from within; the despair, terror, and anxiety are her own, yet some disembodied self
still manages to evade them. Despite the impersonal "you" of
the final lines, she writes, of course, of Alice James in flight
from Alice James; the journal entry provides, indirectly, the key
to its own style. It is hardly surprising that she begins this same
entry by praising William's essay on the "Hidden Self."

By the time she came to record her old breakdown, she had long
since grown expert, after all, at her "complicated eluding."
When William asked that she send back to Boston a lock of her
hair—with his characteristic enthusiasm for experiments in the
occult, he intended to use it to try the powers of a local medium—Alice complied by silently mailing him instead the hair
of a woman who had died four years earlier. "I thought it a much
better test of whether the medium were simply a mind-reader or
not," she wrote in confessing her "base trick"; "if she is something more I should greatly dislike to have the secrets of my
organisation laid bare to a wondering public."[60] As she evaded
even this distant grasp at her hair, so she strenuously resisted all
more immediate attempts on her spirit, the fashionable zeal of
some of her feminine visitors for séances or mind cures. Alluding contemptuously to "the passion women have for rushing
into any distasteful imbecility wh. may arise,"[61] she herself remained aloof from the sisterhood. "It is taken for granted apparently that I shall be spiritualized into a 'district messenger,'"
she noted dryly in her journal exactly a week before she died:

>   for here comes another message for Father & Mother; imag-
>   ine my dragging them, of whom I can only think as a sub-
>   limation of their qualities, into gossip about the little more
>   or the little less faith of Tom, Dick or Harry. I do pray to
>   Heaven that the dreadful Mrs Piper won't be let loose upon
>   my defenceless soul. I suppose the thing "medium" has

60 AJ to WJ (January 3–4 [1886?]). For an account of William's
   experiments with Mrs. Piper, see Allen, *William James*, pp.
   282–285.
61 AJ to WJ (November 25, 1889).

done more to degrade spiritual conception than the grossest forms of materialism or idolatry; was there ever anything transmitted but the pettiest, meanest, coarsest facts & details: anything rising above the squalid intestines of human affairs? And oh, the curious spongy minds that sop it all up & lose all sense of taste & humor! (February 28, 1892)

Beneath the spiritualist fervor of her visitors Alice understandably feared a pressure essentially vulgar and reductive, an alarming eagerness to invade the privacy of others. But so intense was the dread lest her "secrets" be "laid bare," that even anonymous praise could threaten her with terrible exposure: "Imagine hearing that some man . . . here in Leamington whom I never had seen had said that I was 'very charitable!'" she wrote in her diary after giving a sixpence to some poor and prolific neighbors; "I felt as if all my clothes had been suddenly torn off & that I was standing, on the steps of the Town Hall, in the nude, for the delectation of the *British Matron*" (June 13, 1889). Simply to be talked about by someone she has never met is to be made horribly vulnerable. It could be out of Hawthorne, this nightmare of public exposure, but even in Hawthorne, Hester Prynne is pilloried for adultery, not for her subsequent acts of mercy—and Hester Prynne at least was allowed to keep her clothes.

Subject as Alice had been for so long to the probing of countless doctors, exposed for much of her stay in England to the petty indignities of lodging-house life, she perhaps had good reason to fear nakedness and invasion. The diary and letters allude repeatedly to the "intellectual degradation" that the visits of her medical men entailed for her (September 27, 1890), the "fierce struggle to recover one's self-respect" when those visits were over.[62] Feeling herself grasped not "as a whole" but merely "as a stomach or a dislocated elbow"[63] could only have intensified her own detachment, that strategic retreat from her flesh by which she had chosen to save her self. "My new doctor turns out to be a very remarkable & original being quite after my ideal," she wrote of one recent entry in the long succession, "as he never wishes to see me & is quite satisfied to treat me through a third person."[64] For all their irony, her words betray a powerful wish:

62 AJ to WJ (January 3–4 [1886?]).
63 AJ to WJ (July 30 [1891]).
64 AJ to CW (November 15, 1887).

as long as her doctors dealt only with anonymous "third persons," the patient herself could remain free—could preserve in her sickroom a fiercely separate space. She was in fact obsessed by the need for such space, by the architecture of human privacy. The only piece of writing she ever published, a letter to *The Nation* signed "INVALID," is the record of a failed invasion. Her Leamington landlady had turned away a prospective tenant, an American woman who greeted the discovery of the resident invalid by announcing, "In that case perhaps it is just as well that you cannot take us in, for my little girl, who is thirteen, likes to have plenty of liberty and to *scream* through the house." Alice offered the letter, she said, in the "white heat" of her "patriotism"; arriving coincidentally on July 4, 1890, the American lady and her screaming child came as a "transatlantic blast" from her native land, "pure and undefiled."[65] But when a British acquaintance innocently inquired about the arrangements in American boarding houses—"If you lived in one should you have a room to yourself?"—Alice was outraged: "Imagine my emotions on discovering that there was nothing about me suggestive after a yr. of constant intercourse of a practice of the laws of common decency!" she wrote to E. L. Godkin in reporting the exchange.[66] Four months later she repeated the entire incident once again in her journal (April 7, 1890). And after six years among the English she was still registering her shock at the crowded quarters in which they managed to live—"the knowledge of which . . . unfolded itself gradually with increasingly repulsive details" after she and Katharine rented a tiny cottage on Hampstead Heath only to discover that its previous occupants had squeezed five children into its four rooms; their predecessors, nine:

> we long ago abandoned the attempt to solve the problem of how the multifold offspring was disposed of through the watches of the night; but we have been simply appalled by having more & more light thrown in upon the loathsome sleeping arrangements of their servants! I am, of course, speaking only of "middle class" houses. They live in such comfort & luxury, indulge & feed their servants to the last degree, but give them no where to lay their head; for the

65 AJ to E. L. Godkin (July 4, 1890).
66 AJ to E. L. Godkin (January 6, 1890).

butler & footmen actually sleep in pantry & scullery, where the china & glass you eat off, is washed every day. In large houses the butler does it in order to protect the plate: Conceive of having plate with no where to put it, except in the butler's bed-room! The visions which the dullest imagination calls up at these thoughts are too horrible to be hinted! (June 17, 1891)

It is difficult to tell whether the unspeakable threat here is primarily sexual or sanitary, whether Alice identifies most intensely with the servants or with their masters. But if the indiscriminate storage of butlers and dinnerware could conjure up vague horrors, an attempted incursion by a pair of drunken clergymen on her own sleeping quarters late one night evoked terrors whose effects were far more immediate. "They pretended they had been 'discussing theology' together below, & had become excited by so doing," Henry wrote to a friend; "but what they had been discussing was of course whiskey." One of the pair was himself a boarder in the same Leamington house, and in his midnight stupor had apparently mistaken Alice's door for his own. Though the would-be intruders seem not actually to have gotten past her threshold, the ensuing uproar brought on one of her characteristic attacks. "They were perfect strangers to her," Henry wrote, "& the whole thing, including the row & mess after it, made her very ill."

"The incident was a vivid illustration of what horrible little cads & beasts there are in the church of England," the novelist concluded solemnly;[67] it took the victim herself to recognize after the event its possibilities as farce. For several years her hapless fellow lodger continued to figure occasionally in her accounts, making his final appearance in a letter which amusedly recorded his capture in marriage by "a certain Miss Owen": "to secure permanent possession of the rare & precious creature she employed five clergy men & four yards of train," Alice noted; "I myself think that this plethora of satin & ecclesiastics was to divert attention from the exiguity of husband. He is 33 yrs. old & she 48!"[68] When Alice wrote this letter, she was almost forty-one herself, and it is hard not to sense in her allusion to the intoxicated young "clericule . . . who burst, or rather aspired to

67 HJ to Elizabeth Boott (October 18 [1886?]).
68 AJ to Mrs. Morse (June 9 [1889?]).

burst into my room in the middle of the night" and to the desperate spinster who finally caught him an oblique reference to
sexual needs and fears of her own. But the violation that she
seems to have imagined most vividly was not in fact sexual. "I
am very comfortable in my quarters altho' the clerical animalcule of last yr. is still below," she reported to a friend as she
neared the anniversary of the aborted invasion,

> but he has not begun his midnight revelries yet. I am haunt-
> ed however by the fear that I may be suddenly taken ill unto
> death & that before Henry can arrive to protect my little ec-
> clesiastical nurse will introduce the curate to my bedside.
> Imagine opening your eyes & seeing the bat-like object
> standing there! I am sure it would curdle my soul in its tran-
> sit & at any rate entirely spoil my post mortem expression
> of countenance. It is terrible to be such an unprotected
> being as I am.[69]

She is still a sort of virgin and the curate a potential rapist, but if
this continues to be bedroom farce, it has a distinctly mortuary
flavor. Though she is "haunted" by fear, the danger Alice imagines is less to herself than to the ceremony of her dying. Or
rather, Alice's self and her dying have here become imaginatively one. What is most crucially at stake is the threat to her
"post mortem expression."

5

"Pray dearest Fanny don't think of me as a forlorn failure but as
a happy individual who has infinitely more in her life than she
deserves," Alice wrote to her friend Fanny Morse in the spring of
1886. "You know that ill or well one is never deprived of the
power of standing for what one was meant to stand for & what
more can life give us?"[70] Even as a mere formula of consolation,
this is remarkably empty: to possess "the power of standing for
what one was meant to stand for" is to possess a purely rhetorical force, an energy whose ends are wholly undefined. Her language circles back on itself, gathering on its way only a vague
implication of determinism. Indeed, the question of what "friend
No. 1 can possibly stand for," as she put it several years later in
the diary, was still very much an open one:

69 AJ to Sara Darwin (October 4 [1887?]).
70 AJ to Fanny Morse (April 11 [1886?]).

Middle life brings such interest as we see unfolded gradually the destinies of our friends & they take the stamp given
by the end, & it occupies me more than a little to fancy
what friend No. 1 can possibly stand for! A life lifted out of
all material care or temptation to wh. all the rudimentary
impulses were unknown, a collection simply of fantastic
*un*productive emotions enclosed within tissue paper walls,
rent equally by pleasure as by pain—animated by a never
ceasing belief in & longing for *action*, relentlessly denied,
all safety-valves shut-down in the way of the "busy ineffec-
tiveness of women." (November 7, 1890)

Answering her own questions by naming what she is not, she
gives an account of herself whose syntax is revealingly incom-
plete: what begins with "a life lifted out of all material care or
temptation" lacks even a genuine predicate. It is characteristic
of Alice that she should read others' histories in light of "the
end"—and that when she uses the term, she means not purpose
or goal, but simply dying. Again and again she returned to the
idea that only in death could the self achieve definition. "But
what an interest death lends to the most commonplace," she
wrote to William after a friend of his had died, "making them so
complete & clear-cut, all the vague & wobbly lines lost in the
revelation of what they were meant to stand for."[71] Fictional
corpses pointed a similar moral. Reading the climax of a new
play in which an outraged father murders his daughter's seducer
"forces upon one the futile & elusive nature of human means,"
she observed in the diary, "for even the glow of triumph of an
avenging murderer must have but a momentary life, must fade
& flicker out in the presence of his victim, stiff & stark, but yet
complete! whilst he is still the same formless figure, vague &
abortive" (December 16, 1889). The living are "formless," and
their passions "momentary"; what remains is the solidity of the
dead.

"To be able to do something absolutely complete in itself,
what more cd. a human being ask for!" she had exclaimed in one
of the first entries in the journal (July 6, 1889); but only when
the doctor delivered his sentence of death would she hear the
promise of her own longed-for completion. "To any one who has
not been there," she wrote a few days after the event, "it will be

71 AJ to AHJ & WJ (August 21, 1888).

hard to understand the enormous relief of Sir A C's uncompromising verdict, lifting us out of the formless vague and setting us within the very heart of the sustaining concrete" (June 1, 1891). This is not the conventional relief of the mortally ill, the anticipation of escape from pain; there was, after all, "some comfort in good solid pain," as she had once written to William.[72] It is life itself which she wishes to escape—a life experienced as so without substance that no real substantive names it, that it is called simply "the formless vague." In a characteristic inversion, death absorbs the vital terms here, becomes "the very heart of the sustaining concrete." "But what an interesting moment it is," she had written just a year before, "when the familiar figures recede one by one and are seen in the right perspective & live at last."[73]

But however satisfyingly solid was the lump in Alice's breast, she had recorded her desire to *do* "something absolutely complete," not merely to incarnate it. To William's sympathetic comment, several years earlier, on her "stifling in a quagmire of disgust, pain & impotence," her reaction had been vehement: "I consider myself one of the most *potent* creations of my time, & though I may not have a group of Harvard students sitting at my feet drinking in psychic truth, I shall not tremble, I assure you, at the last trump."[74] Her claim to power is, typically, a death-directed one; she can only counter her brother's admiring students by evoking the Last Judgment. Quick to distinguish herself, she would repudiate sympathy even from the brother who had also known "unspeakable disgust," as he once put it in his diary, "for the dead drifting of my own life"—who had narrowly emerged from his own "deadness of spirit" only by a tremendous effort of will.[75] Yet William *had* willed himself free or, at least, had believed himself to do so. "Hitherto, when I have felt like taking a free initiative, like daring to act originally, without carefully waiting for contemplation of the external world to determine all for me, suicide seemed the most manly form to put my daring into," he had confided in his diary in the spring of

72 AJ to WJ (December 11 [1887?]).
73 AJ to WJ (March 16; 1890).
74 AJ to WJ (September 10 [1886]).
75 WJ diary (May 22, 1868); WJ to Oliver W. Holmes (September 17, 1867).

1870; "Now, I will go a step further with my will, not only act with it, but believe as well; believe in my individual reality and creative power." More than a quarter century before the publication of *The Will to Believe*, its future author had chosen to "posit life (the real, the good) in the self governing *resistance* of the ego to the world."[76]

"The only thing which survives is the resistance we bring to life," Alice observed in her own diary some twenty years later, "& not the strain life brings to us" (February 21, 1890). Brother and sister though the diarists are, the echo from one private journal to the other is uncanny. Yet if these are the words of a woman who had also decided to resist the attractions of suicide, they are nonetheless the words of a woman to whom death alone remained a significant gesture, to whom "daring to act originally," as her brother had put it, still meant only dying. "My first act of free will shall be to believe in free will," William had declared,[77] but his sister was never to make the emotional leap of that famous paradox. Alice's "imperious will," as her psychologist brother called it[78]—"the extraordinary intensity of her will & personality," in the words of the novelist[79]—was to exercise itself most directly in the documents and rituals of dying. She too was obsessed with her will, but in her case the noun has primarily its testamentary sense. "I think, really, that half her time in her lonely life is spent in thinking over & planning what she can do with her little property, at the end of that life," Henry wrote to his brother in the summer of 1889.[80] It was a fact of which William himself must scarcely have needed reminding. For several years, Alice's letters from England had been filled with details of a testamentary kind. Orders had been issued as to the disposition of blankets and linen and barrels of crockery, the parlor carpet and the old clock; instructions sent to collect from her cottage in Manchester "a very handsome old mahogany bureau & mirror with brass knobs, two tables, mahogany & four legs with claw-feet, not large, also a small fancy sort of stand with drawers & brass knobs,"[81] to remove her red rug from storage and lay it in William's study, to hang her old pictures on

76 WJ diary (April 30, 1870).   77 Ibid.
78 WJ to HJ (March 7, 1892).
79 HJ to WJ & AHJ (May 28, 1894).
80 HJ to WJ (June 13, 1889).   81 AJ to WJ (March 31, 1889).

their walls. Alice willed her possessions to those left behind and then willed also the means of attaining them. One letter directed William's wife to pick up the keys to the Manchester cottage from a certain "*F. W. Churchill, carpenter*" but to check first with J. B. Warner, the family lawyer; it also reminded her to make an appointment with Churchill lest he be away, even to bring a candle since its boarded windows would probably make the cottage very dark.[82] Little was left to chance—or to the will of others.

She wished to protect the good pieces at Manchester from possible tenants, she wrote, or to save herself the cost of storing her possessions in Boston, but it was not in fact such practical concerns that chiefly moved her. She wanted freely to give her old things away; when William independently chose to pay her storage bill and took the things simply to keep, rather than use, in his own house, his gesture prompted a transatlantic quarrel. Alluding ironically to "the drawbacks of a random & good-natured civilization, where *rights* are not passionately clung to & where affect. relatives permit themselves to rattle round the country with the crockery of their kin," Alice protested her brother's thoughtless generosity:

> I unfortunately, but very transparently, spoke of the storage to make the gift seem less to you. I do not remember to have spoken of it a second time or to have intimated that I felt incompetent to pay for what I considered the proper care of my things. My having chosen so expensive a lodgment for the things showed on the face of it that the objects were precious to me & that I had provided for their safety in a fire- & thief-proof building, as nearly as possible, in a place also where they wd. be accessible & above all concentrated. I made therefore another sad mistake in supposing that what was so plain to my order of mind could not be entirely unperceived by yrs. *I have no words to express my extreme annoyance at yr. having paid the storage.* You doubtless meant to be kind, but you know that kindness imposed upon an unwilling recipient,—and that I *was* an unwilling recipient you can't have had a *shadow of doubt*—is likely to go astray & receive small gratitude in return. . . . If you had not said in yr. letter that the things were *en route* I shd.

82 Ibid.

have telegraphed to Chocorua & Cambridge to try & avert the catastrophe.[83]

The Spoils of Boston, as Henry might have called it, was to conclude with apologetic letters on both sides, but the posthumous exercise of another Jamesian will would soon occasion a new crisis. In the spring of 1889 Aunt Kate died, leaving behind a rather curious document; bequeathing Alice merely a life interest in certain objects and specifying those who must inherit when she in turn should die, it was a will that made her niece feel "singled out," "publicly humiliated"—a will that would effectively prevent her, of course, from subjecting the things to a will of her own. That William and his children would eventually inherit the spoils was never really in doubt, Henry reported to him, but Alice could only cry bitterly now at "the cruelty or at least the infelicity of Aunt Kate's taking from her, in her miserably limited little helpless life, passed in one drawing room in a far-off country, the small luxury of devising *for herself* the disposal of the objects in question—to *you* as a perfect foregone conclusion—& of anticipating the pleasure she shld. thereby give."[84]

Aunt Kate had devoted much of her life to caring for her sister's family, and Alice had often alluded uneasily to having abandoned her for England and for Katharine. "My failing her, after Mother & Father's death, must have seemed to her a great & ungrateful betrayal," she wrote; "my inability to explain myself & hers to understand, in any way, the situation made it all the sadder & more ugly."[85] Whether consciously or not, the deserted aunt had turned her last will and testament into the instrument of a rather pointed revenge. Having parted from her husband after a very brief marriage, Catharine Walsh had presumably never been able to make much use of the family silver she possessed; by the terms of her will, she had seen to it that her niece could do even less. To the forty-year-old invalid and lodging-house dweller, even outright ownership of the silver would have been virtually meaningless—and now she had been denied the last "small luxury" of willing the pieces away. Alice responded by proudly renouncing all claims to them and granting William full possession at once. But if cool dignity would do

83 AJ to WJ (November 4, 1888).
84 HJ to WJ (June 13, 1889).   85 AJ to WJ (March 22, 1889).

for the family silver, only laughter could adequately dispose of a life interest in her late aunt's shawl:

> A life-interest in a shawl, with reversion to a *male* heir, is so extraordinary & ludicrous a bequest that I can hardly think it could have been seriously meant, my desire wd. of course, naturally be to renounce my passing claim to that also, as I can hardly conceive of myself under any conditions, as so abject as to grasp at a life-interest in a shawl! I, however, refrain from doing so fearing to be ungracious to *you* & propose this solving of the problem—viz., that you, your heirs & assigns should give me the shawl, renouncing their rights of reversion in it, & making me its absolute possessor. I may, or I may not, leave it to you in my will, but if I should, it will be entirely a voluntary action on my part & in that way you must look upon it & accept it with any ravages wh. moth & rust may have brought about. I might make a condition of doing so, that you shd. drape yr. manly person in it at my funeral—or, better still, wrap it about you to protect you from the breezes on the wharf when you perform that unaesthetic duty, wh. may some day be yrs., of passing my skin & bones thro' the Custom House. Owing to my unbaptized and ecclesiastically detached condition, I could hardly find burial here—& then what a cruel sell for the British worm, who must, in the frequency of sudden death, have such succulent morsels to feast upon! [86]

The domestic drama becomes, characteristically, a funereal comedy: Alice seizes absolute possession of the shawl only to imagine it ravaged by moth and rust, claims victory in this battle of wills and immediately renders herself a corpse. The troublesome Aunt Kate has been all but forgotten; at center stage are William, his "manly person" draped in the offending shawl, and his sister's mortal remains.

For the "paralysed dictator," as she once casually termed herself,[87] the condition of willfulness was immobility; she could be

---

86 AJ to WJ (April 7, 1889).
87 AJ to Fanny Morse (December 5 [1891?]). Narrowly interpreted, of course, the allusion is merely to her mode of composing letters; this one to Fanny Morse is in the hand of Alice's nurse, Emily Ann Bradfield. "I send thanks from my heart for all the loving words & memories which you have ad-

most fiercely herself when most nearly dead. In the winter of
1890 Katharine Loring summoned the American consul at Bir-
mingham to witness the official signing of Alice's latest will;
when the crucial moment came, the principal actress in the
event promptly fainted:

> The arrival of this august personage the Consul naturally
> caused me to "go off" & I had to be put to bed—when the
> most amusing scene followed. I lay in a semi-faint, draped
> in as many frills as cd. be found for the occasion, with
> Nurse at my head with the thickest layer of her anxious-
> devoted-nurse expression on, as K. told me after, when thro'
> a mist I vaguely saw five black figures file into my little
> bower, headed by the most extraordinary little man, all ges-
> ticulation & grimace, who planted himself at the foot of the
> bed and stroking my knees began a long harangue to the
> effect that he and his wife had both "laid upon a bed of sick-
> ness" wh. seemed to constitute an uncontrovertible reason
> for my immediate recovery. K. with difficulty restrained
> him from reading the Will aloud there & then—he has
> doubtless not forgiven this dam thrown across to arrest the
> flood of his eloquence——It was so curious for me, just like
> a nightmare effect & I felt as if I were assisting at the read-
> ing of my own Will, surrounded by the greedy relatives as in
> novels. After they had filed in and out several times & be-
> come tangled in as much resounding red-tape as the crea-
> ture cd. reel off for the occasion they went off downstairs to
> an "elegant" tea where the Consul entertained them with
> his whole history & the digestive processes of his domestic
> circle, wh. seem to be in a sadly disorganised condition.
> (February 17, 1890)

Half-insensible in the event, comically detached in the telling,
she removes herself even further by transforming the actual
scene into fiction, and its fainting invalid into a heroine thoroughly dead. While Henry worked at rewriting *The American*
for the stage, Alice in turn imagined a private drama of her own.
"I am working away as hard as I can to get dead as soon as possible," she wrote to William's wife in November of that same

---

dressed to my unworthiness," the line in question reads, "& I
should return them multiplied a hundredfold, were I not a
paralysed dictator."

year, "but this play of Harry's makes a sad complication, as I don't want to immerse him in a deathbed scene on his 'first night,' too much of an aesthetic incongruity!"[88]

When Henry's play opened the following January, there was in fact little danger of Alice's upstaging him. "The trouble seems to be," her letter had concluded sadly, "there isn't anything to die of. . . ." But before the year was half out, Sir Andrew had delivered his fatal diagnosis; by the time " 'The American' died an honorable death," in the words of Alice's diary for December 30, the final acts of her competing performance were well under way. "The only drawback being that it will probably be in my sleep," she had earlier written of the anticipated conclusion, "so that I shall not be one of the audience, dreadful fraud! a creature who has been denied all dramatic episodes might be allowed, I think, to 'assist' at her extinction" (September 12, 1890). Now she had been clearly granted that place in the audience: though she would literally sleep away the last hours of her life, Sir Andrew's discovery meant that she was to be cheated less than she had feared. On the morning of her death she finally lapsed into unconsciousness, but "she knew she was dying," Katharine Loring wrote of the preceding hours, "& was very happy in the knowledge."[89]

And if she could never really bear witness to the climactic moment, she could still "assist," in her terms, at the production. Clarissa-like, she had long ago begun making arrangements for her own funeral. Her body was to be cremated at nearby Woking, the ashes shipped back with Katharine to Cambridge. "Of course you know her absolute decision on this point," Henry wrote to William, "—& she had gone into all the details."[90] In addition to Katharine and Henry himself, she wished only two other mourners present at the ceremonies—her faithful English nurse and her old friend Annie Richards. ("Though almost never seeing her," Henry wrote, Annie "has shown devoted friendship to her ever since she [Annie] has been in England."[91] "It is comfortable to think of Annie back in London," had been Alice's characteristic way of putting it some three years earlier, "more attainable for funereal rites in wh. function I am always in imag-

88 AJ to AHJ (November 26 [1890]).
89 Katharine Loring to Fanny Morse (March 12 [1892?]).
90 HJ to WJ (March 8, 1892).
91 Ibid.

ination employing her."⁹²) When she had asked her dying father "what he should like to have done about his funeral," Alice recalled in her journal, he requested that the Unitarian minister "say only this, 'here lies a man who has thought all his life, that the ceremonies attending birth marriage & death were all damned nonsense,' don't let him say a word more." But "having been denied baptism by my parents, marriage by obtuse & imperceptive man," she could not quite manage her father's cheerful contempt for the rituals of dying. The events at Woking were to be her "first & last ceremony"—and silent, "uncompromising" Unitarians would be difficult to find. "In all probability an Anglican priest will supervise my obsequies," she ruefully admitted; "perhaps the impish part of me will hover about, & enjoy the fine & highly decorative rhetoric . . ." (June 24, 1891). Even if it were, as she half-suspected, "damned nonsense," her imagination would still insist on attending.

6

"The difficulty about all this dying is, that you can't tell a fellow anything about it after it has happened, so where does the fun come in?" Alice dictated in her journal on December 11, 1891. Then someone—probably Alice herself—drew a line through "after it has happened"; to "tell a fellow anything about it" was enough. Strictly speaking, the deleted words had been redundant, indeed had betrayed by their very redundancy how impossible was her desire; only after death had "happened" would she possess the requisite knowledge—when it would be, by definition, too late. But the question she allowed to stand was not merely rhetorical. If she could not record death itself, she could at least record her dying—could still have, thanks to Sir Andrew, her "fun." "It is the most supremely interesting moment in life," Alice had dictated to William the previous July, "the only one in fact, when living seems life, and I count it as the greatest good fortune to have these few months so full of interest & instruction in the knowledge of my approaching death."⁹³ "I am being ground slowly on the grim grindstone of physical pain," the last entry in her diary begins, and the formally alliterated words seem to have as much to do with energy and will as with the horrors of dissolution:

92 AJ to Sara Darwin (December 9 [1888]).
93 AJ to WJ (July 30 [1891]).

& on two nights had almost asked for K's lethal dose, but one steps hesitantly along such unaccustomed ways & endures from second to second; & I feel sure that it can't be possible but what the bewildered little hammer that keeps me going will very shortly see the decency of ending his distracted career; however this may be, physical pain however great ends in itself & falls away like dry husks from the mind, whilst moral discords & nervous horrors sear the soul. These last Katharine has completely under the control of her rhythmic hand, so I go no longer in dread. Oh the wonderful moment when I felt myself floated for the first time, into the deep sea of divine *cessation*, & saw all the dear old mysteries & miracles vanish into vapour! that first experience doesn't repeat itself, fortunately, for it might become a seduction. (March 4, 1892)

Katharine's "rhythmic hand" was employed in hypnosis, a newly discovered anodyne to which they had resorted at William's urging; that hand, or its fellow, was also engaged to the very end in taking dictation. "One of the last things she said to me, was to make a correction in the sentence of March 4th 'moral discords & nervous horrors,'" Katharine wrote when it was all over. "This dictation of March 4th was rushing about in her brain all day, & although she was very weak, & it tired her much to dictate, she could not get her head quiet until she had had it written. . . ."[94] On the afternoon of March 5, Alice composed a valedictory cable to William—whispering the words "very distinctly," Henry reported, in his ear.[95] "Tenderest love to all," the message read; "farewell am going soon."[96] "All through Saturday the 5th & even in the night," Katharine noted, "Alice was making sentences."[97] On the afternoon of Sunday the sixth, she was dead.

"Alice just passed away painless," Henry wired to Cambridge.[98] William quickly dispatched his reply—a telegram whose gothic speculations offered a fitting climax to the whole strange performance that had been his sister's dying. The psy-

94 These comments appear as a postscript to Alice's diary immediately after the March 4 entry.
95 HJ to WJ (March 5 [1892]).
96 AJ to WJ, cablegram (March 5, 1892).
97 Katharine Loring's postscript to the diary.
98 HJ to WJ, cablegram (March 6, 1892).

chologist warned his novelist brother that Alice's death might merely prove an illusion. Knowing as he did his sister's fierce will to die, he apparently feared lest her body have simply mimicked the look of the dead. "I telegraphed you this A.M. to make sure the death was not merely apparent," he later wrote, "because her neurotic temperament & chronically reduced vitality are just the field for trance-tricks to play themselves upon. . . ."[99] Henry hastened to assure him that his fears were groundless. "You wouldn't have thought your warning necessary if you had been with us, or were with us now," he wrote on March 8. "She lies as the very perfection of the image of what she had longed for years, & at the last with pathetic intensity, to be."[100] His letter crossed with another from Cambridge that was even then in the mail. "What a blessed thing to be able to say," William had already written, "*that* task is over!"[101]

99 WJ to HJ (March 7, 1892).
100 HJ to WJ (March 8, 1892).
101 WJ to HJ (March 7, 1892).

The
Letters

EDITORIAL NOTE

Notes to the letters appear at the foot of each page or at the foot of a letter that ends mid-page, keyed to names or phrases in the text that seem to call for further explanation. Space prevents full identification of a reference each time it is made; a complete note is given at the first appearance of a figure or event, and the reader who encounters an apparently mysterious allusion, especially later in the correspondence, should consult the index to help elucidate it. Not all information has proved recoverable, however; the dates and even the identities of some of the women in particular still go unrecorded. When a puzzle remains, therefore, readers should not attribute it to some missing item in their own stores of common knowledge, but to the failure of the editor, despite her best efforts, to locate the key.

For a description of the manuscripts of the letters and an account of the principles by which they were edited for this book, readers should see the Note on the Text.

THE LETTERS

....

<to Henry James, Sr. March 11, 1860>

Sunday Mch 11th

My dear Father.
We have had two dear letters from you, and find you are the
same dear old good-for-nothing home-sick papa as ever.
Willie is in a very extraordinary state of mind, composing
odes to all the family. A warlike one he addressed to Aunt
Kate, in which the hero is her husband and dies for her, and
he says, "The idea of any one dying for her"!! And he wants
mother to take them in to Mrs Thomas and Mrs Osbourn
to be read, and admired by them.
We have all come to the conclusions that he is fit
to go to the lunatic asylum, so make haste home before
such an unhappy event takes place.
We are all very well except Mrs Thomas who was not down
to dinner yesterday.
We have given up our play as it is not a pretty one and is too
hard. Good-bye. I will try and be good and sweet till you
come back, and merit the daisy curtains, and get a chance
at your dear old pate again

Your affect daughter
Alice James

hero is her husband. Mary Walsh James's younger sister Catharine Walsh (1812?–1889) had, in fact, been briefly married to a
Captain Marshall; but by the time of this letter she had quar-
reled with her husband, left him, and resumed her maiden
name. Aunt Kate spent much time living and traveling with
her sister's family.
Mrs Thomas and Mrs Osbourn. Mrs. Thomas, whom HJ remembered as a "handsome American widow" (*Notes of a Son
and Brother*, Chap. 1) and Mrs. Osbourne were both com-
patriots of the Jameses and, apparently, fellow-residents at
their Geneva hotel. Like the Jameses, they were educating
their sons at Swiss schools.

All Alice's own composition *except the first sentence. She wanted to be started.*

All Alice's . . . started. In RJ's hand.

. . . .

<to William James. October 13, 1867>

Cambridge Oct. *13th / 67*

My dearest Willy

The photographs were received a few weeks ago and gave great delight to the family. I gave one to Mary as you desired, and she was very much pleased to have it. I enclose a note from her. We have been looking quite anxiously for the last little while for a letter from you. I suppose it will be coming along soon. Mr. Holmes was here a few evenings since and said he had heard from you from Berlin. How does Berlin compare with Dresden? Has Sargy Perry arrived yet or are you still alone? A propos *of alone, Miss Mary Felton anxiously asked father the other day whether you were quite alone, when father said, yes, she exclaimed, "Oh!* what a pity!*" There is a hint for you. The little Bob left for the south week before last. We miss him very much and were very sorry to have him go back so soon, but he was crazy to get back to the farm and to work which he cannot live without. He is a most manly*

gave one to Mary. Probably AJ's friend Mary Lee, who seemed to have—as William himself put it—a *"penchant* for me." "And I dont blame her for it," he'd added (WJ to AJ, November 14, 1866).

Mr Holmes. Oliver Wendell Holmes, Jr. (1841–1935), a lifelong friend of WJ and HJ, was later to serve for thirty years (1902–1932) as associate justice of the U.S. Supreme Court.

from Berlin. For purposes at once educational and therapeutic, WJ had sailed for Germany in April 1867; he was to live and travel there until November 1868.

Sargy Perry. Thomas Sargeant Perry (1845–1928), grandson of Commodore Oliver Hazard Perry, was a friend of all the James children, especially Henry; later a scholar and man of letters, he taught language and literature at Harvard.

Mary Felton. The daughter of Cornelius Conway Felton, classical scholar and, briefly, president of Harvard College from 1860 until his death in 1862.

back to the farm . . . cannot live without. After the Civil War, AJ's younger brothers, Robertson ("the little Bob") and Garth Wilkinson ("Wilky") had purchased a cotton plantation in

fellow and is quite determined to make something of the
place. Wilky will probably come north and leave him there
alone, which will be a most excellent plan, as the plantation
is insufficient to occupy or support them both, and Bob seems
to be most decidedly the one to be left. Mr. Scott also intends
leaving so there will be quite a change. Tom Ward came in the
other evening and said that he had heard from you. He was
very pleasant, but seems most childlike, he uses words in the
most singular way. Mother asked him how he liked your
photograph, he replied that, "it was very astonishing but
looked very genial." What he meant it would be hard to know.
I have been invited by the young ladies of Cambridge to join
the "Bee". Have you the faintest idea of what the "Bee"
consists? I imagine not. It is a sewing society formed at the
beginning of the war by the girls and kept up now for the poor.
Miss Susy Dixwell is at the head of it and all the, Cambridge
young misses go, so I shall have plenty of gossip to tell you.
    Nearly everyone has got back from the country, the Nortons
and Ashburners among others. Miss S. A. and A. J. Sedgwick
dined with us a little while ago. Miss Ashburner laughed

Gordon, Florida, which they intended to work with freed black
labor. "Their object is to make a settlement of northern men
in Florida," Alice wrote to Fanny Morse in February 1866, "in
which way they think they will be doing the country a great
deal of good." The plantation project eventually failed.
Mr. Scott. Colonel Harry Scott, who joined RJ and GWJ in the
plantation venture.
Tom Ward. Thomas Wren Ward, William's fellow student at
Harvard and one of his closest friends. Tom's father was the
banker Samuel Gray Ward; his mother was Anna Hazard (Barker) Ward, whose brother, William H. Barker, had married HJ
Sr.'s sister Jeanette.
Miss Susy Dixwell. The younger sister of Fanny Dixwell, who
later became the wife of Oliver Wendell Holmes, Jr.
*the Nortons and Ashburners . . . Miss S. A. and A. J. Sedg-
wick.* In 1862 Charles Eliot Norton (1827–1908), later well
known as an author, translator, and professor of art history at
Harvard, had married Susan Ridley Sedgwick. The Ashburners
here probably include Susan Norton's two English aunts, Anne
and Grace Ashburner, who had cared for her after the death of
her parents. S. A. Sedgwick is Sara Sedgwick (1839–1902),
later Sara Darwin, Susan's younger sister as well as AJ's friend
and frequent correspondent. "A. J." Sedgwick is Arthur G.
Sedgwick (1844–1915), Susan and Sara's only brother, a lawyer

*at Arthur for sleeping so soundly, and said that the maid
whom she had left in the house had told her that her only
trouble had been all summer, that she had several times
feared that Mr. Arthur was dead. Father said that she certainly
would have had no such fears if Bob had been left under her
care, for he made such a noise in his sleep. "But she would
have been afraid that he was drunk," replies Harry, which was
rather rough upon the poor little Bob who was beside him.
Miss A. (who is the most astonishing and delightful old maid
imaginable enjoying a joke so much, especially when you
think she wont) laughed very much.*

*I will recount to you some jokelettes of the Harriette which
will probably bore you, but which at the time they were
perpetrated amused this innocent family very much. The
scene is laid in the dining-room, time, dinner.*

*Harry to the mother. "May I have some of those brown-rolls
that were left this morning at breakfast."*

*M. "Yes, certainly, but do you wish to eat them with your
soup." H. "You can't certainly expect me to minutely explain
what I intend to do with them." Laughter from the family
& pause. H. "I was coming over the bridge this afternoon and
stopped a run-away horse." You may easily imagine the shouts
of the family at this. A.K. "I hope you did not try and stop
him by the bridle." H. "Would you prefer to have me take hold
of his legs." A.K. "But you should not run after horses and stop
them." H. "Would you rather have me run before them." You
must let your imagination supply the manner of this Harry,
a good deal of eyebrow nostril and shoulder affectation. I read
to mother the other day out of the 'In General' column of the
Advertiser that there was a paper printed in Paris on some sort
of material that could be eaten after read, consequently the
contents would be well digested, whereupon mother remarks
in her charming way, "why thats very true, isn't it?" She was
also heard to say the other day that love-letters were meant
for one eye, whereupon father said that he supposed that the
other eye winked at them. The mother constantly makes these*

and journalist who later served for a number of years as assistant editor of *The Nation.*
the *Advertiser.* The *Boston Daily Advertiser* (1813–1929),
a New England newspaper which had achieved a national
reputation.

delightful remarks, but I forget them all. A Mr. J. M. Howe called here a few evenings ago, he seems a nice man quite amusing; he said that the only remedy he knew of against fleas in Florida was "to take one's wife down with you." The horrid man! There is the longest list of engagements and weddings, all the world seems to be getting married. Has mother told you of May Eustis's engagement to a Mr. Wister of Philadelphia. A very nice man, thirty-seven years old, very handsome and very nice manners they say. I am very glad that she is not going to marry an infant, which seems to be the fashion just now. George McLanahan is engaged to some one, I don't know the name. Louise Wilkinson is married. Mary McKim has just been married to a Mr. Richard Church, and Serena Mason to somebody else, also Ned Lowell engaged to a Miss Goodrich. Kitty Temple's friend Mary Hane has just been married and any amount more only I can't think of them just now. Has father told you of George Cranch's death,

May Eustis's engagement to a Mr. Wister of Philadelphia. Mary R. Eustis was a descendant of William Ellery, a signer of the Declaration of Independence for Rhode Island, and of William Ellery Channing, the abolitionist and preacher; William R. Wister was a Philadelphia lawyer. In 1898 the daughter born of this marriage, Mary Channing Wister, married her cousin Owen Wister, the future author of *The Virginian.*

Serena Mason. A Jamesian cousin on HJ Sr.'s side. In *A Small Boy and Others*, HJ reminisces about his youthful exploration of Paris with her and her three sisters.

Ned Lowell engaged to a Miss Goodrich. Edward Jackson Lowell (1845–1894), lawyer and future historian, married Mary Wolcott Goodrich in January of 1868. Mary was the daughter of author and publisher Samuel Griswold Goodrich, better known as "Peter Parley"—the pseudonym under which he and his staff wrote well over a hundred edifying books for children.

Kitty Temple's friend Mary Hane. Katharine ("Kitty") Temple was a first cousin of the younger Jameses, one of six Temple children early—and for HJ, at least, romantically—orphaned. Kitty's younger sister Minny was the inspiration for several Jamesian heroines, most notably Milly Theale in *The Wings of the Dove.* Mary Hane has not been identified.

George Cranch's death. George Cranch was the son of the painter, poet, and Unitarian minister Christopher Pease Cranch (1813–1892)—a lifelong friend of the Jameses. In 1863 Wilky had helped George obtain a commission in the Union army.

a short time since, he died of consumption. Mr. Godwin and
his daughter Minny were here last week having just returned
from Europe. Minny has improved very much having grown
very much more quiet and dignified in her manners; she
is also quite pretty in the face and in the figure; being arrayed
in a Paris gown who wouldn't have a pretty figure?
Mr. Godwin told father that his income *from the 'Evening*
Post' was seventy thousand dollars! A neat little bit, think you
not? Why don't you start a paper, and have the like? If you had
any strength of mind you would. I called with father the other
day on the Fields; after awhile father & Mrs Fields began
to dilate on the vanity of riches, when Mr Fields interrupted
by saying that for his part he thought it would be very nice
to have some "aunt around whom memory does not cluster"
die and leave one a nice little sum. He said many more funny
things and told some excellent stories. I have been lately
reading somethings of De Quincy's which I found quite
amusing for awhile, but for long rather tiresome. If you ever
read novels just get 'Madame Therèse' by Erkmann-Chatrian,
I read it the other day for the first time; it is the most
adorable little book; I like it as well as any of the others,
I think. The country is looking superbly, and we are having
the most beautiful weather. Every one says that the trees are

Mr. *Godwin.* Parke Godwin (1816–1904), author and editor,
had acquired a financial interest in the New York *Evening Post*
in 1860; the paper was then edited by his father-in-law, the
poet William Cullen Bryant. After Bryant's death in 1878,
Godwin succeeded briefly (1878–1881) to the editorship.
the Fields. James T. Fields (1817–1881), author, publisher, and
for ten years (1861–1871) editor of the *Atlantic Monthly,* and
his second wife, the author Annie Adams Fields (1834–1915).
The Fields home had become a kind of literary salon for their
fellow Bostonians.
somethings of De Quincy's. Thomas De Quincey (1785–
1859), the English author best known for his *Confessions of an
English Opium-Eater.*
'Madame Therèse' by Erkmann-Chatrian. Emile Erckmann
(1822–1899) and Alexandre Chatrian (1826–1890), both Alsatians, collaborated on a number of historical novels about the
French Revolution and the Napoleonic wars. *Madame Thérèse
ou les Volontaires de 1792,* part of a series of *Contes Nationaux,* was published in 1863.

brighter than they have been for a good many seasons,
because we have had so much rain that the leaves dry slowly.
I spent a week at the Clifton House with Aunt Kate before she
came home. We walked one day along the cliffs to Marble
Head and I found what I never before had suspected, that the
rocks on that shore are so fine, fully as bold as the Newport
rocks only without any surf, which makes a great difference.
With heaps of love from all believe me my dear Willy
                                    Your loving sister
                                    Alice James

the Clifton House. A hotel on the Massachusetts coast; the
shore to which AJ alludes is between Swampscott and Marble-
head.

. . . .

<to Annie Ashburner. September 26, 1873>
                                    Cambridge Sept. 26th / 73
My dear Nanny
    I stand convicted of every crime which you may feel pleased
to heap upon me, my conduct has been of the basest I most
readily admit, especially as I have so much to tell you of all
our wonderful adventures of the summer. To begin with
we went through with more than the usual amount of anguish
& despair last spring, to know what to do with ourselves for
the fatal months of July & August, when the family were
inspired with the bright idea of betaking themselves to the
provinces. I was sent off the first of July with Aunt Kate
as an advance guard. We joined en route *some cousins from*
New York & betook ourselves to Quebec, where we passed ten
days very pleasantly at the Misses Lane's boarding house,
wh. has lately been made famous by Mr. Howells story
of "A chance acquaintance," which perhaps you may have
read & perhaps not; if you have you will be interested
to know that I slept in the room in which "Kitty" is supposed

To Annie Ashburner. Annie Ashburner (1846–1909), whom AJ
also calls "Nanny," "Nannie," or "Nancy," was the daughter of
Mr. and Mrs. Sam Ashburner, and a cousin of the Sedgwicks.
Later widowed and settled in England, she was to remain a loyal
friend until Alice's death—and one of the four mourners
whom AJ expressly requested at her funeral.

56 LETTERS

to have dwelt, & wh. looks into the Ursuline convent. Whilst
in Quebec we went up the Saguenay, passing two most
delightful days. I don't know, but I have a vague idea that you
have done all this, but what I know you haven't done,
is, what we subsequently did, that is go down the Gulf
of St. Lawrence, & whilst I have a drop of blood in my veins
you never shall, for its an experience to which I would hardly
condemn my worst enemy. We started from Quebec in a boat
that had previously been a blockade runner. It was only
28 feet wide & there were 130 passengers on board all
Canadians who are by nature several degrees lower than the
lowest middle-class English, & art has yet done nothing for
them. My dear, we were five days & nights on board
& I am alive to tell the tale, a fact of wh. I am prouder than
of anything in my adventurous career.

We landed at Pictou a little town in Nova Scotia at 4 o'cl'ck
of a Sunday morning, in a little sail boat, it had been pouring
pitch forks all night, but fortunately held up at that moment.
There were some twenty or thirty passengers, each trying
to get ahead of the other at a certain Mrs. Taylor's who was
our only hope in the way of lodgings. We at last all met
in Mrs. T's parlor, the front door open but not a soul
up to receive us. There we sat waiting our doom, with Aunt
Kate who was our leader, flourishing very vigorously
& audibly in the face of the others a certain telegram which
she had sent & which wd. of course secure us rooms, when,
lo! a maid of all work made her appearance, saying that
there was not a room to be had in the house, telegram
or no telegram; then you should have seen the stampede
of women in water-proofs, umbrellas & bags tearing through
the desolate little town in the early dawn seeking for where
to lay their heads. We finally found a spot over a gin-shop
which had nothing in itself or its landlady, but necessity

Mr. Howells story . . . convent . . . Saguenay. Kitty Ellison,
the heroine of W. D. Howells's short novel A Chance Acquaintance (which had first appeared earlier in 1873), spends
some time in a pleasant lodging house in Quebec whose rooms
overlook the garden of an Ursuline convent. A representative
of the democratic West who hails from "Eriecreek," New York,
Kitty falls in love with an aristocratic Bostonian. The novel
opens with a journey up the Saguenay.

*to recommend it, but which turned out to be on further
acquaintance much better than it looked. We had with
us a pleasant young Englishman & his wife a Dr.
Tredell by name, who helped to beguile the day, but such a wife!
I may truly say, that never before have I seen feminine folly,
till I made her acquaintance, I hope I shan't forget all about
her before we meet, for my pen is quite unequal to the task
of doing her justice. We went from Pictou to Prince Edward's
Island which we had heard was an Earthly Paradise, but
which we found a* dirty desolate hole, *where we lived for three
nights and days over another (much more odoriferous than the
first)* gin-shop. *From this sweet spot we went to Halifax
& from there to St. John, where I met the parents who came
from Cambridge to meet us, where we stayed for four weeks
enjoying the lovely cool weather & an excellent hotel, but
little else the town being desolate & dreary to the last degree;
but notwithstanding all our hardships yr. humble servant has
flourished like a young bay-tree, & is now enjoying
an amount of strength wh. she has not known for a long time.
We had a good many laughs too over our troubles wh. I only
wish you could have shared (the laughs not the troubles).
I am afraid you have not had a very lively summer, but hope
you will go to Florence for the winter. Wm. sends his regards
& hopes he may have the pleasure of seeing you before very
long. The Ashfield summer seems to have been a success.
Charles, yr. cousin, is less attractive I think than ever. Mother
sends love to yr. mother & yr. self and wishes much that she
could see you sometimes. With remembrances to every one
believe me always*

Yr. loving friend,
Alice James

Ashfield . . . Charles, yr. cousin. Charles Eliot Norton ("yr.
cousin") kept a summer home in the village of Ashfield in
northwestern Massachusetts.

. . . .

<to Annie Ashburner. November 2, 1873>

Cambridge. Nov. 2nd / 73

*My dear Nannie
    I hope you wont be too much alarmed at the frequency
of my epistles of late, but I suppose that if I wrote every other*

day I should still get messages of reproach through Sara,
which to say nothing of their untruthful nature are
discouraging in their effect. But I shall keep on suffering with
all the rest of the world with whom virtue is the guiding
principle! I don't know what I have to tell save a thrilling
event in the family annals, in the erection of a lamp-post, for
which we have waited & petitioned the common-council for
anxiously & long & saw yesterday with breathless interest
put up. You may easily imagine our impatience for the shades
of night to fall, and our disgust when the moment came
& they didn't fall at all, but the moon rose up with
a brilliancy never before imagined in one's wildest dreams
& never a lamp was lighted that blessed night in the whole
of Cambridge. This afternoon looks equally unpromising,
there's not a cloud to be seen & the moon I suppose is making
all her preparation with the greatest satisfaction to pop
up at the earliest possible moment. Isn't it provoking! I went
up this morning to Kirkland St. but found them all flown,
to their devotions let us hope. On my way back I met Lizzie
Boott & we started off on a walk & got as far as the botanical
gardens where we collapsed on one of the green-house-steps
and baked ourselves in the sun for an hour & a most delicious
process we found it. We are having such weather as no mortal
ever saw before or as I am afraid we shall never see again, our
autumn always so fine is this year far surpassing itself. Lizzie
has been off staying in Waltham for a week or two. She told
me some gossip nothing much worth repeating, unless the
following example of the degeneracy of Boston fashion you
may find shocking, if not agreeable or valuable. The ladies
give extensively champagne parties suppers etc, & in some

Sara. Sara Sedgwick, Annie's cousin and AJ's good friend and
correspondent.
Kirkland St. The home of the Sedgwicks and their Ashburner
aunts in Cambridge.
Lizzie Boott. Elizabeth Boott (1845–1888) and her father Francis Boott (1813–1904), an amateur musician and songwriter,
were good friends of the Jameses. Though the Bootts were now
living in Cambridge, almost two decades of Lizzie's life had already been spent in Europe, where the widowed Francis had
transported his infant daughter after the death of his wife in
1847.

cases are found to partake somewhat too largely of this
agreeable mixture & consequently comport themselves
in a way hardly becoming a lady of taste. Mrs. Gordon Dexter
whether more than once or supported by some other fair ones
I know not mounted on the table & danced about holding
up her petticoats as high as you please. Is this the manners
you meet with at Tunbridge? I am afraid that when you get
back you will be quite behind the age, there's no knowing
what we may have got to then!

I don't think I told you of our going down to breakfast one
day at St. John & finding Mrs. Sparks and family arrived.
We became intimate for the first time with the former & our
vague plan of departure for the next day became in the course
of a few hours fixed as fate. Was there ever such a horror? Her
children are marvels of patience and virtue I think, & as for
the noble Pickering what can we do to testify our admiration
of his courage. The only possible explanation must be that
he is in love with Lizzie as few men are with women. They are
to be married it seems to be generally hoped in the spring.
Mrs. S. expressed herself with such admiration of you all,
especially your mother whom she considers one of the rarest
persons—"a person, Mrs. James, whose taste you can always
be sure of, you will find that her taste always agrees with your
own." I could hardly refrain from asking her if it extended,
this congeniality to collars, for if I remember rightly it seemed
to me that it took a different form in your mother's case from
what it does in Mrs. S. But don't let's say another word about
her, she seems to me to be an unholy object. After I had been
home a few weeks from the provinces, I skipped down with
Lizzie B. to Beverly to spend a few days with the Morses.
We had a very nice time. I saw no one new save Mr. Charles

Tunbridge. Annie Ashburner was now in England.
Mrs. Sparks and family . . . Pickering . . . Lizzie. Mary
Crowninshield Silsbee Sparks was the second wife and now
widow of Jared Sparks (1789–1866), editor, historian, and for-
mer president of Harvard. The "noble Pickering" was Edward
Charles Pickering (1846–1919), then professor of physics at
MIT and later an eminent astronomer, who married the
Sparkses' daughter Lizzie the following year.
the Morses. Frances ("Fanny") Rollins Morse (1850–1928), AJ's
lifelong friend and correspondent, lived with her parents.

*Jackson, by whom my affections would instantly have been
captivated had I not been told that his were already engaged
with Miss Fanny Appleton, not openly I believe as yet but
in aspiration. Isn't he lovely & hasn't he got the nicest face
& the sweetest smile you ever saw? I hope I shan't see him
again or I am afraid the illusion will be dispelled. I renewed
my acquaintance with Dr. James Putnam popularly known
as Jim. He has grown an inch or more physically & Europe has
added to his many inevitable Jackson virtues a charm
& attraction which before they possessed not, so that
he is a very pleasing object now. The contrary process seems
to have taken place unfortunately with his brother Charles,
if one can judge by merely passing him in the street, which
perhaps you may say is a superficial method of forming one's
conclusions. Its characteristic at any rate! On reading over
my letter I am somewhat struck with its disjointed nature
no two sentences apparently belonging to the other giving
a jerky character to the whole, but you who know in what
flowing numbers I can write if only I choose will forgive
me, for should I tear this up you wont get another I am afraid
you ungrateful creature for some time. Write soon & tell
me that you keep yr. spirits up & that life has some joys if not
all we shd. wish. Every one sends love to all & believe
me my dear Nannie*

*Always yr. loving
Alice James*

Mr. Charles Jackson . . . Fanny Appleton. Charles Cabot Jackson (1843–1926), a graduate of Harvard Law School and a bro-
ker, married Frances Elizabeth Appleton—a distant relative of
Longfellow's wife—in 1876. (Identification courtesy of Jean
Strouse.)

Dr. James Putnam . . . his brother Charles. James Jackson Putnam (1846–1918), a good friend of WJ and of many of the leading physicians of his time, later known for his pioneering
work in neurology; and his older brother Charles Pickering
Putnam (1844–1914), chiefly remembered for the crucial role
he played in a large number of social and charitable projects in
late nineteenth-century Boston. James's "inevitable Jackson
virtues" were presumably inherited from his grandfather,
James Jackson (1777–1867), an influential physician and professor of medicine and a popular figure in Boston, notable for
his dignified and courtly manner.

. . . .

Cambridge. Feb 1st / 74

My dear Sarakins
    I am going to please myself this morning and I trust not
seriously displease you by sending you a few lines, which
if you are merely just—a base, masculine, habit of mind, you
may take as an answer to the letter with which you were
so good as to cheer my exile, but knowing that you are
nothing if not generous, I shall live in the hope of better
things. I trust that New York is amusing you as much as it did
me, and that in spite of the ash-barrels, old shoes, hoop-skirts
and all the other various objects of art and virtue which
so richly decorate them, you find the streets sufficiently
entertaining. Aren't the women lovely creatures? I wonder
if you are ever torn by pangs of envy and cry aloud as I did,
"why am I not made as one of these!" or rather why are not
my gowns, for my features I have long since ceased
to question as the work of an inscrutable wisdom, but I can't
get reconciled to the peculiarities of my clothes, so that when
I see a maiden arrayed as I am not, I am greatly visited
by hankerings, hankerings which I am sure no woman's
breast is quite a stranger to, be she Miss Abby May herself.
    Cambridge my dear, is in one of its convulsive fits of gaiety,
for no known reason save despair at your departure
manifesting itself in hollow mirth. Last night was a ball at the
Bootts, which went off very pleasantly. We had songs from
Mr. Szimelinyi (in an arsenic green cravat) Mr. Boott and
Lizzy. I had a talk with Dr. Haagen if talk it can be called,
this is a specimen; "You knew Dr. Freund, he has lost three

as it did me. AJ had recently returned from a brief visit to
New York.
Miss Abby May herself. A relative of Louisa May Alcott and a
prominent figure in Boston reform circles, especially those
concerned with women's suffrage and education, Abigail Wil-
liams May (1829–1888) was an ardent advocate of dress reform; in 1879 she was to publish a pamphlet entitled *Dress.*
Dr. Haagen. Hermann August Hagen (1837–1893), physician,
surgeon, and leading entomologist, had come from Germany
in 1867 at the invitation of Louis Agassiz; since 1870 he had
been professor of entomology at Harvard College. The William
Jameses later named their third son Herman (1884–1885) after
him.

children!" "Impossible!" cried I, "yes" said he, and consulted
his wife in German, who turned to me and said "oh! yes, they
had four children in three years!" and thus our souls
communed for half an hour in sweet accord. Baron von
Ostensacken was presented to me and I greeted him affably
as Mr. Ostens:—(I couldn't for the life of me remember the
end of his name) which insult he revenged by turning his back
upon me after only one or two remarks, which may have been
baronial, but was certainly not gentlemanly. I don't believe
he is any more of a baron than the clerk at Tiffany's, his nose
looks at any rate as if it had come very recently into the
family (the baronetcy not the nose). You will be glad to hear
that we have excellent news of the boys Wm's fever was of the
slightest. Please give my kind regards to Mrs. & Mr. Godkin,
come back soon yr. self and believe me as ever
                                                        Yr. loving friend
                                                        Alice James
P.s. I open my letter to protest against your staying away
two or three weeks more as Theodora, who has just been
in says that you contemplate doing. We will have none of that
Miss, just you come home after a respectable fortnight, that
is quite long enough for a modest woman to stay away from
home, so we shall expect you tomorrow week at the latest.
I meant to tell you in my letter, that I had heard that Sargy
& Lilla are to be married in a month or two & to live
on no one knows what, they themselves less than any one
I fancy.
Sargy's philosophy can hardly be of the fashionable positive

Baron von Ostensacken . . . I don't believe . . . a baron. Despite AJ's skepticism, Carl Robert Romanovich von der Osten
Sacken (1828–1906) was indeed a Russian baron; he was also
an entomologist (like Hagen) and a diplomat. Having served as
secretary to the Russian legation in Washington and then consul general of Russia in New York, he was in the United States
in an unofficial capacity when he was "presented" to Alice.
Mrs. & Mr. Godkin. Edwin Lawrence Godkin (1831–1902), co-
founder and editor of *The Nation* and later editor-in-chief of
the New York *Evening Post*, and his first wife, Frances Elizabeth Foote Godkin.
Theodora. Maria Theodora Sedgwick (1851–1916), Sara's
younger sister.

*school exclusively or he would never run the risk of assuming
the entire responsibility of Lilla's solid proportions in addition
to his own six feet of muscle, on such slender expectations
as a summer to be passed in the sylvan shades of Park
Sq. in Dr. Cabot's house, which is the only tangible provision
for the future with which they seem to be provided. Isn't
it wild? I wonder what they'll make of matrimony between
them. They seem to be such an impossible couple. Lizzie
Sparkes told me yesterday that she was to be* guillotined *the
first week in March! Mind about the coming home or you'll
not find us wh. perhaps wont terrify you greatly however.*

      Lilla . . . Dr. Cabot's house. In 1874 Thomas Sargeant
("Sargy") Perry married Lilla Cabot, the daughter of Samuel
Cabot, surgeon to the Massachusetts General Hospital.

. . . .

<to Sara Sedgwick. February 16, 1874>

Cambridge. Feb. 16th 74

My dear Sara

    *Why, oh! why, dont you come? we're perishing without you!
You are the most wretched fibster, that I have met in a long
time. Didn't you promise that you were not going to stay more
than a fortnight, and here its months that you have been gone!
If you don't come soon I shall in desperation elope with the
handsome butcher-boy, with whom I have an interview every
morning for the purpose of telling him that Mrs. J. does not
wish anything. He must think that we are a curious race,
living on our own fat, unless he knows that madam, only has
him come for looks and galavants herself to market every
morning. He is very good-looking & is filled with emotion
whenever he sees me, so you had better fly to the rescue. Your
letter came & caused deep joy, it was like your excellent self
to send it to such a miserable sinner from amidst all your
superior and millionairy friends. What does a millionaire look
like? You must tell me all about them when you get home.*

    *I had a letter from Bessy Ward two days ago announcing her
engagement to a Saxon Baron Ernest von Schönberg. I think
that if I condescended to a title I should draw the line*

    Bessy Ward. The daughter of Samuel Gray and Anna Hazard
(Barker) Ward, and sister of W J's friend Tom Ward.

*at a duke. Aren't you sick of these flimsy Baron's who are
always on hand to be converted into husbands? How much
more respectable a good solid shoemaker would sound, even
better than a butcher boy! The Ward family are very much
pleased I hear, so I suppose they imagine he is a somebody.
Bessy says that it has been very hard for her to give
up America & that she "smiles through her tears", which
is a very good occupation for the present, as long as she
doesn't in the future weep through her smiles. There is nothing
new. I took tea last night at the Bootts to meet the Ned
Lowells, but only Mr. Ned appeared. He is an unattractive
youth possessed of concentrated Boston qualities, with a sad
resemblance about the back of the neck to Harry. He paid
Mr. Howells a very great compliment, by insisting
in a frenzied manner that Arbuton could not possibly have
behaved otherwise than he did & introduced the Boston
ladies, for the piazza on which they were was only three feet
wide! Poor creature! if he takes novels so hard, what does
he make of history, to say nothing of his wife's flirtations.
Your dear friend Mr. Anderson popped in to call on Lizzy;
he sat on the edge of the sofa tight and compact, like a neat
little parcel drawn up at Metcalfs and talked for about ten
minutes, and almost in the middle of a sentence, popped out
again. He treated me with his usual contempt. What is the
opposite to elective affinities? whatever it is, he is one and I'm
the other! A propos of elective affinities I have been reading
Mérimée's letters, a dozen of which are much better than
three hundred, notwithstanding their excellence of style, they*

Arbuton . . . Boston ladies . . . the piazza. Ned Lowell's frenzy
concerns the climactic scene of W. D. Howells's *A Chance
Acquaintance* (1873), in which the snobbish Miles Arbuton
fails to introduce the unstylishly dressed and "countrified"
heroine, Kitty Ellison, to two elegant Boston ladies of his acquaintance whom they happen to meet on a piazza in a village
near Quebec. Though Kitty has just agreed to accept Arbuton,
the incident on the piazza convinces her of the gulf between
them, and she rejects him.

elective affinities. An allusion to Johann Wolfgang von
Goethe's novel of erotic and spiritual attractions, *Elective Affinities* (1808). Its German title—*Die Wahlverwandtschaf-
ten*—originally had reference to chemical rather than human
"affinities."

are awfully monotonous, treating of his personal relations
alone with the fair unknown, of whether she will take a walk
with him or whether she wont, usually she wont. It is hard
to imagine how a man could write year after year
to an intelligent woman, letters which were not simply love-
letters, about such trifles. But such are men! french ones
especially I imagine, from my vast acquaintance with them,
I judge. But what a string of nonsense I have treated you
to, when I began I only meant to show you the base,
blackness of your conduct, but my usual intemperance has
as ever disgraced. Come, oh! come or you will have another
dose! What do you suppose I heard the other day? nothing less
than that those dreadful Loverings had had no end of offers!
It was insulting, but satisfactory as explaining the mystery
of why the article had been so scarce in Quincy Str, for if such
ragged growth as the Miss L——s are what's courted, its
no wonder that a rare exotic like—modesty forbids my saying
who—is left unplucked upon its stem, to reach a bloom
bordering, to put it delicately, on the full-blown. But to come
to business, A. K. says she thinks the chocolate an imposition,
if you think the same pray leave it behind, as its no sort
of consequence. I fancied it wd. be a small parcel or I shd.
never have suggested your bringing it. My paper is all gone &
you must be glad. Every one sends love & prayers that you
will soon make yr. appearance. Believe me

Ever yrs.
Alice James.

Mérimée's letters . . . the fair unknown. Lettres à une incon-
nue, the letters of the novelist, historian, and archeologist
Prosper Mérimée (1803–1870) to his "fair unknown"—Mlle
Jenny Dacquin (1811–1895), had been published the previous
year (1873). Mlle Dacquin had originally written to Mérimée
under a pseudonym, and only later did he discover her identity; though he wrote to her almost daily from 1831 until a
few days before his death, they met rarely. As AJ implies, the
correspondents do not appear to have been lovers.
those dreadful Loverings. The two daughters of Joseph Lovering (1813–1892), professor of mathematics and natural philosophy at Harvard, and his wife, the former Sarah Gray
Hawes. Though Lovering himself was generally well respected
and liked, his occasional witticisms and somewhat odd habits
made him a slightly comic figure in Cambridge circles.
. . . .

<to Annie Ashburner. October 11, 1874>

20 QUINCY ST

CAMBRIDGE

Oct 11th / 74

My dear Nancy

*I have at last returned, I hope for good, from
my wanderings, having got back day before yesterday from
Brattleboro, whither Aunt Kate and I went to pass a week
with the Bootts. We had heard that there were very good
saddle-horses to be had there, so we thought, Lizzy and I, that
it would be pleasant to verify the statement. We found that
it had some foundation in fact, but as, owing to fatigue,
weather and a strict observance of the Sabbath, I was unable
to take more than four or five rides altogether, the first two
or three being devoted to inducing the wretched stable-keeper
to give me a decent horse and an endurable saddle, & the last
two or three to developing a spirit sufficiently superior to such
trifles as legs scraped to the bone & the consciousness
of looking like an animated meal-bag to the jeering natives
of the village, the equestrian side of our expedition was not
surrounded by the glory with which my fancy had fondly
clothed it. Brattleboro itself, however, was charming
& we made acquaintance with some of the people who were
quite characters in their way. First & foremost I came near
having an offer! One old gentleman who came to see us one
evening, asked one of the ladies the next day whether she
thought Miss James wd. have him. Imagine the flutteration
within my bosom! At last I was to have the privilege
of declining matrimony & of escaping the mortification
of descending to the grave a spinster, not from choice of the
sweet lot, but from dire necessity. But, alas! no such fate for
me, the man was a wretch, it being his habit to destroy the
peace of any maiden who might come along, by this airy little
remark. My fate, which if he had only spoken I should look
upon as rapturous, is as humdrum and hopeless as ever.*

*We also consorted with some friends of the Bootts, the
Wells, who trace their descent from the English kings before
Jesus Christ. Mr. Boott questioning Anglican B. C. royalty
received for answer, "oh! you know those old northern
creatures, Fergus, Thor etc etc." Now I don't believe*

*Devonshire aristocracy can beat that! certainly you don't find
it in lodgings. I was delighted to find that you were in Devon, for if there
is an earthly paradise there it is, in my opinion. Not lodged
in Ilfracombe, however, but in Lynton, which if you haven't
been to, I shan't speak to you when you get back. Such a spot!
one can hardly believe its true at first. I have been out taking
a little walk this afternoon. I went first to see the Nortons
& then to the Sedgwicks. Theodora I found alone. Sara has
gone off to Naushon. I am so sorry that Theo. shdn't have had
an invitation too, she has been so shut up all summer & has
behaved so beautifully about it that she deserves some
amusement. But Sara is much the greater favourite of the two,
and I am afraid it will always be so. There does not seem
to be any cause for immediate anxiety from Charlemagne,
I don't think anything is going on at present.*

*I wish I had something new and exciting to tell you the only
thing of interest for us has been the birth of nephew
no. 2! Wilky's wife presented us with this addition last week.
Everything is very prosperous so far. I am so glad that
it is a boy and not a miserable girl brought into existence.*

*Harry's return has been another source of pleasure to us, but
we shan't keep him long, he already talks of spending the
winter in New York or Washington.*

*Theodora told me that they had not very good news from
yr. mother that she had some trouble in her foot. I hope that
it is all over by this time. Write soon and tell me yr. winter
plans. I have made the most virtuous ones for myself on the*

Naushon. An island off the Massachusetts coast near New
Bedford, owned by the Forbes family into which Emerson's
daughter Edith had married.

Charlemagne. AJ's ironic way of referring to Charles Eliot
Norton. Susan Sedgwick Norton had died in 1872, and the fear
that Norton would remarry one of his late wife's sisters—either Sara or Theodora—is a recurrent theme in AJ's letters
around this time.

nephew no. 2! Wilky's wife. The child, Joseph, was Wilky's
first; he and his wife, Caroline Eames Cary, had been married
the previous year. AJ's first nephew was RJ's son Edward
Holton James, born in 1873.

Harry's return. From Europe, where he had been since he had
conducted Alice and their Aunt Kate on their trip in the summer of 1872.

*score of letter writing to the world in general and to your fair
self in particular. So expect to be bored. Tea awaits
me so good-night with much love to all*

*Ever yrs
Alice James*

. . . .

<to Annie Ashburner. December 26, 1875>

Dec. 26th / 75

*My dear Nancy
    I suppose that by the time that this reaches you all your
Christmas festivities will have been almost forgotten. But
if I am too late with for a "Merry Christmas," I can surely
wish you a "Happy New Year." I only wish that I might have
some hope of seeing you before the new year has worn itself
into an old one, but if I had even a faint hope I am afraid that
it would prove so very delusive a one that I fancy I am better
off as I am, without any. I got your last letter with much
pleasure, also the Academy for wh. please thank your father
with my love. We were very glad to see the notice of Harry, its
altogether the best that he has had in any English paper.
    What sort of a Christmas have you had? it could not have
been quieter than ours. But we have had one good present
in the shape of a little niece born on the 24th making the
fourth grandchild. When I last wrote I think that father
& mother were gone West, perhaps Sara has told you about
our having had to send for them home on account of Aunt
Kate's sickness. The day I wrote to you was the first of it, I had
little notion how sick she was, thinking that it was nothing
more than an influenza. She has got well over it now
& is almost as strong as ever. I went on with her to New York
about a month ago, & stayed a few days & did my winter's*

the Academy . . . notice of Harry . . . English paper. Presumably an allusion to a favorable review by H. G. Woods of HJ's *Transatlantic Sketches* (1875) in the October 16, 1875, issue of *The Academy*. After noting that James's title implied that he was "apparently too modest to look for readers out of America," the reviewer went on to hope that his work would "have a wider impact" and to praise "the freshness and individuality of his remarks" (p. 398).
a little niece. GWJ's daughter Alice.

shopping, I shall make more of a visit later I suppose. It is too
bad that Theodoras plans should be so unsettled. I wish that
they had some one to ask them every now & then to make
a visit. I should think that staying in a boarding house with
a brother wd. be far from interesting. The journalist I believe
has finally arrived, they have been expecting him for several
days. Wm. & I were invited to dine with him on Thursday
last, but we were disappointed & I had to console myself with
Mr. Godkin & Mr. Charley Jackson, the former as uproarious
& the latter as beautiful & seductive as usual. My passion
grows, its fortunate I see him rarely for I am told that
it wd. be altogether wild in me to nourish the faintest hope,
Miss Appleton still reigning supreme over his affections. I saw
her the other day at the Morses. She does not attract me in the
least, but I am forced to confess that she is not bad-looking,
its painful, but true. I refrained from looking in the glass for
some time after I got home. Its most inconvenient
to be possessed of so tender and apparently undesired
an organ as mine. It was seriously threatened again the other
night at Ellen Gurneys dinner-table, & it was only through
immense self-control & the knowledge of his married
condition to which I couldn't shut my eyes for a minute, but
what they would open upon his stout washer-womany wife
who sat like a great sun-flower opposite me, that I preserved
any tolerable equanimity. Perhaps you will be surprised when
you hear that my charmer was Mr. Moorfield Story. I used
to know him slightly long ago but never then understood
my advantages, perhaps if I had I might have sat in the place

the journalist. Probably Arthur Sedgwick, then assistant editor of *The Nation* and living in New York.
Ellen Gurneys dinner-table. Ellen Hooper Gurney (1838–
1887), wife of Ephraim Whitman Gurney (1829–1886), professor of history at Harvard and editor of *The North American
Review.*
Mr. Moorfield Story. The lawyer Moorfield Storey (1845–
1929) later combined a very successful litigative career with a
considerably less successful one as a pamphleteer in a number
of controversial political causes, crusades against imperialism
and on behalf of blacks and American Indians among others.
His "stout washer-womany wife" was the former Gertrude
Cutts, whom he had married in 1870.

of the sun-flower! Now what under the sun did he want
to go off to Washington for that creature! its a mystery
of mysteries! But he is an adorable creature at any rate. But
to return to sense——Have you ever heard of Miss Ticknor's
society for Studies at home? If you haven't the enclosed
circular will enlighten you, & you will be edified I trust
by hearing that I have become one of the Managers. The
society has grown so much the last year that they have been
obliged to add managers, & Fanny Morse who has had
to do with it from the beginning came out the other day
& said that I must be one of them, so after violently declining
I finally meekly succumbed. I am with Miss Katharine Loring
& have charge of the historical young women. I think I shall
enjoy it & I know it will do me lots of good. Don't you want
to become one of my students? I will write you the wisest
of letters about any period of the world you choose. You can
laugh and think me as much of a humbug as you choose, you
can't do so more than I have myself. My work has not fully
begun till the first of January when I shall have about twenty
letters pouring in from all parts of the union. Some of them
are very entertaining & some very poor, but the best of the
joke is that in June the students come to Boston, those that
are able, & one has to go and be introduced at a yearly
meeting, don't you think they will be impressed when they
see me & Sally Russell. You must treat me mercifully when

Miss Ticknor's society for Studies at home. The Society to Encourage Studies at Home, founded in 1873 by Anna Eliot Ticknor, met regularly in the library of the Amory-Ticknor house
at No. 9 Park Street in Boston. Writing letters on various intellectual subjects and recommending further reading, the female members of the society ran what were in effect charitable
correspondence courses for women all over the country.
Miss Katharine Loring. Katharine Peabody Loring (1849–
1943), later Alice's closest friend and companion. In a letter to
Fanny Morse after Alice's death, Katharine herself dated their
friendship from December 17, 1873, when the two women
met at a lunch given by Fanny—"& from the moment of that
festivity is dated the great happiness of my life." "It is an anniversary which we always kept unknown to any," Katharine
wrote nineteen years to the day after the event; "but I feel that
now it would be a joy to thank you for it" (Schlesinger).
Sally Russell. Sarah ("Sally") Russell, daughter of George and

you write on the subject. I told Sara the other day in fear
& trembling.
Did you hear through Kirkland St. of Mrs. Greenough's
receptions? Well Mrs. J. has been inspired to have some too,
so she is going to be at home on Thursday evenings in January,
I wish you would look in upon us on one evening at least.
I hope they will be successfull, I am sure. If they are I suppose
we shall have to have them every year. They are to be very
informal & sociable. I have it quite on my mind to tell you
that I have seen Miss Louise Minot several times lately
& have got to like her very much better than I did at first one
gets used to her absurdities. I have also become a bosom
friend of Lillian Horsford at whom we used both to rail, she
is a most excellent creature. I am dying to know who the
mysterious man is whom you allude to in yr. last, the ex-lover
of Sara. Do tell me. I am so glad to send this to London I like
much better to think of you there than in the country
notwithstanding the fogs & the smoke. Have you as good
lodgings as last winter. Write soon & believe me

                                                 Always
                                              Yr. loving
                                                   A.J.

Sarah (Shaw) Russell, and later the wife of James Barr Ames
(1846–1910), who as professor and then dean of Harvard Law
School substantially helped to shape twentieth-century meth-
ods of legal education.
Mrs. Greenough's receptions. Probably an allusion to Frances
(Boott) Greenough, Frank Boott's sister, the wife of architect
and painter Henry Greenough (1807–1883), and sister-in-law
of the noted sculptor Horatio Greenough (1805–1852).
Lillian Horsford . . . we used both to rail. In an earlier letter to
Annie (November 7 [1874]), AJ reported that she had "cut"
Annie out entirely with one of her "admirers"—Lillian Horsford: "such kissing & hugging & general gushing as goes on
between us, you never saw. She is an excellent girl but sadly
wanting in the power of perceiving that her affections are not
as vehemently responded to as she imagines, an amiable weakness however!" (National). At one time the president of the
"Bee" to which AJ belonged, Lillian Horsford later married
William Gilson Farlow (1844–1919), professor of botany at
Harvard.

. . . .

                    20 QUINCY ST
                    CAMBRIDGE

                                           April 12th '76
My dear Nancy
    It seems to me that it is an age since we communed one
with the other. How does it strike thee! I am getting to feel
as if you had turned into a regular British maiden & to fear
that you are growing to despise yr. humble American friend.
If such be the case, pray oh! pray never let me know, for
it wd. afflict me deeply, my sentiments for thee, being
unalterable! How strange it will be after all these years
to meet & have a regular talk once more, such as we were
wont to indulge in on those Sunday afternoons when you used
to come & sit with me whilst I lay on the bed. I do not pine
for the lyings on the bed, but I must say that an occasional
confabulation wd. be refreshing to the soul. I have just been
having one of an hour & half with Lizzy Boott who as you
may have heard is off once more in a month for Europe.
We shall miss them greatly, Mr. B. especially, who keeps one
in a continual state of irritation either of pleasure
or displeasure one hardly knows wh. predominates.
He is more of a child than most infants of six, but then
he is very nice too. He is so handsome & frank & honest that
one can't but forgive him all his absurdities till the next time
he provokes you, when you make up yr. mind that you will
never speak to him again. Lizzy hopes to study with Couture
in Paris. I wish that her work wd. come to more than it does.
She gives so much time to it & it seems so the main interest
in life for her that I am afraid that as yrs. go on & it comes
to nothing more decidedly good that she will be disappointed.
Feminine art as long as it only remains a resource is very
good but when it is an end its rather a broken reed.
Matrimony seems the only successful occupation that
a woman can undertake. This reminds me of the most idiotic

> *Couture in Paris.* Thomas Couture (1815–1879), the French
> academic painter of portraits and historical subjects, had ac-
> quired an especially strong reputation as a teacher, numbering
> among his pupils Fantin-Latour, Manet, and Puvis de Cha-
> vannes. Lizzie did, in fact, study with him for several years.

*conversation I had the other evening with Miss Jane Norton
with whom I dined at Mr. Godkin's. She said that she thought
all these Boston women instead of devoting themselves
to painting, clubs, societies etc. ought to stay at home
in a constant state of matrimonial expectation. They were all
so happy together that men said to themselves oh! she's
so happy we wont marry her! wh. was a new view that men
were attracted by depressed & gloomy females, & also that
they generally married them from compassion. She also
abused their habit of wearing water-proofs—her own gown
as she was speaking was of so hideous a description that
I shd. have been only too thankful if I had only had a water
proof to cover her up with. Whether it was all palaver
to please Mr G. I do not know but whatever it was it was
awfully foolish. Don't you think its despicable for women
to run each other down before men? I always have thought
it the shabbiest sort of sycophancy. But to turn to a pleasanter
subject I have just got the most enthusiastic letter from Fanny
Morse announcing Bessy Lee's engagement to Dr. Fred
Shattuck. There has been lots of talk about her & Ned Lowell,
who there seems to be little doubt wanted to marry her. The
Frank Lee's started the business & now she has had a great
triumph in taking them entirely by surprise. They or none
of her family expecting it. It seems that eight yrs. ago when
Bessy was abroad with Mrs. Edward Perkins, Mrs. P. when*

Miss Jane Norton. The older sister (1824–1877) of Charles
Eliot Norton. Neither she nor their younger sister Grace
(1834–1926), HJ's lifelong friend and correspondent, ever
married.
*Bessy Lee's engagement to Dr. Fred Shattuck . . . talk about
her & Ned Lowell.* Elizabeth Perkins Lee, the daughter of Henry Lee of Brookline, married Dr. Frederick Cheever Shattuck
(1847–1929) the following June. Shattuck, a very fine diag-
nostician, was later (1888) named James Jackson Professor of
Clinical Medicine at Harvard. The "talk" about Bessy and Ned
Lowell was presumably occasioned by the death of the latter's
first wife in 1874; Lowell remarried in 1877.
Mrs. Edward Perkins. The former Jane Sedgwick Watson, now
married to the Boston lawyer Edward Perkins. AJ had been
much less enthusiastic about the announcement of Jenny Watson's engagement than she was now about Bessy Lee's: "Is it
not funny, he is more than five years younger," she had written
to Fanny Morse at the time; "can you possibly imagine marry-

*in England wanted to go into retreat & she left Bessy with Mrs
Shattuck & her daughter & Dr. Fred. who were there at the
same time. The impression was then made upon the youth
who has been constant ever since, but not in circumstances
to declare himself. The moment has now come & all the
world seems delighted. She is too pretty & attractive
a creature to be unmarried & beside she wd. have
no meaning as an old maid. Don't you love to hear
of successful engagements, it always sends a thrill of joy thro'
me, altho' my own turn I am afraid will never come on this
side of the grave. I am deeply hurt at yr. ridicule
of my professorial character I assure you it is not a thing
to be laughed at some day you may be only too happy to sit
at my feet. Theo. dined here yesterday. Her visit to N.Y. has
worked a marvellous transformation she is as cheerful as she
used to be before Charlemagne exhausted all her vitality.
I only wish she might permanently keep house for the
journalist I think that she wd. be quite happy if she
cd. & then I think N.Y. a much healthier atmosphere for her
than this. For she is not an intellectual being & it does not
agree with any one to try to be what they are not. All fears
from Charles with regard to her are quite over we all think
I am only sorry that I shd. have communicated them to you.
Sara is still in N.Y. we miss her awfully. What joy
it wd. be to have her engaged wdn't it. This is a horribly
shabby letter but if I don't send it I know not when I can
write again so here goes*

Ever yrs. A. James

ing a boy so much younger than yourself? It would not be so
strange if Ned Perkins was not so immature, but he always
seemed to me to be a perfect infant" (July 22 [1866?]).

. . . .

<to Annie Ashburner. February 28, 1877>

*Cambridge
Feb. 28th '77*

My dear Nancy

    *I was delighted to get yr. last letter & to hear that you had
seen the young Henry. A day or two after yrs. came one from
him telling how much he had enjoyed seeing you & how*

friendly & pleasant you had all been. I cannot tell you how
strange it seems to me to hear of yr. being homesick for these
barren shores. I should be ashamed to have you know how
I long for some of that picturesqueness & beauty on the face
of nature, in wh. you are perpetually wallowing.
I am frightened sometimes when I suddenly become
conscious of how constantly I dwell in the memory of that
summer I spent abroad. I suppose, however, that you will say
with Lizzy Boott, that man liveth for people & not things,
& that you are not pining for the rocks, boards & wooden
shanties that so plentifully bestrew this blessed land. But for
its delectable natives, who, to be sure, are excellent creatures,
but then there are not more than half-a-dozen whom
it wd. cost one much of a pang never to see again but then,
again, you will say, that these half-a-dozen make up life
& that without them beautiful scenery nourisheth not the
soul. But is there not some one young woman with whom you
can commune? What & where are the maidens, to whom
I hear constant reference made in Kirkland St., as very
attractive, whose names I know not, but I think they are
nieces of Miss Travers? Are they not to be consorted with?
or mayhap is my Nancy difficult to suit? Would you like
to know what would fulfill, at the present moment,
my highest ideal of earthly happiness?——Nothing more than
to be driving thro' the streets of London town, with thee
by my side, in a hansom-cab! Now, this consummation
of bliss, with the exception of one trifling element,
is constantly attainable by you—so why, oh! why, are you not
happy? It can't be possible that the absence of the few
molecules, which go to make up the person of yr. humble
servant, shd. poison all yr. joy. I am too modest to think that!
Talking of friends I have had it on my mind to tell you several
times how much I am getting to like yr. ancient crony Mrs.
Cora Peabody. I have seen her at the Bee lately & have had
long talks with her. You know we always have a fruitful
& most harmonious theme in thee—comingling our sorrow
for your absence, our hopes of yr. return & our joy

that summer I spent abroad. The summer of 1872, when AJ___
traveled in Europe with HJ and their Aunt Kate.

in yr. virtues. I have never met her husband, but I think she seems to be thoroughly married to him. He shines through much of her talk. They have both behaved very nicely *to a friend of ours, who has lately had a very disagreeable experience thro' a busy-body of a mischief-maker. As the mischief was* a propos *of Mr. P. he took pains to relieve the mind of our innocent friend & did it very nicely as did also his wife. All this I need hard say is, of course, strictly private.*

I wish that you had some work to do that amused you half as much as my society work does me. I suppose it seems to you like an awful humbug, but it is not half so much so as it seems, & I in attempting to teach history *am not half the fool that I look. You may laugh as much as you please, but I am nevertheless speaking the truth. In the first place we attempt very little, & the little we do attempt we entirely accomplish, that is so far as our own part of the business goes. You see it can do very little harm to a poor uneducated maiden in the wilds of California, Kansas, Missouri Michigan Kentucky Florida Iowa & Illinois (I have students in all those states) who has never seen but half-a-dozen books in her life, to get a letter once a month from a semi-educated being in Boston who recommends & sends her good books to read & who has a very beneficial effect upon her spelling.* We who have had all our lives more books than we know what to do with can't conceive of the feeling that people have for them who have been shut out from them always. They look upon them as something sacred apparently, & some of the letters I get are most touching, girls who write to say that they have longed always for just such help & never hoped to get it, & the difficulties that they will overcome to join the society are incredible. Now this is the sort of being that we want to help & that we do help, so I do not see that there can possibly be any harm in it, if we are willing to take the*

Mrs. Cora Peabody . . . her husband. Cora (Weld) Peabody was the wife of Francis Greenwood Peabody (1847–1936), then minister of the First Parish Church (Unitarian) in Cambridge and later professor of theology and dean of the Divinity School at Harvard; Peabody's interest in nineteenth-century German religious thought and in the question of Christian social ethics significantly influenced the course of twentieth-century American theology.

*trouble, & it is a good deal, I have to write between thirty
& forty letters every month, but I have nought else
of importance to do. Perhaps you may wonder at my sudden
onslaught upon yr. innocent self, but I feared it must seem
very silly to you, & as it is what I care most about just now,
I did not want you to judge it without a hearing. My paper
is gone, so fare thee well & write often.*

Ever yr. loving
A. J——

** Mind I don't say grammar, so you needn't laugh at my hers
& theirs being somewhat mixed.*

> my hers & theirs . . . mixed. The sentence to which this note
> is attached originally read in part: "You see it can do very little
> harm to a poor uneducated maiden . . . who have never seen
> but half-a-dozen books in their life, to get a letter once a
> month from a semi-educated being in Boston who recom-
> mends & sends them good books to read & who has a very
> beneficial effect upon their spelling." AJ crossed out and cor-
> rected the erroneous plurals and then added her self-conscious
> note. The confusion was presumably prompted by the long
> string of states and the parenthetical "students" who inter-
> vene between the singular "maiden" and the clause that modi-
> fies her.

. . . .

<to Frances Rollins Morse. November 25, 1878>

Cambridge
Nov. 25th '78

*How can I thank you, my dearest Fanny, for all your
goodness to me this summer?——It seems absurdly
presumptuous in this little sheet to think that it is competent
to navigate the seas burdened with such a weight of gratitude
as it must carry. Your letters have been most delightful and
I do not know what I have done to deserve them in such
bountiful measure when your time must be so constantly
filled up, pray never write when it is a tax. I am afraid that
you may think that this is all very well if I had only said
it some months ago, but it is only within a short time that
I have begun to write letters and I find that I have to pay
my debts much more slowly than I want to, for my friends
have all been so kind that they have greatly accumulated
during my long idleness.*

*I am very glad to hear that Mary is able to go about a little
in Paris, I have been so sorry that she should have been
so shut up through the summer & losing so many of the
beautiful sights that you were all enjoying. But how much
I envy her!—convalescence in Europe seems such an easy
process, where there are so many helps on every hand. When
one can only take a passive part in life, the bare, crude,
blankness of nature here with nothing to call one out of one's
self preys upon the soul, and makes the process of getting well
a task and not a pleasure. But I hope that this does not sound
like a lament over my own circumstances, for, I assure you,
I am no longer an object of compassion. I shall have to admit,
however, that I was pretty wretched through the summer
& gave my poor family an immense amount of trouble, but
for the last couple of months I have been learning to behave
myself better & better all the time. My physical sufferings
would have given me no concern, but my patience, courage
& self-control all seemed to leave me like a flash & I was left
high and dry. For a young woman who not only likes
to manage herself but the rest of the world too, such a moral
prostration taxed my common sense a good deal. But,
I suppose I needed the lesson greatly and I only hope that
it will bear some of the fruits that it ought.
   Why, my dear Fanny, have you never congratulated me upon
the great joy that has been brought into life by William's
marriage? A happiness which grows day by day as we get
to know our dear Alice better. How William can have been
so fortunate a man, we cannot any of us understand, and
he himself less than the rest of us. She is a truly lovely being
so sweet and gentle & then with so much intelligence besides.
I do not believe there ever was a marriage that gave so much
satisfaction as this, to one side of a house at any rate. It was*

Mary. Mary Morse, Fanny's sister.
William's marriage . . . our dear Alice. On July 10, 1878,
William James had married Alice Howe Gibbens (1849–1922),
the schoolteacher daughter of Dr. Daniel Lewis Gibbens and
Elizabeth Putnam Webb. Despite AJ's tone here, Fanny's silence may have been prompted by the fact that the summer of
WJ's marriage coincided with the summer of AJ's most devastating breakdown—a crisis so severe that she was apparently
unable to attend the wedding.

entered into too by both of them so seriously and deliberately
that I cannot but feel that the years will justify them. They
have rooms very near us in Harvard St—— so that they are
constantly with us & a little call upon them makes
a delightful stroll at dusk.

A propos of marriages of a happy description, I have
so often wanted to tell you, of how much I am getting to like
Margaret Warner. I have seen a great deal of her this autumn,
as she is very fond of driving & is always a willing
companion. Her intelligence & sense make her more & more
estimable the better you know her, and then she is so very
entertaining. Her cheerfulness & happy way of taking life,
must make her an invaluable mate for a solemn being like
Mr. Warner.

We were all more than pleased with Mr. Darwin, and think
that Sara has had most uncommon good-luck in her
matrimonial venture. Her visit, however, was a great
disappointment for she looked so wretchedly forlorn
& unhappy at first that one did not know what to make
of it. I suppose the truth is that we have taken Sara's troubles
too hard in the past & that they were always physical & not
moral. But I cannot take up the burden again, and lament
with the others over the "dulness of Sara's neighborhood," for

*Margaret Warner . . . an invaluable mate for a solemn being
like Mr. Warner.* Margaret Storer, the daughter of Robert B. and
Sarah (Hoar) Storer, had married the lawyer Joseph Banges
Warner (1848–1923) in 1876. Warner's solemnity is perhaps
best illustrated by "the most Boston arrangement," as AJ had
termed it in a letter to Annie Ashburner, through which he
courted his future wife: "What do you suppose they do? why,
they read Constitutional History & meet once a week to dis-
cuss it! Doesn't it savour of the soil, if it had been any thing
but Constitutional one cd. conceive of it, but thus are the
youths & maidens made in these latitudes!" (February 11,
1874) (National). Warner frequently acted as lawyer for the
Jameses, later taking an active part in the management of
Alice's small estate and serving (with Katharine Loring) as ex-
ecutor of her will.

Mr. Darwin . . . her matrimonial venture. On a journey to England in 1877, Sara Sedgwick had met and married the banker
William E. Darwin, Charles Darwin's eldest son. "She is in a
densely English milieu," Henry wrote to William, "and has a
densely English husband" (January 28, 1878).

I cannot, just now, at any rate, forgive her for not being able
to make some enthusiastic expression about her delightful
husband, for how is existence possible unless we resolutely
make the most of all our blessings. I am afraid that this may
sound very brutal to you but it was such a disappointment
to find that she was not doing her best. But how wrong
it is to judge other people by our own foolish little standard.
That is what you don't do. Pray give a great deal of love
to your father mother & Mary. I hope it wont have
to be so long again before I write to you.

As always

Yr. loving

A. J.

. . . .

<to Sara Sedgwick Darwin. August 9, 1879>

Cambridge

August 9th '79

My dear Sara

I have two very agreeable letters to acknowledge and thank
you for. For not having done so before I have no excuse to offer
save that natural depravity with which you have been so long
familiar. I have been very glad to hear from time to time that
you are feeling somewhat stronger, a strength which I trust
will continue to increase uninterruptedly, for ill-health though
not an exceptional or tragic fate inevitably brings a certain
monotony into the lives of its victims which makes them
rather skeptical of the much talked of and apparently much
believed in joy of mere existence. But your life now is so full
of new joys & interests that an occasional head-ache or a little
graceful languor is merely a decent tribute which you ought
willingly to pay to your mortal state and single sisters.

If all that the newspapers say is true the summer has not
gone as pleasantly with you as with us, for with the exception
of two or three hot spells the weather has been deliciously
cool & the frequent showers have kept the grass & trees
as green as possible.

The first of July I made a bold push and started off with
Katharine Loring for the Adirondacks to try William's
panacea for all earthly ills the Putnam shanty. We had meant

the Putnam shanty. An old farmhouse in the Keene Valley of

*to spend a month but I found that the air did not suit
me at all so we left at the end of a fortnight, having found
that the bosom of nature was just about as much of a humbug
as I always knew it was. You will never find me being taken
in again by any of her snobbish votaries who are half of them
only too craven to say how squalid it all is. We made a very
thorough trial for between ourselves the shanty lacks nothing
in the way of discomfort and is no doubt after camping the
next worst thing. We stumbled gracefully over the stones
in the brook and K. bathed therein, but I assure you that for
purposes of cutaneous refreshment a tub in the hand is worth
fifty brooks in the bush. We perched ourselves on the sharpest
stones we could find and religiously spent endless hours
in listening to the babbling water, the gentle hum of the
musquito, giving joy untold to the sportive midge who found
me quite the loveliest production civilization had as yet sent
to him. The beauty of the sylvan scenes was sadly marred
by the excellent but prosaic K. who would insist upon
inserting a hideous rubber blanket between my fair form
& all the mossy logs upon which I wished to extend it thereby
putting a cruel barrier between me and all the dear little
crawlers I had come so far to feel and who would no doubt
have found me as delectable & succulent a feast as did their
wingèd brethren. We had the shanty fortunately all
to ourselves and the only romance in the situation was
at night when we sat by our bonfire the woods all round
us and no one else within a mile, save some lively cows who
in the middle of the night with that unreasonableness
characteristic of their sex would charge the shanty with their
horns driving K. to her revolver & me under the bed. But this
joy was soon denied to us for a male protector presented
himself in the person of the virtuous Dr. Charles Putnam who
stayed a few days. He ate and consorted with us through the
day but when the deeper shades of night fell he with great and
unexpected propriety betook himself to the other house. It just
occurs to me that perhaps those new friends of yours*

New York, which WJ and his friends Henry Bowditch and
James Putnam jointly purchased and converted into a vacation
retreat. The William Jameses spent their honeymoon there in
the summer of 1878.

in Basset, for whom you have so easily abandoned the old,
might be shocked to hear of two virgins of thirty summers
living alone in the woods with a bachelor, but I think if they
were to see the piety of his mouth his virtuous spectacles and
the general maiden-aunt like turn of his figure the veriest prig
of them all would fall back abashed. Our food was sent
to us from the other house under the auspices of "Si Ware, the
gentleman-cook, & a hired girl," which shows you that the
same inequality between the sexes exists in the wilderness
as that which disgraces the effete civilizations to which you
so passionately cling. We were not so well off as we should
have been had we had Hat Shaw the factotum of last year
to look after us. She was a delightful creature. She had a sister
who much to her disgust had aspirations after "culture"
& having been through the High School wanted to go to the
Normal School. Hat got Katharine L. to examine & discourage
her for she said that it made no sort of difference after you
were married whether you were a "lady-graduate" or not. The
girl turned out to be a semi-idiot and has since sought refuge
in matrimony—like yourself.

   I wish you could know Katharine Loring, she is a most
wonderful being. She has all the mere brute superiority which
distinguishes man from woman combined with all the
distinctively feminine virtues. There is nothing she cannot
do from hewing wood & drawing water to driving run-away
horses & educating all the women in North America.

   But how mercilessly I am running all about my own affairs
without telling you anything about any one else, but you
know at this season we are very much divorced from the rest
of the world, so that I have absolutely no news to give you.
I had a very kind invitation from Nanny the other day
to make her a visit. I was so sorry to miss her when she was
in town. I am delighted to hear that she has got back her old
life and spirits and that she is no longer the pale shadow
of her former self that she was when she was here last.

   William and his family are off at the White Mountains.
Alice is very well & the infant is a dear little man though
I am sorry to say he is entering life through a good many

Basset. A residential suburb of Southampton, the home to
which William Darwin had brought his new wife.

stomachic tribulations, but those will pass in a few months
I suppose.
   If Miss Ashburner is with you pray give her my love
& to Mr. Darwin my kindest regards. I only wish that I were
going to have the pleasure of making his acquaintance this
autumn, for I feel as if I had got a very indistinct glimpse
of him through the maze of wretched feelings in which I was
sunk last autumn. Father & Mother join me in a great deal
of love to yourself dear Sara & believe me
                                        Always yours very affectly
                                                 Alice James.
. . . .
<to Frances Rollins Morse. October 7, 1879>
                                              Cambridge Oct. 7th '79
My dear Fanny
   I had a dream the other night at once amusing and
distressing in which your Mother came into the room & said,
with wrath and indignation in her face and voice, that you
must not write to me again until I had answered your letters
that my conduct was past forgiveness, which shows you that
I am haunted with remorse by night as well as by day for the
evil of my ways. But notwithstanding that appearances are
so much against me I am deeply grateful for your letters
which always give so much pleasure though I have one fault
to find with them, that you devote yourself too exclusively
to what you are seeing and say nothing of what you are feeling
& being. If you would apply your admirable literary skill
to a few physiological and psychological details your letters
would be perfect. I should also like to have a little light
thrown upon your plans which in my mind are still shrouded
in mystery for you seem to be taking it very coolly for granted
that we are all going to give our consent to your staying away
indefinitely. You will please to remember that when you went
away this autumn was to be the extent of your tether.
   Your last letter reached me at Cotuit whither I had gone
to spend ten days with the ever faithful Katharine, and
a delightful ten days they were, we should greatly have liked
to have made them twenty but K. had an engagement which
obliged us to leave. It was doubly pleasant to hear from you
in such a charming spot and to have such good news of dear
Lucy and Lizzy, the latter of whom we learn from Mr. Boott

you must have since seen in Munich. What is Duveneck doing for her?

I found on getting home from Cotuit a volume addressed in your hand-writing by an author to me unknown. Many thanks for it though I have not been able yet to read it, but I suppose it must be something you have been enjoying and that I have got a treat before me. And now I have something else to thank you for and that is the very pretty little sacque you sent the baby. Alice was going to write you a letter of thanks but I knowing she was unfit told her that I would tell you how pleased and grateful she was, but I would not have her know how tardy I had been in giving you her very grateful message. The sacque was characteristically pretty and the little man has already found it serviceable. Alice got up rather slowly from her illness & is still not as strong as she ought to be for the baby has given her rather an anxious summer owing to the unsatisfactory state of his little stomach which gives him much tribulation. The last few weeks he has picked up very much and seems much better. He is a dear little soul and we have a delightful visit from him every day, the day seems quite lost if we don't see him. We have no domestic news, we are all well, Father unusually so. I am growing stronger all the time though I cannot do much or walk much yet. I was a good deal knocked up the first of the summer by a crazy expedition to the Adirondacs, a place only fit for the most robust in health to whom perpetual tramping is possible, but the last place for a degenerate being like me who needs to spend most of her time in padded seclusion. I am very glad however now that I went & have been consoled for all disappointments by the revelation of Katharine Lorings virtues whose depths I had thought I had sounded long ago but I found that I had only stirred the surface thereof. She is a phenomenal being and no one knows what she has been & done for me these trying months I have been through.

Our great interest of course is in watching the European

Duveneck. Lizzie Boott was now studying painting with the American expatriate Frank Duveneck (1848–1919); they later married.

the baby. WJ's first child, Henry ("Harry"), had been born May 18, 1879.

*news. The spectacle of poor England's ignominy is truly
a melancholy one it seems almost as if her sun might have
set. Did you see the question of the French paper asking
whether Miss Braddon and Ouida were not to be in the next
Cabinet?
Have you read such a pretty story "Cousins" by the author
of "Mr. Smith?" If you have not I should think that it would
be a delightful book to read aloud. The little brain that I ever
had has all run utterly to waste the last two years, as I spend
my time reading the trashiest of novels. I hope when the cool
weather comes to be able to make a reformation but I doubt
my success.
Pray give a great deal of love to all your circle, and
remember that though I do not write I think of you all the
time.*

> *Believe me my dearest Fanny
> Always your loving
> A. J——*

*poor England's ignominy . . . Miss Braddon and Ouida . . . in
the next Cabinet.* The news from Europe concerned troubles
in Afghanistan, where the murder early in September of the
British envoy and his escort had recently prompted an invasion of British troops. The invasion was not going well, pros-
pects for internal stability in Afghanistan looked poor, and the
Liberal opposition at home was blaming the interventionist
policies of the prime minister, Lord Beaconsfield (Benjamin
Disraeli) and the viceroy of India, Lord Lytton.
    The French newspaper's sarcasm about the popular British
novelists Mary Elizabeth Braddon (1837–1915) and "Ouida"
(the pseudonym of Marie Louise de la Ramée [1839–1908])
was an allusion, as *The Nation* reported, "to the rôle which
two 'second-rate novelists' (Lord Beaconsfield and Lytton)
have played in the catastrophe"—though both the French paper and *The Nation* seem to have confused Lord Lytton, the
viceroy who was also a poet (1831–1891), with Bulwer-Lytton,
his novelist father (1803–1873). See *The Nation* for October 2,
1879, p. 217.
"Cousins" by the author of "Mr. Smith." Novels by the popular Scottish-born novelist Mrs. Lucy Bethia (Colquhoun) Wal-
ford (1845–1915). *Cousins* had just appeared; the very successful *Mr. Smith, a part of his life,* which had been published in
1875, was reputed to number Queen Victoria among its many
fans.

. . . .

My dear Fanny

*I told you the other day that I had got your sweet note, but
it did not seem an appropriate moment to add that it had for
me a melancholy side in that it revealed what a burden I had
been upon your friendly spirit all summer. Pray do not let this
be so for I assure you I have not more to do than I can
manage—now that the moves are all over & this little box
is pretty much in order the paddling of the domestic canoe
through the placid waters of Mt. Vernon St—will be child's
play.*

*The last seven months have brought such changes
in so many ways & to me so many new responsibilities that
I feel at times that I may not be equal to them, but I find
I am from day to day & I try to keep in mind as much
as possible the invaluable thought that one has only to live
one day at a time & that all the vague terrors of the future
vanish as the future at every moment becomes the present.
I used to think that I loved my dear Mother & knew her
burdens, but I find I only knew half them, & that in losing her
I am only nearer to her than I ever was before; it is such
a happy thought that her dear, tired body is at rest & that the
blessed memory of her beautifull spirit will never grow dim.
Remember dearest Fanny that if ever I want anything that you
can do, I never should hesitate for a minute to ask your help.
So do not let me prey upon your mind.*

Always yr. loving

A.J.

Sept 11th

the moves are all over. After the death of her mother, AJ and
her father moved from the old house in Quincy Street, Cambridge, to a smaller one at 131 Mt. Vernon Street, Boston, then
spent several months of the summer at a cottage in Manchester, Massachusetts. They had now returned to Mt. Vernon
Street.

. . . .

Wednesday
20th

My darling Harry
   Darling Father's weary longings were all happily ended
on Monday at 3 P.M. *the last words on his lips being "There*
is My Mary!" For the last 2 hrs. he had said perpetually
"my Mary." He had no suffering but we were devoutly
thankfull when the rest came to him, he so longed to go, the
last thing he said before he lost consciousness was,
"I am going with great joy!"
   The end of life had come for him ⅋ he went ⅋ I am sure
you will feel as thankfull as I do that the weary burden of life
is over for him. I have no terrors for the future for I know
I shall have strength to meet all that is in store for me, with
a heart-full of love ⅋ counting the minutes till you get here.
                                            Always yr. devoted A——
   The funeral is to be tomorrow Thursday 20th at 11 A.M.
There seemed no use in waiting for you the uncertainty was
so great——

   Monday at 3 P.M. HJ Sr. died December 18, 1882.
   Thursday 20th at 11 A.M. Thursday was in fact the 21st, as the
   dating of Alice's own letter indicates.

. . . .

<to Anna Hazard (Barker) Ward. January 7, 1883>

131 Mt Vernon St
Jan 7th

My dear Mrs. Ward
   How could you for a moment think that your affectionate
sympathy could seem to us an intrusion? I have learnt this
last year, what I little suspected before how infinitely
to be valued any human sympathy is, even from mere
acquaintances, at these times, how much more therefore
to be prized is yours bound up with all those precious, never
to be forgotten memories of the past, all that is left to us now
of our dear Father ⅋ Mother. All the affection which you
express for dear Father I am sure he fully returned; he had the
greatest pleasure a couple of months ago in hearing all about
you from Mrs. Storer, who came to see him shortly after her
return from Clifton.

His death was no surprise & no shock to us for ever since
dear Mother went we looked for it at any moment & we are
all only too thankfull that his weary time of waiting was
no longer & that their good souls are forever reunited. He was
ill just a month & had absolutely no suffering but that
of weakness and exhaustion at the very end. There were
no signs of disease about him of any sort, it was simply that
the end of life had come for him & his body knowing
it resolutely refused food so that he gradually sank away.
A happier or more beautifull death it would be impossible
to imagine & what is so precious to us his children, is its
perfect consistency with all that he has thought & said
& lived so that by the manner of his death his life's work was
consummated actually showing to us that life not death had
come to him.

Our dear home is gone from us & a new leaf in life will
have to be turned by us, but how blessed is our lot with its
priceless memories! & I have no fear but that the burthen
of loneliness, so heavy now, will be lightened for us by that
Help which comes to all who really need it. Harry sends you
his warmest love & when he goes to New York will surely see
you. He is, as I am, deeply grateful for your loving words. Pray
give my love to Mr. Ward & also to Tom.

Yours affectly & gratefully
Alice James

. . . .

<to Alice Howe Gibbens James. [February?] 1884>
My dear Alice

A thousand congratulations upon your happy deliverance.
The young man seems to have shown the most happy alacrity
in entering life, I hope it is a prophecy that he means to take
and make life easy.

I am sorry that he has chosen the inferior sex, though
I suppose it is less on one's conscience to have brought forth
an oppressor rather than one of the oppressed, and you wont
have to look forward to evenings spent in Lyceum Hall

deliverance. Herman James, the William Jameses' third son,
was born on January 31, 1884. He died less than two years later
after a bout with whooping cough and pneumonia.

*trembling lest he should not be engaged for the german or left
dangling at supper time.*

*I shall not come out to see you until I hear from your good
mother that it is well for me to do so, as I have no confidence
in the discretion of the "bundle of fleas."*

With a great deal of love

As ever yours

A——

Sunday

Lyceum Hall . . . the german. Lyceum Hall stood where the
Harvard Coop now stands. The German cotillion was a popular dance.
the "bundle of fleas." Probably WJ.

. . . .

<to Frances Rollins Morse. [Spring 1884?]>

5 E. 56th St.

Sunday

My dear Fanny

*You must not measure my satisfaction in getting your letter
by my delay in answering it. I was more glad than I can tell
you, with this stump, to have news of you in this alien, odious
spot. How any one can live here and lead a virtuous
& reputable life amidst the Jews, the tawdry, flimsy houses
and the ash-barrels seems hard to understand, but I suppose
there is some domestic existence somewhere. That blessed
hamlet, Boston, seems like a shrine of all the virtues.*

*I am very glad upon other than moral and aesthetic grounds
that I came, the place would be a failure indeed if it could not
do something for one's base, physical necessities! The first ten
days I was here I felt a wonderfull change quite as if I had
been transformed, and I came to the conclusion that I was the
lowest of organism with absolutely no insides but a stomach,
if that were in order the universe might crumble and I should
be found dancing a jig on top of the heap. This state of things
has not continued, however & the last ten days I have had
every reason, either on account of the atrocious weather or the
misconduct of the doctor, to consider myself as belonging*

the doctor. William Basil Neftel (1830–1906), a Russian-born
specialist in female nervous diseases, which he treated by the

*to the highest form of created thing; which means nothing
more tragic than that I have had a long indigestion, owing
to my having been obliged to walk too much when I first
came, I suppose. The doctor is as kind and easy to get on with
as he can be and the only thing I have to complain of is that
"Rome was not built in a day;" as I have known this fact for
a month or two I was foolish to allow my hopes to rise
through the specious representations of a non-Puritan
temperament, to put it mildly. I am beginning to sympathise
with the lady who died and found Heaven delightfull "only
it was not Boston." I am delighted with your suggestion
of telling me something about your work. Your silence on the
subject has always made me feel very much left out in the
cold as if I were not worthy to be taken in to your confidence.
I have delightfull quarters & Mary's virtues increase every
day. I expect to come home a pauper, & hope that you will
bend all your energies to helping Lizzie with the concert she
is going to get up for me when I return, which blessed
moment I am all in the dark about, not for a fortnight,
at least. There is a lady upstairs who talks about the "nerve
tone" of negroes being so delightfull! Write me just a word
if you can dearest Fanny. I miss your dear face more than you
suspect.*

> *Love to the Parents*
> *Yrs. A——*

---

then-fashionable method of electrotherapy. AJ had come to
New York to put herself under his care.

your work. Engaged in charitable and social work, Fanny
Morse was to be involved for many years with the Associated
Charities of Boston—one of the earliest (1879) of the so-called
charity organization societies in America. These nonsectarian
societies, which had begun in London about a decade earlier,
attempted to coordinate the efforts of all existing relief organi-
zations in a particular area; typically, they operated by divid-
ing a city into districts and sending out trained visitors like
Fanny Morse to make house-to-house calls on all the needy
cases.

Mary's virtues. Mary was a recently acquired servant.

Lizzie. Presumably Lizzie Boott, who had temporarily returned with her father to the United States.

. . . .

131 Mt. Vernon St
May 5th

My dear Sara

*I have left your kind letter of January '83! so long
unanswered that it may seem as if I had forgotten your
existence, but I am sure that your benevolent mind has not
allowed you to harbour any such thought. I have been so ill
for the last year and a half that I have done nothing in the
way of letters excepting what was absolutely necessary and
that is why I have not thanked you for the sympathy and
affection you expressed after dear Father's death. We were
so glad to have him go & that he was not kept in weariness
& desolation any longer after Mother's death that we could
give no thought to our own loss. It has fallen most heavily
of course upon me, but I am gradually getting used
to my loneliness and I find as every one else does that
no burden is given that one cannot fit one's self to, after the
necessary hewing & hacking. I have every consolation
in having so many kind friends & brothers, Boston surpasses
itself, you know, when trouble comes. I am having a more
than usually strong sense of its excellence now as I have just
got back from two months spent in that wilderness of Jews
& ash-barrels, New York, where I am willing to allow that
there may be a sporadic instance, here & there, of domestic
virtue, but absolutely no civic ones. Boston looks like
Nuremberg architecturally and like—Bassett shall we say?—
morally and socially. I ought not to be too hard upon New
York, however, for my visit did me a great deal of good. I went
to test the skill of a Russian electrician, a Dr. Neftel, of whom
I had heard great things & who certainly either in spite
or because of his quackish quality has done me a great deal
of good in many ways. I was charmed at first with the Slavic
flavour of our intercourse but I soon found myself sighing for
unadulterated Jackson. To associate with and to have to take
seriously a creature with the moral substance of a monkey
becomes degrading after awhile, no matter how one may have*

unadulterated Jackson. Presumably an allusion to James Jackson (1777–1867), the old Boston physician.

been seduced by his "shines" at the first going off. His
electricity however has the starching properties of the longest
Puritan descent, & I wish very much that you might try
it some of these days. I am sorry to hear that you are still
bothered with your head, it has not been all climate with you
and the British absence of "snap" is not all that you want.
I see on re-reading your letter that you speak of my going
to England to live. Two friends called to see me the other day
to say good-bye, they having seen in some newspaper that
I was on the eve of going. I have no intention of doing
so myself at any rate for a year or more to come. I have been
anxious to solve the problem first as to whether I could not
make a home for myself here and to my great satisfaction
I find that I can. Some of these days I shall be bothering you
for information about ways & means in England & the feeling
that you are there, dear Sara, will strengthen my hands very
much to undertake what would otherwise seem a very forlorn
venture. Pray give my kindest regards to Mr. Darwin & believe
me always very affectly yours

                                                        Alice J——

....
<To Catharine Walsh, William James, etc.
November 22, 1884>

                                            40 Clarges St—
                                              Picadilly W.
                                            Nov. 22nd 1884
Dear Aunt, brothers & sister.
    I am sorry that so many days have passed without
my writing, but you have heard that I have not "passed away"
yet, from Kath. & Harry. We had for the season a very fair
voyage, tossing most of the time but only one storm. The most
comfortable state-room & ship I ever was on for though the
ports were only open twice there were absolutely no smells.
Excellent service, a stewardess worthy of her name, Devine,
& a devoted and innocuous doctor who unmurmuringly
obeyed all Kath's. behests. Our miseries began however
immediately for by 10. A.M. the morn we started we were both
in our berths sweetly carolling. K. revived somewhat at the
end of a couple of days and afterwards made the best voyage
she ever did, which she attributes to the fact of her having had

one of William's blisters suspended to a wisp of hair four
inches from her head, for 48 hrs. I was not, I am sorry to say,
so fortunate for after the sea-sickness subsided all the winds
of the firmament took possession of that omniverous Organ
of mine & I was rent by perpetual & violent indigestion which
is only now gradually subsiding. Even sea-sick Katharine was,
of course, equal to the occasion & only gave out once when
throwing herself into her berth she called out to Mattie
Whitney (a perfect sailor) "do come and hang on to Alice's
head," & there was such an incubating fervour in her voice
that that amiable young woman's embryonic protestations
were brought to life and she came & hung, instead of letting
the poor thing lollup off. But it is all a horror of the past
& though I swore I should not return for 30 yrs. & then only
as a corpse to enrich the soil having done so little for the
history of my native land, I am now ready to go in six
months. Through the agency of Mrs. Stanley Clarke Harry
brought an excellent maid with him to Liverpool. Her banged
& bugled definiteness is in amusing contrast to that soft mass
of formless virtue Mary, she is an excellent servant & as kind
& devoted as she can be & her conversation constant
& comic. She has been my one study as my observation has
been limited to four walls except during my journey from
Liverpool, the most of which took place after dark. I sadly find
on looking out of the window that all sense of novelty
& excitement has worn off, it all seems as if I had been here
yesterday. I have a pleasantish little parlour with a tomb-like
closet for bed-room attached in which one cannot see to read
two feet from the window "on a very fine day" but I feel
as if I had been there all my life & it is just the place to spend
the day in bed with a head-ache. I enjoy the dusky darkness
greatly it is like living in a tunnel. I shall hope to go out a bit
next week in a bath-chair in the Park which is only five
minutes off. One or two people have called but I have not
been well enough to see them, my only social excitement
has been Bob's friend Mrs. Van Rensselaer who has been

Mrs. *Stanley Clarke.* Mary Rose Clarke, the daughter of Sir
John and Lady Rose—the latter a Temple by birth and thus a
distant relative of the Jameses.
Mrs. *Van Rensselaer.* "A pincushion of a woman," as HJ called

*in London the last year much sought by the aristocracy! Harry
says that she is nothing but a little round ball that has rolled
about in the dust all its life—if half her tales of the turpitude
of her present associates are true she is in the dustiest place
she ever was in before. I have heard of more horrors from her,
from Harry, from Campbell & the newspapers than I ever
heard in all the rest of my life put together. It makes one cry
out for the burnished purity of Mt. Vernon St—— The last
week there have been five or six families of high degree
figuring in the Police Court, for libels, assaults divorces
& murders, a more horrible state of society one cannot
imagine.*

    *I am looking for Katharine & Mattie Whitney this afternoon
who are coming to town to see the sights for a week. I shall
stay on here as long as I am comfortable & until I get
decidedly stronger. Sara has asked me to stay on the 10th
through Christmas but I am too flabby yet to engage myself.
I shall go later.*

    *Mrs. Lowell asked me to the Thanksgiving dinner, but she
wont get anything so precious. I am much obliged to the aunt
for her letter, but why did you let Charlotte King loose upon
me, I have had two notes already from her inviting me to stay
in Versailles, it is all owing to Wm. I shall write again soon.
With lots of love*

                                Yrs as ever A—— J——

P.S. *Campbell considers it included in her functions
to administer moral support & consolation for the feebleness
of my body, her latest is—"you are indeed very delicate, Miss,
& it is hard to be so ill, but then you ought to be thankfull
that there is nothing repulsive about you & you have no skin
disease, as long as I have no skin disease & my body is whole*

---

her elsewhere, Mrs. Van Rensselaer was an expatriate American widow who spent a number of years in Italy and England.
Campbell. The "excellent maid" described above.
Mrs. Lowell. Frances (Dunlap) Lowell (1823–1885), second
wife of the American poet and man of letters, James Russell
Lowell (1819–1891), who at the time of this Thanksgiving dinner invitation was minister to the Court of St. James.
Charlotte King. A maternal cousin, Charlotte King lived
much of her life abroad and spent her last years in Versailles.

I feel that I ought not to complain of anything!" Forward
to Cambridge. Give best love to Cousin Helen

> *Cousin Helen.* A first cousin of AJ's mother and her Aunt
> Kate, Helen Wyckoff Perkins had been raised virtually as their
> sister and was, in HJ's words, "scarcely less a stout brave pres-
> ence and an emphasized character for the new generation than
> for the old" (*A Small Boy and Others*, Chap. 9).

. . . .

<to Alice Howe Gibbens James. December 8, 1884>

London. Dec. 8th
1884

Dear Alice
   I was delighted to get your letter a few days ago & to hear
of the great land purchase. It is of course terra incognita
to me, but a settlement anywhere with a family on one's
hands seems like the first necessity of life. I am glad that you
say it was a bargain & that you have some trees already
started. I suppose John Gray sold to you cheap as a bait
to future purchasers. Perhaps its being more or less countryish
will simplify the summer question. I have nothing new
or interesting to tell you. Katharine & Miss Whitney were here
for a fortnight, & though they were out literally from morning
to night it was a great pleasure to have occasional glimpses
of them. Although the thermometer has only been about
30° the cold has been intense owing to its damp quality,
by constant stoking day & night my little apartments have
been kept habitable. Kath. says it is warmer here than
Bournemouth, with unremitting care she could only get
Louisa's room up to 65°. They say you feel the cold out much
less than in the house. The only new person I have seen is Mrs.
Stanley Clarke who very kindly came one afternoon when

> *the great land purchase . . . John Gray.* The land in question
> was probably that on which the William Jameses' 95 Irving
> Street house later stood. WJ's friend John Chipman Gray
> (1839–1915), lawyer and for nearly forty years professor of law
> at Harvard, was a specialist in real property.
> *Louisa.* Louisa Loring, Katharine's younger sister, was at the
> time of this letter an invalid. It was to accompany Louisa in an
> attempt to cure her "weak lungs" that Katharine had originally
> come to Europe.

*I was well enough to see her. I had often heard of her charms,
but I was in no way disappointed, it is a delight to see such
firmly moulded features, speech & manner after our
accidental & slipshod personalities. I am much impressed
by the expensiveness of everything, as soon as I am able
to I must move or I shall be ruined. The only cheap things
I have seen are a pair of gloves & a package of envelopes.*

*House rent is quite as high as in Boston unless you go to some
distant quarter where you would die of loneliness, people not
having the time to go & see you, & where your rent would
soon be doubled by cab-fares. Italy I imagine is the only
cheap place unless you are willing to bury yourself in some
provincial town. I give Campbell $1.50 less a month than
I gave Mary, but she does just half the work, and has brought
the science of dawdle to perfection. Besides being the thing
servant she is an excellent creature however & gives
me a dose of robust comfort every morning, such as "your
illness is a very pleasant one, Miss, with some ladies it isn't
pleasant at all," so you see I have my consolations. You would
think so if you could see my head for when it is not upon the
pillow it is elaborately coiffée in Camp.'s last "idea," so that
although I am thinner & more mildewed of tint than ever
I never have had such varied & dressy locks before. As I did
not seem to mend & had another bad attack of gout in the
stomach which kept me in bed for nine days I consented
against my conscience & my purse to send for Dr. Garrod,
whose whereabouts Kath. of course knew by instinct. We read
his book two years ago & Beach said that he was the only*

heard of her charms. "She is delightfully good-looking," HJ
had earlier reported to AJ, "& has, among other advantages,
the finest 'form' in London" (January 30, 1881).
Dr. Garrod. Alfred Baring Garrod (1819–1907), later physician
extraordinary to Queen Victoria, specialized in the chemical
investigation of disease and is best known for the discovery
that gout is associated with increased uric acid in the blood.
He was knighted in 1887. The book AJ refers to is probably his
Treatise on Gout and Rheumatic Gout (1859), whose third
edition had appeared in 1876.
Beach. Probably Henry Harris Aubrey Beach (b. 1843), a
Boston physician and member of the Harvard medical faculty.
Dr. Beach, whom several of the Jameses consulted, was the
first to diagnose AJ's trouble as "rheumatic gout." "He told her

man in the world who knew any thing about suppressed gout.
I have since heard that he is the supreme authority.
On Saturday afternoon therefore a round, genial ball
of seventy rolled into the room with whom I passed the most
affable hour of my life, an old fellow all rounded & smoothed
by tradition, with all the graces of the mendacious Slave
& the honesty of the angular Oliver. He listened with
apparent interest & attention to my oft-repeated tale, which
by the way to save breath & general exhaustion I am going
to have printed in a small pamphlet, he understood without
question or explanation all my symptoms, especially the
emotional ones. He said of course he could say nothing until
he had seen me again & given me a thorough examination.
I do not expect any thing very satisfactory, but he may give
me some hints as to diet. These details, medical, are for
William's delectation. Give him my love & tell him that
I shall hope to surpass even my "Boston level" giddy
as it was. My present collapse is no mystery to me, so many
long months have led up to it.
    Dec. 10th I have seen today a Nation a month old & feel
as if I was once more in the current of human life having
learnt more from it of European events than I have in the
whole month that I have been here, though I see two daily
papers. I have decided to move on Saturday—& shall
go to 7 Bolton Row upon which Bolton St abutts. You had
better send this to Aunt Kate as I shall not be able to write
again in sometime as I have a large number of claims upon
me. With love to all

Ever yours affectly
Alice J——

---

that there was something lying back of her nervousness, and
the cause of it, and he was bound to find it out," Aunt Kate had
reported to HJ in the winter of 1882 : "A three weeks investigation has persuaded him that it is *gout*, rheumatic gout! and he
promises her exemption from her nervous attacks. Alice's experience, as she now looks back upon it confirms this diagnosis fully and she is full of hope for the future. She thinks
that this may shed some light upon your head-aches. Of
course this [is] a constitutional trouble. If the gout were to
come out in her joints she would have no nervousness" (CW
to HJ Jr., December 2, 1882).

*Tell the artist philosopher with my love that he is kept green
in my memory by the waiter whose tragic solemnity
of demeanour only equals his own*

> *the artist philosopher.* Presumably an allusion to WJ.

. . . .

<to William James. December 23, 1884>

40 Clarges St——
Dec. 23rd
1884

Dear William
*I was delighted to hear such good news of your eyes & of the
prowess of the "human turtle," that your letter brought. I was
much amused and entertained by your description of the
"aureate darkness." It is a perpetual pleasure and I dread the
time when I shall have to come to the surface. We have as yet
had no fog & much less rain than I had expected. It pours all
the time at Bournemouth, Kath. writes. My life passes with
clock-like regularity. I have seen one or two people, no one
new except Mrs. Humphrey Ward, a niece of Matthew
Arnold's a scribbling lady, belonging to the middle-class,*

> *the "human turtle" . . . the "aureate darkness."* The "human
> turtle" was WJ's baby Herman, whose progress in "creeping on
> the floor" the proud father excitedly reported in his letter of
> December 7: "I have rushed up and seen the phenomenon—a
> wonderful human turtle with nothing on but a diaper, pitching
> himself all about the room. Congratulate us!" In the same let-
> ter he had also commented sympathetically on AJ's surround-
> ings: "I should think you would indeed get a sort of nutritious-
> ness from being in those dusky gleaming quarters with the
> rich sombre conflict of the light with darkness going on all day
> before your eyes, and with nothing to do but rest, and respon-
> sibilities 3000 miles behind you. . . . I hope you will often
> think of me as I was winter before last immersed in the same
> aureate duskiness. Those were strange days indeed when I was
> suddenly plunged there alone, to await more and more news of
> poor Father's death. They are stamped indelibly upon my
> memory."
> *Mrs. Humphrey Ward.* Mary Augusta Ward (1851–1920), later
> the author of the best-selling *Robert Elsmere* ("one of the most
> beautifull books for purity & moral elevation I have ever read,"
> as AJ then reported to Sara Darwin [April 5, 1888]), had just
> written her first novel in 1884. The writer's cramp to which AJ
> alludes in this letter was to afflict Mrs. Ward for the rest of her
> life.

woolen type. She, as well as Mrs. J. R. Greene, are afflicted
in the most melancholy manner with writer's cramp in both
hands & arms. She told me that her sister-in law wrote for her
for three hours every day "and though I am very fond of her
she irritates me dreadfully, at moments." The emotions of the
sister in law not given! But I had a truly delicious call from
Mary Wilkinson, no pen can describe it & although it only
lasted for twenty minutes, or so, I was more done up than
I should have been by Mrs. Morse, Grace Norton & Anna
Palfrey rolled into one. "Are you fond of history, Alice!"——
"Do your brothers live anywhere near you in America, Alice!"
but the funniest thing she said was, a propos of Emma's
misfortunes, about people being able to bear anything that
came, or something of that sort—"Oh! yes I have found that
out by experience. I have always feared that if my husband
should be very ill I should not be able to keep awake, but last
winter he was very ill and I did not sleep at all!" She looked
very smart & invited me to drive in her carriage a very neat
brougham I saw her getting into, the proceeds probably
of Jamie's rail-road that her husband, according to Mrs.
Wilkinson, has stolen. Mrs. W. told Harry a little while ago
that Jamie had gone off on a holiday for three weeks & left
this precious rail-road in care of Mr. Matthews & when
he returned Mr. M. would not give it up & they did not "know
what to do about it!"——I look back & long for my salon

Mrs. J. R. Greene. Alice Stopford Green, wife of the historian
John Richard Green (1837–1883), served for a number of years
as his amanuensis and co-authored with him a *Short Geogra-
phy of the British Isles* (1880). In 1888 she brought out a re-
vised edition of her late husband's immensely popular *Short
History of the English People*.
Mary Wilkinson. The daughter of James J. Garth Wilkinson
(1812–1899), physician, fellow-Swedenborgian, and good
friend of HJ Sr. (AJ's brother "Wilky"—Garth Wilkinson
James—had been named after him.) Mary's husband, Frank
Mathews, was a London solicitor. "Mary is in fact lovely," HJ
had earlier observed to WJ, "but the dullness, small provin-
ciality, and 'lower middle class' quality of the conversation
and the *milieu* are incompatible with close relations" (May 1,
1878).
Emma. Mrs. James J. Garth Wilkinson, née Emma Anne
Marsh.
Jamie. James J. Garth Wilkinson.

in Boston, as doubtless from her perch in purgatory Mme
Dudeffand is longing for hers. It seems like the centre of all
wit & wisdom, with those excellent beings all permeated
& perfumed with goodness!

My doctor came last week & examined me for an hour with
a conscientiousness that my diaphragm has not hitherto been
used to. When he came to the end he was as inscrutable
as they always are & the little he told me I was too tired
to understand. He is coming next week when as there wont
be as much percussing & stethescoping to be done I can get
more out of him. I shall not tell you till then what he told
me. I think he takes the gout as a foregone conclusion simply
& is deciding what other complications there are. Meanwhile
he has left me a pill of which he thinks all the world
& I am to have my spine sponged with salt-water, I was much
disappointed by his lack of remedial suggestions, all great
doctors are chiefly interested in the diagnosis & don't care for
anything else apparently. They ought to have a lot of lesser
men, like tenders, to do their dirty-work for them, curing their
patients etc. I shall let you know if he tells me anything
interesting, I am much afraid that it wont be immediate
dissolution, but on the contrary a long drawn out process.
I sent some cards to the children, I hope they will go safe, give
them lots of kisses, also much love to Alice & Bob. Don't
write except just when you feel like it.

Always affectly
Alice——

P.S. It occurs to me that I have never mentioned Harry. His
kindness & devotion are not to be described by mortal pen,
he shows no outward sign of impatience at having an old man
of the Sea indefinitely launched upon him, I am afraid that
he will find me attached to his coat-tails for the rest
of my mortal career.

I sent out to a chemist to have some powders put up

Mme Dudeffand. Maria Anne de Vichy-Chamrond, Marquise
du Deffand (1697–1780), whose celebrated salon in Paris was
frequented by a number of noted aristocratic and literary figures, Voltaire, Montesquieu, and the philosophe D'Alembert
among others. Separated from her husband, she was reputedly
for a brief while the mistress of the Regent.
My doctor. Garrod.

in cachets, they came back in papers, when remonstrated with
the man said he supposed cachet was an American form
of a latin word. This in the heart of Mayfair!!
H. seems very well & is much less stout.

cachets. Medical term for capsules.

....

<to Catharine Walsh. January 31, 1885>

Bournemouth
Jan. 31st

My dear Aunt Kate.
I don't know when I last wrote to you but it must be a good
while ago as so many weeks have gone by since I wrote to any
one. I was glad to hear from your last letter that you felt
yourself again & that you were going to Newport. I was
getting so incrusted with grime in my London quarters that
I felt a change to be absolutely essential, of course I had
no alternative but Bournemouth, Harry & Kath. being
my only anchorages. I am sorry to come to the sea but I shall
never have to see it as my windows don't give on it at all.
Kath. comes in of course every day & does all my marketing
for me. They seem to be quiescent for the present but
I tremble every time I see her lest their plans change. Louisa
seems to be doing well & of course from my point of view
seems like an Amazon, but she may take a fancy to move
at any moment. I have not seen her but I hope to be strong
enough to see Mattie Whitney next week, who is a nice little
body. I have very pleasant rooms & infinitely better food
& cheaper than in London where I was greatly over-spending
my income. I am on the high ground-floor which gives upon
a busy but noiseless road so that as I lie in bed I can see the
passing, & I feel as if I were more in the world than I have felt
since my progress in the arms of two stewards thro' the
emigrants on the deck of the Pavonia. My doctor turned out
as usual a fiasco an unprincipled one too. I could get nothing
out of him & he slipped thro' my cramped & clinging grasp
as skilfully as if his physical conformation had been that
of an eel, instead of a Dutch cheese——The gout he looks

the Pavonia. The ship that had brought AJ to England.
My doctor. Garrod.

upon as a small part of my trouble, "it being complicated
with an excessive nervous sensibility," but I could get
no suggestions of any sort as to climate, baths or diet from
him. The truth was he was entirely puzzled about me & had
not the manliness to say so. I got from him however a very
thorough examination. He said I had no organic trouble, that
my organs were simply disturbed in their functions. My legs
are produced by a functional disturbance of the lower half
of the spine. "Is this produced by gout?" "Oh! dear me yes
I have seen people with their legs powerless for years from this
cause!" He assured me that it did not lead to paralysis, a grim
spectre which has been staring me in the face for a long time.
My legs have been entirely useless for anything more than
hobbling about the room for three months & a half & most
of the time excessively painfull. I asked the doctor whether
it was not unusual for a person to be so ill & have no organic
trouble & he said, "yes, very unusual indeed."——I should
have thought he would therefore have liked to do some thing
for me—but it was only my folly in going to a great man
their only interest being diagnosis, & having absolutely
no conscience in their way of dealing with one. I have very
cheerfull accounts of my health from Boston, a letter from
Mrs. Lodge who hears that I have "completely recovered."
A delightful letter from Mrs. Kellogg wondering why I don't
write. If you should be writing to her, please tell her
of my condition as I don't know when I shall be able
to answer her, & will therefore not write again unless she
knows why. I have been very sorry not to write to Wm. but
I have been too nervous & feeble. I saw Sara for a few minutes
in London—quite a transformed being, in her appearance,
at any rate she has been extremely affect. & kind since
I arrived proposing all sorts of friendly offices. She proposes
coming here to see me, but I hope not for some time as I dread
any excitement, my nerves having been so shattered by that

Mrs. Lodge. Probably Anna Cabot Mills (Davis) Lodge, wife of
Henry Cabot Lodge (1850–1924), author, editor, and for more
than thirty years senator from Massachusetts.
Mrs. Kellogg. A Cambridge acquaintance of whom AJ was
fond—"so handsome, elegant & American," as she noted
gratefully when Mrs. Kellogg later visited her in England (AJ to
CW, October 8, 1888).

horrible night five weeks ago. I am sorry to send so dull
a letter but I have no annals but those of a sick room. Give
my best love to Cousin Helen. Tell Elly V. Buren how sorry
I am not to be able to write to her. Let me know the Ripleys
Paris address as soon as you know it.

Yrs. as always
A.

Elly V. Buren. Ellen James Van Buren (b. 1844), AJ's first
cousin, was the daughter of HJ Sr.'s youngest sister, Ellen King
James, and of Smith Thompson Van Buren, a son of President
Martin Van Buren.
the Ripleys. Maternal relatives.

. . . .

<to Catharine Walsh. November 21–24 [1885?]>

7 Bolton Row. W.
Nov 21st, 23rd & 24th

My dearest Aunt.
  You may have observed a considerable hiatus in our
correspondence on my side, I shall not however waste
my energies upon trying to whitewash the past but expend
them, as you will doubtless prefer, upon a pencil sketch of the
present. You know of course that I have pitched my tent
at No. 7 Bolton Row, where, as it faces Bolton St. & overlooks
a vast sea of mews behind, I have all the light vouchsafed
by Heaven at this season of the London year. The rooms are
very good & as our landlady is a Swiss she is possessed
of a larger repertory for the manipulation of the potatoe than
were her origin British. Miss Ward, my fourth keeper,
promises, & until now has performed very well, but the
standard of morals is so low & human nature so debased
on this side of the water that I am prepared for the darkest
revelations at any moment. She is a "reduced lady"
& consequently cheap, she is as intelligent as any creature
can be stultified by the Church & Toryism. She goes
to Celebration on an empty stomach between eight & nine
A.M. & a gloom is cast over the Sabbath by an exclusive
devotion to "Lenten Lessons" & the "Christian Year," but
as she rarely moves or turns a page I am in hopes that the
labours of the day are lightened by a good deal of soporific
refreshment. I am going to provide myself with a weekly

*Zola to cheer up the Lord's Day. Katharine's sudden flight was
a great shock as you may imagine. We had counted upon six
or eight weeks more. Poor Louisa is still very ill, I have great
doubts (between ourselves) myself about her ultimate
recovery. Her lungs are said to be perfectly sound now ℰ that
it is only nervous prostration. I am afraid that being the case
that she wont gain much this winter as they have got
to go to the Riviera for her chest ℰ that is found to be very
bad for nervous troubles. The present break-down all came
from six inches of snow at the end of Sept! I should think that
my experience ℰ hers would make, if it were known, the
European climate maniacs pause ℰ consider. Don't for the
world repeat what I say about Louisa's condition it is only
my own impression, Kath. is as optimistic about her as ever.
I am gradually working the Bournemouth poison out
of my veins—was it not extraordinary my planting myself
in a spot to which the doctors say you have only to go to find
out whether you have rheumatism, or not! Whether
I am much better or not, I don't know, I am gradually getting
stronger ℰ am able to do a great deal more, but as always
happens as my physical strength increases my nervous
distress ℰ susceptibility grows with it, so that from an inside
view it is somewhat of an exchange of evils. To have
a tornado going on within one, whilst one is chained
to a sofa, is no joke, I can assure you. I get into the sitting
room about 12 o'clck ℰ stay until between 5 ℰ six
ℰ I manage to get about the room half a dozen times a day
which is a great gain. I have much less severe ℰ constant pain
ℰ my legs feel almost as comfortable as they did before I left
Bournemouth ℰ got them so dreadfully bad by the journey.
I suppose you have heard of my "invalid chair"—a variety
of the Bath family—presented to me last summer by the
munificent Kath. It has rubber tyres ℰ bicycle wheels so that
there is absolutely no jar ℰ one can lie out in it like a bed
if necessary. I got out in it about a dozen times in Hampstead
ℰ you may imagine, after six month of the British bed-room,
how I enjoyed the glimpses of that enchanting spot. I have*

a weekly Zola. Emile Zola (1840–1902), French naturalistic
novelist, whose numerous novels focus on the dark underside
of nineteenth-century French life and emphasize the deter-
mining power of environment and heredity.

only got out once since we came to London, it is very difficult
to regulate the weather & my various attacks at the same
moment, after the New Year things will be better doubtless.
I see H. every day, he is as good as good can be, of course.
He looks & seems very well, barring an occasional head-ache,
the frequency and severity of wh. he says are much reduced
by guarana. I only wish I could take it but it always makes
me faint.

I was very glad to see Helen R—— & much amused by her
unqualified surprise at "finding me the same," whether she
expected to find me developed into a higher or lapsed
to a lower organism I could not make out. What a sad break
up for poor Mrs. Gibbens to lose Mary & her health too at her
age. I have written this bit by bit as you see, please forgive all
shortcomings & send it to Wm. I shall write to him soon, but
I have lot of debts to pay off as I can. Much love to C. Helen
& any receptive cousins.
    Address here.

Always very affectly yr
A——

guarana. An extract from the crushed seeds of a South American plant whose principal agent is chemically identical with
caffeine, guarana was chiefly used in the latter half of the century as a headache remedy. Also prescribed as a nervous tonic
and stimulant, it might well have induced rapid heartbeat and
even faintness.
Helen R. Helen Ripley, a relative of AJ's mother and Aunt Kate.
to lose Mary & her health too. In December 1885 Mary Sherwin Gibbens, one of AHJ's two younger sisters, married
William M. Salter (1853–1931) and moved to Chicago, where
Salter wrote and lectured about ethics for the Ethical Culture
Society. Later that same month Mrs. Gibbens was to set sail
for Italy to recover from a serious affliction of the lungs.

. . . .

\<to William James. January 3–7 [1886?]\>

7 Bolton Row W.
Jan. 3rd, 4th

Dear William
    I hope you wont be "offended," like Frankie, when I tell you
that I played you a base trick about the hair. It was a lock, not

Frankie. Francis Boott, whose sensitivity to emotional injury
the Jameses had noted before.

*of my hair, but that of a friend of Miss Ward's who died four
years ago. I thought it a much better test of whether
the medium were simply a mind-reader or not, if she
is something more I should greatly dislike to have the secrets
of my organisation laid bare to a wondering public. I hope
you will forgive my frivolous treatment of so serious a science.
I have a great many very kind & sympathetic letters to thank
you for with many amusing & Venner like predictions
as to the date of my recovery, I am glad to observe that you
have grown wily by experience & deal of late altogether
in years instead of months, as at first—it is safer.* While
I am on the subject I may as well add that, as you know, the
tendency of the age is rather to overdo the sympathetic & that
there is a fortunate provision of nature which keeps one from
seeming as flimsy and dismal to one's self as one does to one's
affectionate friends. My ill-health has been inconvenient
& not aesthetically beautifull, but early in youth I discovered
that there were certain ends to be attained in life, which were
as independent of illness or of health, as they were of poverty
or riches, so that by turning my attention exclusively to them,
even my torpid career has not been without its triumphs
to my own consciousness & therefore not to be pitied for. This
is meant not as biographical but simply to cheer you
up, in return for all your like efforts in my behalf. It may seem
supine to you that I don't descend into the medical arena, but
I must confess my spirit quails before any more gladiatorial*

the medium. Leonore Evelina (Simonds) Piper (1859–1950), a
famous Boston medium, whose apparent ability to communi-
cate with the dead was to interest WJ for more than twenty
years. When his mother-in-law first visited Mrs. Piper in 1885,
WJ, like his sister here, was skeptical; but subsequent visits of
his own and others at least partly convinced him of her
powers. Later in 1886 he would publish an account of her séances in the first volume of the *Proceedings of the American
Society for Psychical Research.*
Venner like predictions. An allusion to the elder Oliver Wendell Holmes's novel about heredity and predestination, *Elsie
Venner: A Romance of Destiny* (1861). The eponymous heroine is cursed by a snakelike nature, traced to the influence of a
prenatal snakebite. Her father's hopes that she will outgrow
her affliction are only fulfilled after Elsie is rejected by a
lover—when the curse briefly lifts, she sickens, and dies.

*encounters. It requires the strength of a horse to survive the
fatigue of waiting hour after hour for the great man & then the
fierce struggle to recover one's self-respect after having been
reduced to the mental level of Charlie Möring. I think the
difficulty is my inability to assume the receptive attitude, that
cardinal virtue in women, the absence of which has always
made me so uncharming to & uncharmed by the male sex.
The days of the week roll by as like each other as peas
in a pod. It is a very curious & disciplining process, in view
of my privileges of the past, to live shut up to little Wardy's
centimetre of mind, to whom every thing from Warwick
Castle to a gas-fire is "pretty & sweet." But it has its
consolations & I simmer with a Goethian like sense
of my own superiority. A few virtuous matrons have come
to nibble at me but no one worth recording, they all seem like
the tamest of tame Boston, Boston minus a capacity for
understanding one's jokes or one's misguided flights
of rhetoric. Annie Richards is as good as possible & Sara came
in the other day on her way to Cambridge for the holidays.
She looks* dreadfully *& seems more lifeless than ever so that
one feels like a flea beside her. A. Richards thinks she is very
much hipped, but that is all nonsense, any one looking as she
does must be really ill. She was very kind & affectionate. Poor
Clover Hooper's death is sad indeed, a dreadfull shock—
it has enabled Ellen, however, to write to me, as Kath. says*

the mental level of Charlie Möring. Charley Moering was a
Cambridge acquaintance who died several years later "a complete idiot" (WJ to AJ, July 23, 1890).
Warwick Castle. Standing on a rock which rises sheer out of
the river Avon not far from Leamington, Warwick Castle is
celebrated for its collection of pictures and antiquities and for
its beautiful park and gardens.
Annie Richards. The former Annie Ashburner had married an
American, Francis Gardiner Richards, in 1879. Annie was now
living in England, where she had settled after her husband's
death in 1884.
hipped. Suffering from hypochondria; depressed (a British col-
loquialism; shortened variant of *hypochondriac*).
Clover Hooper's death . . . Ellen. On December 6, 1885,
Marian ("Clover") Hooper Adams (b. 1843), wife of Henry Adams (1838–1918) and pioneer woman photographer, committed suicide while her husband was out for a walk. She had
been depressed since her father's death the previous April.

*it evidently takes an immense emotion to make it possible for
her to express a lesser one.*

*Jan. 7th This scrawl has been written at various moments
& meanwhile yrs. of Dec. 24th has come in. I shall be curious
to hear what the woman will say about the hair. Its owner
was in a state of horrible disease for a year before she died—
tumours I believe. I am glad to hear that you are all well,
Harry writing & drawing! Give my love to Alice, but don't
let her know you address me as "dearest Alice" it may
complicate our relations. I am sorry about the Childs, but still
more sorry that you have the support of them on your hands!
Where is the Valario-Washburn child? & has Mrs. Washburn
mère died? I have vainly striven to learn for a year. Fanny
Morse writes to me about the sky & the leaves & the dear
knows what invalid pap. It seems to be taken for granted
by many that as soon as one is ill one has necessarily become
an imbecile to be fed on skimmed-milk. Your discovery that
the climate has largely to do with my condition amused
me extremely & throws a curious light upon Harry's & Kaths.
letters if they have given no impression of the poisonous effect
of the deadly, damp, raw, nerve exacerbating chill of the air.
Until lately every joint in my body was constantly pierced
with rheumatic pains flying from my head to my feet, from
my stomach to my hands, how I should have lived without
salicene I don't know. The same* betterment *has taken place
since I came to London that was so* wonderfully marked *when*

Though the circumstances of Mrs. Adams's death were generally kept secret, HJ appears to have known at least that she
killed herself; whether AJ shared his knowledge is not wholly
clear. Ellen (Hooper) Gurney was Clover's older sister.
the Childs . . . on your hands. Francis James Child
(1825–1896), philologist and professor of English literature at
Harvard, and his wife, the former Elizabeth Ellery Sedgwick,
long good friends of the Jameses. Worried that Child was in
straitened financial circumstances and that he had been over-
working, WJ had been talking about trying to arrange a leave
of absence for him in Europe the following year.
the Valario-Washburn child. Presumably the child of Mr. and
Mrs. William Washburn; the latter, *née* Sedgwick-Valerio, was
a relative of AJ's Sedgwick friends.
salicene. Salicin, formerly used as an analgesic, is a bitter
glucoside obtained principally from willow bark; it was
thought to be effective in counteracting "rheumatic poison."

*I was here four yrs. ago. I think it is the lessening of the damp
through the pavements & houses, & being so much more
protected from the East wind wh. blows perpetually. London
is anything but depressing to me, I adore the darkness & the
roar of the city is a constant satisfaction. The only thing
I dislike is the layers of grime with wh. one is incrusted. You
know that statistically it is the healthiest city in the world.
I never felt cold until this yr. All through the summer
at Hampstead as well as now I have my couch within three
feet of the fire, I have 2 suits of winter underclothing a flannel
lined wrapper, 2 very warm shawls over my shoulders a very
heavy rug over my legs & these constantly supplemented
by a duvet & fur cloak, it is simply the chill of the tomb
wh. penetrates to the marrow of one's bones. But enough you
see you get enough of me when I once start. Give lots of love
to Alice & the chicks. Let me know about the hair.*

Always
Yr. loving sister
A.

Tell A. to send me one of her good letters when she can.
** There is however the same finality of tone, as if you
had been exclusively surrounded by the receptive,
wh. is delicious!!*

> when I was here four yrs. ago. Accompanied by Katharine Lor-
> ing, AJ had spent the late spring and summer of 1881 traveling
> in England and Scotland.
> duvet. A quilt stuffed with eiderdown or swan's down.

. . . .

<to Catharine Walsh. February 11–15, 1886>

7 Bolton Row
Mayfair W.
Feb 11th 12th

My dear Aunt Kate.

*You have doubtless lived long eno' in the world to know
that people within sight & sound of the battle field don't
generally know anything about the scrimmage until every*

> the battle field. AJ alludes to disturbances that had broken out
> in Picadilly a few days earlier, after police charged a crowd of
> about ten thousand who had assembled in Trafalgar Square to
> protest the condition of the unemployed; the crowd dispersed
> through adjacent streets, and stoning and looting followed.

thing is over, & have consequently not been alarmed about
H. & me. H. happened to be in Bournemouth or he wd.
have heard at least what was going on as the house on the
corner of Picadilly next to No 3. had its windows broken.
I shd. very likely have heard the shouting too if it had not
been one of my bed days so that I was at the back of the
house, with the sitting room door shut & occupied just at the
moment with violently ringing my bell for the house-maid
having discovered that smoke was rising up from under the
fender owing to the carpet & rug being on fire from having
been judiciously laid close up to the grate! Wardy was calmly
enjoying herself at the Pantomime at Drury Lane; & said
when she got in "I think there must have been some trouble
as I see that the windows in the house on the corner are
broken & the shops are all closed along Picadilly." And
trouble enough there had been! The next two days, especially
Wednesday, London looked like a city that was besieged, they
say all the shops shuttered & barricaded. It has been dreadfull
for the poor tradesmen many of whom have lost their little all,
& who are as badly off comparatively as the workingmen.
It seems pretty sure that none of the working men had
to do with it, nothing but roughs & thieves who were
evidently upon a lark, from their reckless & random conduct.
The most astonishing thing was that no lives were lost with
such a shower of missiles of every description flying in all
directions. There were numberless poor ladies dragged from
their carriages & robbed of their jewells & frightened
to death, the footman in many cases running away!!! The
conduct of the police was absolutely disgracefull, tho' Wardy
thinks it was very natural that they did not want to get
themselves hurt! Things are all in order again except the
broken windows wh. are all boarded up, but great anxiety
remains I think in the minds of every one, wh. is proved from
the fact that 100,000 gentlemen have enrolled themselves
to act at any moment they may be called upon as special
constables in the City. A lively little lady who comes to see
me, Mrs. Montague Cookson, whose husband is a lawyer
& a defeated Radical candidate, was here yesterday
& I asked her whether there was wide-spread anxiety that the

Wardy. Miss Ward, AJ's hired companion.

British workman wd. turn at last & she said that there was
the greatest simply from the fact that there was not work
to give him & that whatever relief there was could only
be temporary. She goes every week to the East end & works
under some clergy-man who told her that he never had known
such destitution in his life, that thousands of families were
living in one room who had tasted no food all winter but
"sop" which consists of crusts of bread wh. they get from the
parish & wh. they soak in water & these the families
of cabinet makers, etc honest hard-working men who are only
crying out for work, & "how can you wonder!" as she
exclaimed. Wardy & I jog on together comfortably enough,
the former as serenely sapient & infinitesimal as ever,
& I stronger from month to month & with less constant
physical distress, tho' at best it is a weary ache. Since H. gave
me a screen I have had less rheumatism. Wardy used
valiantly to take command of expeditions in search of the
sources of the drafts, & one morning she made 3 but was
unable to discover that the window on the landing had been
surreptitiously opened an inch & the consequence was that
I was laid up the next day with rheumatism in my head,
unable to move or breathe for twelve hrs. The thermo.
at my right elbow next the fire will be 72° while at my left
2 ft. off it is 59°, if you put a candle near the crack of the hall
door it blows right out even when the landing window is tight
shut, so you see the desirability of a screen. H.'s friend Lady
Clark told him she was afraid I did not get air eno' in Bolton
Row! Sir John came to see me & was struck with my youth
& beauty, I wish it had been my mind for the former must
fade. I am afraid he is not an accurate observer, for
9 or 10 yrs. ago when H. first knew them & he was about 34
yrs. Sir J. told him he thought he was about 52 & this before
he was bald. Wardy has just come in & I asked her if the
shops were getting repaired "Oh, I have never been to see
them!" On Tuesday she found herself in a great crowd
in Tralfalgar Sq. & in the middle there were men haranguing

H.'s friend Lady Clark . . . Sir John. Sir John Forbes Clark
(1821–1910) and Lady Clark, the former Charlotte Coltman;
HJ was a frequent visitor at their home in Tillypronie,
Scotland.

& shouting I asked what they looked like workmen or roughs,
"Oh, I wd. not for the world have looked at them!" her ideal
is to reduce the field of one's speculation, observation
& reflection to a minimum, she has an indulgent contempt
for my erratic mental orbit, but I cannot flatter myself that
I have developed her in the least I think I have only stupefied
her. Feb. 15th I have not been able to write for a couple
of days. The blackness continues & I feel exactly as if I were
a perpetual Rembrandt, but the afternoons are lengthening
suggestive of the dread approach of summer & the rural
districts. Sara D. came in yesterday, it is pleasant to see her
but after five minutes talk that deathly "gone" look comes
over her face & you feel as if you had sapped her life blood.
She retains all the rigidity of Kirkland St. & her old
pretensions to elevate the tone of the conversation,
wh. produces a ludicrous effect in this atmosphere fetid with
scandal & the voice of the evil-tongued. Every now & then
some new being comes to see me, but they are mostly still
struggling, some of them began in Oct. & when they do arrive
most of the call is passed in an elaborate acct. of the
difficulties wh. they have overcome to get here. It is amusing
to find Boston's favorite graces so perfectly reproduced. Mrs.
Cookson is quite the most amusing person from her being
of a nervous organisation & having a strain of hyperbole like
a refreshing transAtlantic blast. Their au pied de la lettre
nature is inconceivable, the other day I said something to one
of them about things being more or less chaotic at home,
"Why, I thought there was very little that was wild about
Boston now." I also ventured to another into the subtlety
of saying that So & So had no moral nature, "Why, what
a very odd person, how very peculiar." It rather arrests the
flow of analytical & rhetorical gymnastics. Farewell, forgive
the length of this. Love of the warmest to C. H. I have not
invested my Xmas presents yet as they pay me interest at the
bank, there is no hurry. Send this to Cam.

Yr. loving niece
Alice

Their au pied de la lettre nature. Their literal nature.
C. H. Cousin Helen (Perkins).

. . . .

London
April 23rd

My dear Aunt Kate
I have been hoping for some time past to get one of your
graphic letters telling all about your visit to Wm. & Alice.
Two days ago I received a delightfull letter from the latter
saying how much they had enjoyed your visit & what good
friends you had become with the boys. I am sadly afraid that
the Great-aunt will entirely cut out the lesser one! I was very
sorry to hear about your bad cold, what a victim you seem
to be to them. All goes well here. I grow gradually stronger
from month to month and have fewer "attacks" & less
constant pain. My nights are not the periods of terror that
they were for fifteen months, owing to the improvement
in my digestion, having got rid of a well known form
of trouble produced by the contraction of the pleuro-gastric
nerve wh. takes place with the act of falling asleep, and which
produces all manner of horrible sensations. I find too that
I can see people with less ghastly fatigue than I did at first,
tho' they are very fatiguing still owing to the curious law
of nature which obliges them always to come at one & the
same moment. I have two or three intimates who show
a more than Boston absorption in me, they come two or three
times a week, stay for a couple of hrs. in a, to them, very hot
room, becoming from moment to moment more apoplectic,
without any tea & bread-butter wh. they would naturally
at that hour be consuming by the quart & the loaf, & then
write me a note the next day to explain away all that they
said. There are two views taken of me that rather neutralise
each other, unfortunately, one "so subtle, just like your
brother," the other "& above all so original," this by a lady
who every now & then finds a little refreshment in Plato
& Emerson, don't you think I must have put on a good many
frills since we parted?——It may sound fatuous but I divine
from a certain greenish tinge which is coming over Harry's
features, that after the manner of canines, a little modest day
is dawning for me, rather late, to be sure! Nothing more
absolutely elementary than the British feminine mind as far
as I have observed it could not be conceived of. But enough
of myself, of which I am afraid you have had more than

enough. *I have had flowers twice from Mentone from Mrs.
Duveneck, whose emotional centres cannot have been
greatly disturbed by recent events as she is "calmly happy
& sketching." I should think a little delirious joy, at any rate,
for a week or two, to blind her to the terrors of her situation,
would have been gratefull, but then Lizzie has a happy way
of not seeing the terrors that she does not want to see, so there
is no use making oneself wretched about her of all people.
Harry seems to be very well and happy, he enjoys his new
establishment extremely, and all seems to go smoothly.
He pays Mr. & Mrs. Smith for wage & board, no more than
I paid Mary & Margaret, of course, the washing is all extra.
He told me of dining somewhere the other night where Lord
Derby introduced himself in order to compliment him upon
the Bostonians which he had been reading with great delight
& exhibited the most intimate knowledge of Boston & things
Bostonian. Although he never has been there, he said, that
every European diplomatist shd. marry an American woman
to wh. H. replied "they almost all have," which he allowed
to be the case. H. tried modestly to divert his attention
from "The Bostonians" by discoursing on other matters
to wh. he listened very politely but made no other reply
than to say with the utmost gravity "Miss Birdseye
is Shakesperian." H. was invited awhile back to Lambeth
Palace where he was received with great enthusiasm by the
Archbishop of Canterbury who told him that he was*

Mrs. Duveneck. The former Lizzie Boott, the "recent events"
to which AJ refers being chiefly her marriage to her painting
instructor, Frank Duveneck.
new establishment . . . Mr. & Mrs. Smith. HJ had moved into
his new flat at 34 De Vere Gardens on March 6, 1886, and had
recently hired the Smiths to keep house for him—he as butler
and she as cook; they were to remain until 1901, when their
worsening alcoholism finally compelled him to dismiss them.
Lord Derby. Edward Henry Stanley, fifth Earl of Derby (1826–
1893), statesman, and for almost two decades (1875–1893) an
active president of the Royal Literary Fund.
"The Bostonians" . . . "Miss Birdseye is Shakesperian." In *The
Bostonians* (1886), HJ's satirical novel about reformers and
feminists in post-Civil War Boston, Miss Birdseye is an elderly
reformer who "belonged to the Short-Skirt League, as a matter
of course; for she belonged to any and every league that had
been founded for almost any purpose whatever" (Chap. 4).

an immense admirer of his works and had copied page after
page of Roderick H. into his notebook. They ask him to dinner
very often but he does not go, for dinner is at eight & "Chapel
at half past seven." He had another amusing experience
a short time since he went to the Roseberrys & found the
people all standing in a circle shoulder to shoulder in terror
lest they should turn their backs to the Prince & Princesse
Beatrice & the Countess Erbach who were standing in the
middle. After awhile Mr. Phelps, who had been presented
to the Countess, who is the sister of Prince Henry, came
to him & said she wished him to be presented, so H. was led
up & found the Countess possessed of an intimate knowledge
of his works, & she went on to say that the English novel had
entirely died out, that when they wanted an English novel
they always turned to the old ones & when they wanted
a new book they always got an American *one. This in a little*
German court! H. departed from her as soon as possible, but
was sent for again as she wished to present him to Beaty,
who curtseyed very low & made some infantile remarks
to him, during wh. H. observed the German ambassador
backing himself up to the supper-table, for fear his back shd.
be seen by H. & his young woman. Can you imagine anything
so inconceivably dreary as the existence led by "Royalty,"
how they must long to see a back! *Americans have got it all*
in their own hands socially, at any rate.

This long story has been somewhat long in the telling
& I am afraid it will be longer in the reading. I am trying

Roderick H. The first of HJ's novels to be published in book
form, *Roderick Hudson* (1875) traces the brief and troubled
history of a young American sculptor abroad.
the Roseberrys. Archibald Philip Primrose, fifth Earl of Rose-
bery (1847–1929), Liberal statesman, author, and later briefly
(1894–1895) prime minister; and his wife, the heiress Hannah
de Rothschild (1851–1890).
the Prince & Princesse Beatrice. "Beaty," the youngest daughter (b. 1857) of Queen Victoria, and her husband, Prince Henry
of Battenberg, had been married less than a year. Beatrice had
long been her mother's companion, and after the marriage the
couple continued to reside with the queen.
Mr. Phelps. Probably William Walter Phelps (1839–1894), con-
gressman, lawyer, businessman, and for a brief time (1881–
1882) the American minister to Austria-Hungary; in 1889 he
was to be appointed minister to Germany.

to use a "reservoir" penholder instead of a smutty pencil, but
it has great variations and is at moments very anaemic and
trying. I shall probably go to Leamington at the end of May
but the time is not settled. I decided upon Leamington last
autumn having heard of some excellent lodgings in the busiest
street with a band in front of them every day, where Nature
is not and where Man is! Kath. has a wild plan of coming
to transport me but I very much doubt her being able
to accomplish it. If she has not a crown of Glory somewhere
I don't know who will have! Her whole life & occupations
broken up having to give up all she most wants to do and all
taken as a matter of course. I wonder how much of courseness
there would be about it if she happened to wear trousers!
Oh, the goodness of women!! But you certainly don't need any
instruction so I shall stop my chatter. Give my best love
to dear C. Helen & to any Cousins who may desire it. Address
until you hear from Leamington Care of Brown Shipley & Co.
                                              Always
                                       Yr. loving niece
                                                A. J.
When writing give my love to the Tweedies

> the Tweedies. Edmund Tweedy and his wife, Mary (Temple)
> Tweedy, a "quasi-relative," as HJ termed her in *A Small Boy
> and Others* (Chap. 20). Mary Tweedy's brother, Captain
> Robert Emmet Temple, had married HJ Sr.'s sister Catharine;
> when the Temples died, the Tweedys adopted their four or-
> phaned nieces, among whom was the younger Mary ("Minny")
> Temple.

. . . .

<to William James. September 10, 1886>
                                       Leamington Sept. 10th
My dear William
     I have two very fraternal, sympathetic and amusing letters
to thank you for. The fraternity & amusingness are very
gratefull to my heart and soul, but the sympathy makes
me feel like a horrible humbug. Amidst the horrors
of wh. I hear and read my woes seem of a very pale tint. Kath.
& I roared over the "stifling in a quagmire of disgust, pain
& impotence," for I consider myself one of the most potent

> "stifling in a quagmire of disgust, pain & impotence." "You
> poor child!" WJ had written, after learning of what he called

creations of my time, & though I may not have a group
of Harvard students sitting at my feet drinking in psychic
truth, I shall not tremble, I assure you, at the last trump.
I seem to present a very varied surface to the beholder, Henry
thinks that my hardships are such that I shall have a crown
of glory even in this inglorious world without waiting for the
next where it will be a sure thing, Mrs. Cookson, who saw
me in all my greenery, yallowy shades of last winter never can
imagine that I am invalid at all & the landlady says, "You
seem very comfortable, you are always 'appy within yourself,
Miss,"—this may seem to you a small area within which
to rejoice but it has the advantage of always being at hand.
I heard a while ago that contrary to my strenuous injunctions
Harry had written to you that I had consulted Dr. Townsend.
I did not want any report of the engagement to be spread
abroad except from myself, but I had not the energy to write
at the time. The excellent Henry's pathological apprehension
is as vague as his financial & both apparently a direct
inheritance from Father, so that any account of his
of my insides, or rather what may have been said about them,
by the time it had reached your distant shores, could hardly
have much scientific accuracy, it will be a consolation
therefore to myself, though I fear boresome to you, to say just
what is the matter with me. I thought it wrong, being so ill
as I was last autumn, not to see a physician & find out
whether my legs were getting to be a habit or not, so I called
in Townsend who gave just the same diagnosis as Drs.
Torrey & Garrod, a gouty diathesis complicated
by an abnormally sensitive nervous organisation, the legs
neurosis brought about by anxiety & strain. He assured
me that they could not, the legs, be hurried that time would

AJ's "poor unrelieved condition"; "You are visited in a way
that few are ever called to bear, and I have no words of consolation that would not seem barren. Stifling slowly in a quagmire
of disgust and pain and impotence! 'Silence,' as Carlyle would
say, must cover the pity I feel" (WJ to AJ, July 8, 1886).
Dr. Torrey. After the diagnosis of her fatal breast cancer in
1891, AJ was wistfully to recall John Cooper Torry as the only
one of her physicians "who ever treated me like a rational
being, who did not assume because I was victim to many
pains, that I was, of necessity, an arrested mental development
too" (Diary, May 31, 1891).

do it, assisted by his medicines, but I found that they were
very strong tonics *&* that it was going to be only the old Neftel
system, drugs instead of battery so I gave him up. I was very
glad that I went to him however, as he gave me much good
advice *&* relieved my mind about the genuiness of my legs.
He said what I have been told often before that I should
be much better at any rate, when I reached middle life, this
seems highly probable as I have had sixteen periods the last
year. Dr. Townsend is personally the flower of that type
wh. makes the Briton valuable. I never came in contact with
a more beautifull soul, manly, impersonal, intelligent, kind
as a nursing mother, but with too pale-eyed a purity
& unhumourousness of being to thread the mazes of trans-
Atlantic neuresthenia. But it is a gain to know such creatures
exist in the world—there is an awfull possibility they say, that
just that type may be horribly penurious! in the old world
there seems a canker in every flower, but perhaps it is only
on the tongue.

   I have no excitements, occasionally a new old-maid adds
herself to my circle, but my main stand-by is a Miss Palmer,
who has a tumour *&* an income of 10/ a week! She has the
conversational methods of old Geo. Bradford, is perpetually
trying to escape from the terrors of the sentence in hand,
or rather on tongue, to fly to those she knows not of, in the
next, but George is a perfect woman of the world as compared
to her, tho' she does read her Testament in Greek. Though
I have no human excitements, I have been having the last
month some very serious entomological ones, owing to the
appearance in my bed-room of black-beetles—euphuism for
cock-roaches, they are 1½ inches long ¾ inch wide *&* half
an inch thick with endless number *&* length of leg—a truly
British edition of our diaphanous water-bug. They are odious
& some houses are so over run with them that they have them
in the beds. Wardy returns from her matutinal repast having
"partaken of the Spirit of our Lord" *&* has no more drastic

old Geo. Bradford . . . Testament in Greek. George Partridge
Bradford (1806?–1890), a lifelong friend of Emerson (to whom
he was distantly related) and "*the* flower of New Eng. maid-
enly bachelorhood," as AJ later noted in her diary, "the very
last . . . of his very special kind" (Feb. 13, 1890). In the early
1860s Alice had attended Bradford's school in Newport.

measures to propose than to stand in the middle of the room
with her petticoats gathered up & say "Oh, I'll keep my eye
upon him!" the reckless invertebrate unimpressed by the
potent orb, goes gaily upon his career, whereupon I rise from
my bed, go down upon my ricketty knees & extinguish the
creature with a towell & the landlady exclaims "Whatever
shall we do, how I wish Miss Loring were here to tell
us!" A moribund Yankee is worth twenty of the deadly,
stupid, lazy, doughy lumps, when there is anything to be done.
They make me feel, just the look of them sometimes, -
as if I must shriek & scream or be stifled, it is perpetually like
running your head into a feather-bed. The minds of the most
intelligent even are simply cul-de-sacs, more or less long
of course, but the dead wall you will always come to in time.
They are absolutely without the Irish brain cell & they have
consequently a structural inability to conceive of an Irishman
as having the ordinary human attributes.

Sept. 11th Since I began this the well ventilated Kath. has
arrived to spend a couple of weeks & I am happy. I had a call
yesterday from Helen Paine an ancient friend sister-in law
to Mrs. Julia Bryant P. who said she would go out
to Cambridge & tell you about me; so do not be surprised
if she turn up. All the information you will gather from her
will be that "she is just the same!" I have been considering
& deciding upon my probable future for the next three or four
years, & I see no chance of my being well enough for the
journey for a long time to come, the jar of the voyage coming
out having had such a disastrous effect upon my back I shall
have to be very well before I run the risk again, in view of all
this I want you & Alice to go to the store-room in Boston
& take all or any of the furniture wh. you may need or like.
I suppose you have some of Mrs. Gibbenses things which she

Helen Paine . . . Mrs. Julia Bryant P. Julia Bryant Paine was
the wife of the capitalist and yachtsman Charles Jackson Paine
(1833–1916); Helen Paine was his sister. The Paines were de-
scendants of Robert Treat Paine, a signer of the Declaration of
Independence, and of the jurist Charles Jackson. "Why under
the sun do you call Helen Paine amiable?" AJ later wrote to
Fanny Morse, "She is possessed of all the solid virtues but of
the gracefull who could have fewer?" (June 24, 1888).
Mrs. Gibbens. Elizabeth Putnam Gibbens, mother of WJ's
wife Alice.

will want. The carpets especially, I think there are only two,
the red rug & the parlour rug, are only in danger of being
destroyed. The red-rug will do I shd. think in some way for
yr. study & the other perhaps Alice might use. The beds you
may have use for, take every thing & call it if you like a loan,
it will be a help to me as what is left you will doubtless
be able to have put in a smaller room & I shall be at a less
expense——I have to pay now almost $100 storage
wh. I greatly grudge. The only thing you will have
to do in return will be to see to it all yr. self as I do not want
Mr. Warner to have anything to do with it. He will give you
the keys. The keys of the trunks are in the safe at Higs.
Mr. W. will give them to you. Tell A. that the contents of the
trunks are marked upon them, & she can take all the blankets
& linen of which there is a very small supply. The blankets
may be all gone by this time.* The only thing I shd. like
to leave untouched are the barrells of crockery, as you have
a set you will hardly want it & I feel rather sentimental about
it, I will slough it off in time. The pictures will be better
on yr. walls if possible. The old clock needs to be so much
over hauled that it wd. be quite an expense so you had better
leave it dormant. You must not regard this as a favour to you
it will be one to me. The enclosed letter from Mrs. Gurney
will interest as telling about Mr. G.'s mishap. Love to Alice
& the babies

> *Yr loving sister*
> *Alice——*

I shall go to London about the 15th of Oct.
* & anything else she wants

Higs. Probably the Boston banking house of Lee, Higginson &
Company. The Higginson and the Lee families were friends of
the Jameses.
Mrs. Gurney . . . Mr. G. Kate (Sibley) Gurney and her husband,
the British psychologist Edmund Gurney (1847–1888), who
was a co-founder of the Society for Psychical Research and a
friend and correspondent of WJ.

. . . .

8, GLOUCESTER ROAD,
PALACE GATE. S.W.

Dec 8th

My dearest Alice.

*1000 thanks for your beautifull letter wh. reached me day
before yesterday. I was much thrilled of course by the news
with regard to posterity. I shall approve & congratulate only
upon one condition & that is that you show yourself able
to produce one of the nobler sex. She must have your eyes
moreover & a Gibbensian softness of outline, unalloyed
by that James asperity which has led to sour spinsterhood
in the one feminine blossom wh. the race rose to bringing
forth. I have another delightfull letter to thank you for, which
came I think since I last wrote, but it is hard to remember.
Your letters are always an immense pleasure both
to H. & me. What you say of Ellen Gurney gladdened
me greatly, I thought what I heard could not possibly be true.
I felt as if some sacred thing had been desecrated, I had just
had such a beautifull letter from her! I am glad to have
dropped a consolatory quotation into Edwin's consciousness,
I remember the quotation but not the fact. You had not told
me about Florence James I am very pleased that you found*

the one feminine blossom wh. the race rose to bringing forth.
AHJ was pregnant with her fourth child, who did indeed prove
of "the nobler sex"; the William Jameses' only daughter, Margaret Mary ("Peggy") James, was born March 24, 1887.
Ellen Gurney . . . could not possibly be true. "I was horribly
depressed yesterday, by a call from Mrs. Mason," AJ had earlier
written; the caller "gave such a melancholy account of Ellen
Gurney having been in such an unbalanced state, as my mind
had been full for two days of her letter which breathes so calm,
strong & beautifull a spirit, I was greatly shocked. I am sure it
cannot be as she says" (AJ to AHJ, November 7, 1886). AHJ
had presumably reassured her. But Ellen (Hooper) Gurney—
whose father's death the year before had soon been followed by
the suicide of her sister Clover (Hooper) Adams, and whose
own husband had recently died of pernicious anaemia—was to
grow increasingly distraught. Letters below document her
worsening state.
Edwin. Probably Edwin Godkin.

something to like in her. I should think, however, that the
High Church tendencies of her family was their least evil.
I am delighted that the furniture came so à propos,
do anything you want with it. The old kitchen traps will
be usefull in the country. I am sorry about Bob but what else
could have been expected? Harry had a most characteristic
letter from him in wh. he announces in the end with the
greatest pride & unction that he "knows nothing *of the rest*
of the family." Poor Mary perhaps has to follow suit, such
is the case often in the Holy bonds of matrimony, sweet
& seductive bondage! I have just been consoling myself this
morning with some pages of Father's book. It makes him
so actually present! Wm can have no haunting thought
of having inadequately fulfilled his filial function! Mrs. Ed.
& Mrs. Russell Gurney (Aunt) Mrs. Cookson, & Mrs. Stanley
Clarke are all devote readers of the volume. The last
alternates her perusals with converse with the Prince of Wales!
I am so happy that Wm. is so well & working so much. There
is a great interest here in the Harvard occasion. I see plenty
of people, eno' for my amusement & strength, but no one very
interesting. A Mrs. Wm. Sidgwick, sister-in law of Henry,

Poor Mary. Mary (Holton) James, Robertson's wife. They had
been married in 1872.
Father's book . . . filial function. The Literary Remains of the
Late Henry James, edited with an introduction by William
James (Boston: Houghton Mifflin, 1884)—a posthumous collection that included HJ Sr.'s autobiographical fragment and
other extracts from his writings. "You need be in no anxiety
about your literary remains," WJ had written to his dying father, "I will see them well taken care of, and that your words
shall not suffer for being concealed" (December 14, 1882).
Mrs. Russell Gurney. Emelia (Batten) Gurney, wife of Edmund
Gurney's uncle Russell (1804–1878), a former recorder of
London.
the Prince of Wales. Albert Edward (1841–1910), oldest son of
Queen Victoria and later Edward VII of England.
the Harvard occasion. Harvard University had celebrated its
two hundred and fiftieth anniversary with four days of ceremonies in November.
A Mrs. Wm. Sidgwick, sister-in law of Henry. Henry Sidgwick
(1838–1900), an English philosopher best known for his work
on ethics, shared with WJ an interest in psychical phenom-
ena; he was one of the founders and first president (1882–
1885) of the Society for Psychical Research.

is by far the most intelligent person whom I see. She has a fine
mind & threatens to bring Mr. Henry S. but Heaven forbid,
my nerves are not robust eno' for a stammer yet. This is only
a line of love & greeting to acknowledge yr. letter. Hoping
that your stout heart will stand you in the good stead it has
hitherto, believe me with love to all
                                                   Yr. loving sister
                                                          A. J——
Harry went five days ago to Florence, but I have not heard
from him yet. I am afraid I did not thank Wm. eno' about the
photo.
. . . .

<to Alice Howe Gibbens James. April 3, 1887>
                                                   34 De Vere Gardens
                                                      London W.
My dearest Alice
   This morning comes the thrilling post card from William
giving the happy news of "la belle fillette!" & your consequent
deliverence. I have been eagerly & anxiously waiting to hear
& I am correspondingly rejoiced. You have my warmest
sympathy & congratulations. That "he is a girl" delights
me, it will be so good for the boys, elevate the tone of the
house and be some one for me to associate with in the future!
You & she will be two against three, Mother & I, however,
maintained the fight more unequally still, two against five
& I think I may add not altogether unsuccessfully. Your
beautifull letter came three or four days ago & I was waiting
for this news to answer it. Your stories of the boys were
exquisite & you never can give too many. Your acct. of little
Billy shocked me, his health I mean, I had no idea that the
trouble had been serious. Children out grow those difficulties
in the most wonderfull way. You will have an anxious mind
about him, I am afraid, for some time. You will be sorry
to hear that Henry has had a light attack of jaundice
in Venice. I hear from him & from an outside source that the
attack is a light one, but jaundice is a depressing & tedious

"la belle fillette" & your consequent deliverence. The birth of
Margaret Mary ("Peggy") James, March 24, 1887.
little Billy. WJ's second son, also named William James, was
called "Billy"; born June 17, 1882, he was now nearly five years
old.

*infliction & he has had a bad time with his head, but a note
this* A.M. *says he is sitting up & eating a mutton chop. He has
an excellent doctor & an impassioned Gondolier taking care
of him, Mrs. Bronson in the foreground & Miss Woolson in the
background at Bellosguardo upon whom he is going to fall
back when he is able to travel to Florence wh. will be in a few
days from now, so I think we may have no anxiety about him.
I am enjoying his beautifull rooms of course immensely, at
first it was like an Arabian nights transformation after the
squalor of my two years. Alas! the magic has gone, but the
comfort remains. The Smith's are a rare but not a rich study,
such perfection as servants & such poverty-stricken human
beings! I well understand Harry's groans over them & if I were
shut up to them for a year I should without the slightest doubt
kill either myself or them. Hug your Irish to your bosom!*

*All you tell me of Ellen Gurney interests me deeply,
my heart aches incessantly for her. What a battle she must
be fighting! Wm. says "the heart is a tough organ," which
is true enough but the following form of the same idea appeals
more to the feminine mind—"À force de s'élargir pour
la souffrance l'âme en arrive a des capacités prodigieuses,
ce qui la comblait naguère ai la faire crever, en couvre à peine
le fond maintenant." Be sure & give her, Ellen, my love
whenever you see her also to the Childs and any one who*

Mrs. Bronson. Mrs. Arthur Bronson, the former Katherine De
Kay, had left the New England of her youth for Venice, where
she presided as hostess in the old Casa Alvisi and made it
something of a salon for distinguished visitors. HJ was staying
with her when he came down with jaundice.
Miss Woolson . . . Bellosguardo. Constance Fenimore Woolson (1840–1894), the American novelist and grandniece of
James Fenimore Cooper, was living in a villa on Bellosguardo,
a Florentine hill that had been the temporary home of a number of literary expatriates, including Cooper, Hawthorne, and
the Brownings. HJ would later join her there, taking separate
apartments in the same building.
"À force de . . . maintenant." "As a result of being stretched to
accommodate pain, the heart achieves prodigious capacities;
that which lately filled it to bursting now scarcely covers the
bottom." In her commonplace book, AJ attributes this passage
to Gustave Flaubert. AJ's French contains two slight errors;
the text should read: "l'âme en arrive *à* des capacités" and "ce
qui la comblait naguère *à* la faire crever. . . ."

seems appropriate. I was glad to hear good news of Bob tho'
the purchase of a house sounds rather dangerous as it usually
brings about a necessity, in the case of rolling stones, for
an instant move. Harry had a characteristic & literarily
excellent letter from him a short time since. I have knit
a little plain *shirt and Nurse has knit 3 wh. will be sent you*
au fur et à mésure. I have settled down with little Nurse for
a long tête à tête, much the best thing I can do. She is a good
creature but any hermetic attachment is a discipline. She
is as peculiar in her way as Kitty Prince but the British
element in her keeps her simply un*worldly not compact*
of other*worldliness. I was delighted to see on the p.c. that*
the little maid was the "portrait de sa mère," may she
be so within as well! Although it is not always the fairest that
have the fairest lot here below. The Miss Lawrences were
telling me a pretty story of Sir James Paget the great surgeon
& his wife, who were engaged nine yrs. & have been married
forty, & he told them the other day that he could not conceive
of existence without her, & she is phenomenally *ugly*
& he very good-looking. Mr. Geo. Meredith the novelist said
a picturesque thing about her, she has an enormous *running-*
back forehead & a long pendulous nose & some one was
descanting upon her goodness when he said, "But that brow
like the skull of a camel which has been bleaching for long
ages on the sands of the desert!" The Misses Lawrence are
twin ladies aged 50 yrs. who dress in bright green suits with
scarlet flowers in their bonnets & are excessively lively
& absolutely inseparable, they say "Oh! that always disagrees
with us!" "We have got such a head-ache" etc, etc, one day
a friend hearing of the death of Mrs. Geo. Meredith

Nurse. A young Englishwoman named Emily Ann Bradfield
served as AJ's nurse for the last six years of her life.
will be sent you au fur et à mésure. Will be sent you in good
time.
Kitty Prince. A cousin, Katharine Barber (James) Prince, the
recent widow of Dr. William Henry Prince, first superinten-
dent of the State Hospital for the Insane in Northampton,
Massachusetts.
the death of Mrs. Geo. Meredith. Marie (Vulliamy) Meredith,
the novelist's second wife, had died in 1885. (His notorious
first wife, the daughter of Thomas Love Peacock, had deserted
him in 1858 and died three years later.)

*&) knowing they were very intimate with Mr. Geo. said "Why
one of you must marry him" "Oh! we never could do that!"
These simple andecdotes will not be too exciting food for you,
I trust, but eno' is as good as feast so I wont bore you further.
I shall anxiously look for a letter &) trust to hear that the
report on the post-card was more than fulfilled. I am as*
                                   Always your loving sister
                                              Alice J——
    April 3rd
    I am going to answer Wm. shortly.
. . . .

<to William James. April 24, 1887>

                                              April 24th
My dear William
    *Your letter, date unremembered, but number three since
I wrote to you came yesterday, I sent it and its enclosure
to Henry, off directly to Florence. I am very glad that the
furniture comes in at an appropriate moment but I insist that
you take* nothing *that you are not likely to use &) want,
merely for the sake of storing. The barrels of china &) two
boxes of books wh. I want to keep had* much better *be left,
also the trunks in the store house. The china consists only
of the dinner-service for wh. I have an especial affection
&) wh. wd. be too handsome for you to use in the country.
There are no toilet-sets. I want Alice to look into the trunks
&) extract there from any blankets &) linen etc, wh. she could
use. There is not much but it may be usefull to you &) will
otherwise probably become if not already the prey of moth.
But remember not to take anything to store simply. I am quite
able to pay the cost &) should feel much easier to have
it so. The trunks have their contents marked upon them,
I think.*
    *I am more &) more delighted with the sex of the babe your
"affectional-side," as Aunt Kate wd. say will have a chance
to develop in your relations with her, I feel as if I must hurry
home &) protect the innocent darling before she is analyzed,
labeled &) pigeon-holed out of existence. I am surprised
to hear that her name is doubtfull. I supposed that her sex
made that a spontaneous &) undiscussed homage to Mrs.
Gibbens's maternal &) grand-maternal devotions.*

I am indeed distressed to hear about Bob. Poor, poor Mary!
She has need of all her courage, how bad it must be for the
children now they are getting so old. As Bob has
been drinking ever since he was in the army, off
& on, my unpsychic intelligence leads me to decide that his
"progressive nervous degeneracy" is effect & not cause, the
result however is equally distressing & disastrous. The poor
creature seems to have no inner existence of any kind, he has
always made upon my mind the impression of a human
bladder. My heart is wrung for poor dear, dear Ellen Gurney,
how can you be so cruel as to wish her to live, nothing would
rejoice me more than to hear that she was gone. I am sorry
that Alice still keeps weak but I hope that by this time she
is herself again. I do not see how I came to forget the photo.
in my letter, I mean to speak of it. I think it is lovely & I prize
it greatly. One of these enclosures will please you the other
amuse, I hope. I sent Father's book to Mrs. Gurney, having
heard from Mrs. Edmund that she hankered after it greatly
& I was glad to find that it had not gone amiss. The paper
wh. you sent for Mrs. Ed. Gurney I am sorry went astray in the
move. I have only seen her once this winter she has been
in Brighton. If it was a joke she lost nothing, her gift lies not
in that direction. The absence of the humourous quality
in the people I see is something extraordinary. Altho'
American humour is the fashion I have only dared once
to read those comic cards you sent from the hotel
at Nantucket and then I tried them on Mrs. Andrew Lang
whose passion & profession is American humour and they fell
flat & I felt flatter. It is a horrible moment politically, but you
know quite as much about it as I do. Nearly all my friends are
imbecile Unionist abortions. Their hideous, patronizing,
doctrinaire, all-for-Ireland's-good, little measured out globules
of remedies make my blood boil so I never speak on the
subject. Their stoopidity, the impossibility of their ever
suspecting that the situation is one to be treated
imaginatively makes them on this subject as hopeless

Mrs. Andrew Lang. Leonora Blanche (Alleyne) Lang, wife of
Andrew Lang (1844–1912), the Scottish man of letters and
folklorist who had also been one of the founders of the Society
for Psychical Research.

*intellectually as the beasts of the field. The out & out Tories
one can respect. Lady Playfair told me she had seen great
strong men at dinner fairly shake & tremble with rage
in talking of Gladstone! Upon certain organisations his name
is like a red-rag. I do not know whether to feel flattered or not
by yr. saying that you had had so "many pages" from
me. I had hoped you were wondering at and pining under
my long silence I having only written, when you wrote, once
to Alice & once to Aunt Kate since before the 15th Jan. I have
written again to Alice since the young one came. I shall take
it as a veiled compliment showing how the richness of the
quality had to be accounted for in yr. memory by quantity.
I have not thanked you for 3 charming letters of yrs.
wh. arrived in due time. The wealth of sympathy they
revealed in yr. nature was very beautifull to me & was
received most gratefully, reverently, not to say moistfully.
I only took exception to yr. saying that no matter how ill one
was, "This is life," & consequently of value & to be clung to.*

Lady Playfair. The former Edith Russell of Boston was the third wife of Sir Lyon Playfair (1818–1898), Scottish scientist and statesman. A Liberal, Lord Playfair had been a member of Gladstone's short-lived Home Rule ministry the previous year.

Gladstone. William Ewart Gladstone (1809–1898), Liberal statesman and four times prime minister of Great Britain. Gladstone's relatively recent conversion to the cause of Home Rule for Ireland had badly divided the Liberal party, antagonizing many of its wealthier members. The "horrible moment politically" to which AJ refers was occasioned by the publication in the *Times* several days earlier (April 18, 1887) of a letter purportedly written by the Irish leader Charles Stewart Parnell (1846–1891), which condoned the so-called Phoenix Park murders of 1882—the fatal stabbings of the British secretary and undersecretary for Ireland by terrorists supporting Irish independence. Though Parnell protested his innocence, it was over a year before the letter was clearly established as a forgery.

yr. saying . . . "This is life" . . . to be clung to. In his letter of February 5, 1887, WJ had written: "When, as occasionally happens, I have a day of headache, or of real sickness like that last summer at Mrs. Dorr's, I think of you, whose whole life is woven of that kind of experience, and my heart sinks at the horizon that opens, and wells over with pity. But when all is over, the longest life appears short; and we had better drink the cup, whatever it contains, for it *is* life. But I will not moral-

As, vivre c'est sentir la vie *I never expect to be deader than
I am now, nay, not even after the worms have gorged
themselves, I breathed a gentle remonstrance or feeble
protest. I have however to thank you for a moment of vivid
life called forth by yr. unaccountable want of having in any
way* felt *or* perceived *the "Princesse". I was vehemently
indignant for 24 hrs. but now I shrug my shoulders, the
Princesse being one of those things apart that one rejoices
in keeping ⅋ having to one's self. It is sad however to have
to class one's eldest brother, the first fruits of one's Mother's
womb among those whom Flaubert calls the* bourgeois, *but
I have been there before! having had a holiday I was
unnecessarily shocked at finding myself there again. There
is some East wind for you! a striking contrast to the mild
Southern zephyr in wh. your own Alice bathes you.
    Give her lots of love ⅋ kisses to Harry ⅋ the babe*
                                             *Always yr. loving
                                                    sister A. J——*
Henry *is* quite well *again!*

---

ize or sympathize, for fear of awakening more 'screams of
laughter' similar to those which you wrote of as greeting my
former attempts."
vivre c'est sentir la vie. To live is to feel life. A J had copied the
same phrase, unattributed, into her commonplace book.
the *"Princesse."* The *Princess Casamassima* (1886), HJ's novel
about a man torn between the claims of art and those of social
revolution.
Flaubert. Gustave Flaubert (1821–1880), the French realistic
novelist and master stylist. Alice quotes him several times in
her commonplace book.

. . . .

<to William James and Alice Howe Gibbens James.
June 16, 1887. Dictated to Emily Ann Bradfield>
                                              *34 De Vere Gardens
                                              Kensington W.
                                              June 16th '87.*
Dear William ⅋ Alice
    *Hearing through Aunt Kate, that Mrs. Gibbens' name is not
liked, I send a line, from a bed of illness, to ask why you
do not choose the name of "Margaret?" There could not*

Mrs. Gibbens' name . . . *"Margaret."* The William Jameses
had apparently decided not to name their daughter after her

*be a prettier name, or a worthier aunt. The name is entirely
new in our family, and in infancy she could have that most
delightful of nicknames "Peggy." Please do not send my letters
to New York, unless expressly told to do so, also please
remember to charge me with four of Father's photographs,
Mr. Warner will pay you. Kindly remember to tell him about
the furniture insurance being lessened for another year. I have
been running down very much the last six weeks, and had
a bad little illness last week ; but Katharine is come to the
rescue, and I shall get off to Leamington as soon as I can pull
myself together for the journey. Before K. arrived I fell so low
as to send for an M.D. who had been variously and highly
recommended. After examining my heart, which he seemed
to consider an unnecessarily vivacious organ, he looked
at me and asked, "Does the protruberance of your eyeballs
increase rapidly?" I am only sorry, not to be able to gratify
William, by saying that my reply was "Yes" ; but truth
forbids. He also remarked, "You won't die, but you will live,
suffering to the end." The last gentleman of the trade I saw,
was going to make me perfectly well in four months! Farewell
with lots of love to all*

Your's as ever

Alice.

(EAB)

---

maternal grandmother, Elizabeth Gibbens. As AJ here partly
urges, they eventually chose to call the new baby "Margaret
Mary" after her two maternal aunts—Margaret (Gibbens)
Leigh and Mary (Gibbens) Salter. The nickname "Peggy"
stayed with her well past infancy.

. . . .

<to Sara Sedgwick Darwin. October 4 [1887?]>

II, HAMILTON TERRACE,
LEAMINGTON.

Oct 4th

My dear Sara

    *I have been long in answering your pleasant letter but since
it came my little world has had many convulsions—digestive,
mental & sentimental. I was very glad to hear from you that
you had enjoyed your visit so much & that all had gone well*

whilst you were there. I hear that you have been to Spa since
you got back, your venturing so far afield again makes
me hope that you are more robust than is your wont.
I am getting on famously for me. I saw a new physician last
spring whose advice I have followed with great benefit, so far.
He holds out the hope that in eighteen months or two years
time I shall be strong enough to have some special treatment
for my poor spindles, but we shall see, it does not do to hope
for extravagant results. He is a very interesting & peculiar
being & I have not decided whether he is a genius
or a maniac, he seems to have the qualities of both. For many
small reasons I have decided to spend the winter
in Leamington. Entire quiet & a reducing of myself,
if possible, to a lower level of imbecility even than that
already fixed by nature, has been decreed for me—intercourse
with the bovine native I find most conducive to that result.
In London the friends are rather many & altogether too
stimulating for jangled nerves. I shall be densely dull
& lonely of course, but the sands of my little hour-glass will
run out as swiftly here as anywhere.

I am very comfortable in my quarters altho' the clerical
animalcule of last yr. is still below, but he has not begun his
midnight revelries yet. I am haunted however by the fear that
I may be suddenly taken ill unto death & that before Henry
can arrive to protect my little ecclesiastical nurse will
introduce the curate to my bedside. Imagine opening your
eyes & seeing the bat-like object standing there! I am sure
it would curdle my soul in its transit & at any rate entirely
spoil my post mortem expression of countenance. It is terrible
to be such an unprotected being as I am.

My soul was rejoiced to get a box from the U.S. today,
containing sweet potatoes & Indian meal—& some
diaphonous hot-water bags. My diaphragm has been lying
crushed for the last six months under one of British
manufacture, as dense & solid as the Empire. Did not you
palpitate over the yacht race? but you are a degenerate

the clerical animalcule. See above, pp. 33–34.
the yacht race. The allusion is to the two victories of the
American sloop *Volunteer* over the Scotch cutter *Thistle* in
the America's Cup races of September 27 and 29, 1887.

daughter I am afraid. With kind remembrances to Mr.
Darwin

Always affectly yrs.

A. J——

....

<to Catharine Walsh. November 15 [1887?]>

11, HAMILTON TERRACE,
LEAMINGTON.

Nov. 15th

Dear Aunt Kate.

*Thank you for two letters, the last received yesterday. I have
been having a bad siege with my head or I should have
written before to say how grieved I have been to hear of poor
Cousin Helen's "stroke". It is an immense relief to hear that
the dear, good soul does not suffer. I was of course immensely
touched & gratefull for her kind thought of me. I hope that
Helen Ripley got her share. Tell me when you write, she is the
one who needs it most. I wish I were where I could be of some
service, but the most I can ever hope to do in this world
is to keep out of the way. I have constant "attacks" of all
descriptions, more frequent than ever, but not so bad at the
time & I get up from them quicker & feel stronger in the
intervals. They are extremely inconvenient & I much prefer
the rarer kind. My new doctor turns out to be a very
remarkable & original being quite after my ideal, as he never
wishes to see me & is quite satisfied to treat me through
a third person. He gave a very remarkable diagnosis of my
case & nature after seeing me once for 20 ms. during wh. time
I lay with my eyes shut in explosions of laughter owing to the
comicality of his manner. I shall give him a good trial. I have
been delighted to hear of you from K. who gives charming
accts. of your blooming condition. I am glad the umbrella
is to your taste. Silver tops are all the rage & have the
advantage of durability. Don't you think K. looks older?——
Her existence must be a mild purgatory. Some day the rights
of women will be respected, I suppose.*

*I am glad also that the photo. pleased you. My room is very
pleasant & the most comfortable in the way of temperature
of any that I have had. It has no sun however being North.
The bed-room is South & I get all the sun there is in the morn.*

before I rise as I do not get up until 12.30. "Little Nurse" is not little, her figure is exactly like a book-marker & her face like a sheet of note paper, as Fanny Morse said. She is a good healthy creature & I look back upon my year with the diseased jelly-fish as something heroic. "Father thinks you have improved me very much, Miss, that I am much more intellectual than I was." "Oh! I am glad to hear it, Nurse." "Yes, Miss, I made several remarks about books the last time I was at home." She is on a microscopic scale a perfect illustration of her race, abrupt and arbitrary streaks of supreme intelligence traversing a bog of absolutely, passive imbecility. My solitude is almost complete an anaemic Yankee appealing not at all either to the taste or the compassion of the Leamingtonites. After my London experiences my disgust & fatuous amazement are great at being so suddenly let down to my natural level. About once in 3 weeks an old maid comes to tea & such an old maid! dressed in my cast off things which I send her to give to the poor & which she intercepts to adorn her own decrepitude. It is weary work having to suppress all but the one syllabled reflection, but owing to my extraordinary capacity for maintaining the sane perpendicular I am not likely, "likeunto" to Bowles's butler to assume the horizontal in the river Leam. "Whatsomever, Miss, 'is Lordship died, & it was likeunto this, Miss, thank you, Miss, thank you, the butler became un'appy in 'is mind & put 'imself in the Leam, Miss, thank you, it was likeunto that, Miss, thank you." The only news in the 'ouse is that the curate lately took unto himself a dog who chose of all places in the house for his midnight misdemeanours the rug outside my bed-room door. After a second performance he was h'ordered out of the ouse & the craven Clerk had as usual to succumb before the militant old-maid in the "droring-room."

Please send this scribble to Cambridge, with my love to all & thanks for an excellent letter from William wh. I shall shortly answer. Let him meanwhile rest assured that no race to which I belong is an inferior one. If there is any means

the *diseased jelly-fish.* Miss Ward, AJ's previous hired companion.
Bowles. The current bath-chair man, later dismissed as a drunkard.

of saying anything to Cousin H. which she can apprehend you
will surely give her my heartfelt thanks & love for all her
goodness to me, of a life-time. Also give my love to Henry
W. You never speak of Ellen V. Buren Morris! Is she well.
                                   Always your loving niece
                                              A——

Henry W. Henry Wyckoff was Aunt Kate's—and Mrs. HJ
Sr.'s—cousin. For the story of "the odd, the eccentric, the at-
taching Henry," see *A Small Boy and Others*, Chap. 11.
Ellen V. Buren Morris. AJ's cousin Ellen James Van Buren had
married a Dr. Morris.

. . . .

<to Alice Howe Gibbens James and William James.
November 20 [1887?]>

                    II, HAMILTON TERRACE,
                         LEAMINGTON.
                                                   Nov. 20th
My dearest Alice & William
     At the risk of oppressing you by a too prompt reply
to yr. charming letters I must unburthen my soul of its load
of gratitude. They equal each other in quality but Alice
manages to enclose more of the domestic atmosphere within
an envelope than any one else. The "echoes of the little men"
are my delight. I am glad that my photo. was acceptable, but
I am sorry to see by Wm.'s that Time has laid its mark upon
his "thoughtfull & noble countenance," but the genial Lodge
who saw it, says it gives no idea of his beauty, wh. beauty,
by-the-way, seems to be one of the facts in the progress
of the race, a solid gain about wh. there is no dispute. Your
Cambridge news is very interesting, but what a horror about
Ellen Gurney, was ever a man so heavily weighted as Edw.
Hooper? & when one looks back at their youth, when we first
knew them, who could have conceived of such an end! And
poor Elly Emmet what a purgatory life must be to her! Being

Lodge. Presumably Henry Cabot Lodge (1850–1924).
Edw. Hooper. Edward William Hooper (1839–1901), brother of
Ellen (Hooper) Gurney and Clover (Hooper) Adams.
poor Elly Emmet. Ellen James (Temple) Emmet (1850–1920),
Minny Temple's younger sister, had married a cousin, Christopher Temple Emmet, and moved to California; widowed in
1884, she had recently returned to Cambridge with her six

with Alice this winter must do her good, her strong and gentle spirit must soften her. To think of having no other armour than "grimness" with wh. to meet "the stings & arrows etc." with all its cracks & crevasses for letting in despair. Surely there is nothing so true as that we are simply at the mercy of what we bring to life & not at what life brings to us. May God help her. I am disgusted with what you say of Marg. Warner. She seldom writes but when she does she is always very friendly & she used to be very admiring of Harry. How extraordinary it is that that brazen instrument of a Lydia Perry should have brought forth those charming verses, so full of such tenderness & grace. A propos of Grace, I am amused to hear that the ancient houri of Kirkland St. is still sowing her belated crop of wild oats. I suppose her mouthing ineptitudes, her 3 century old anecdotes & her snobbish pretentiousness are as great as ever. Instead of Froude why does not Charles expurgate her?—was there ever any thing so exquisitely delicious as Charles pruning Carlyle! Aunt Kate

---

children. In 1891 she was to remarry—much to AJ's disgust: "How surprised & shocked I am to hear that Ellie Emmet whose heart, I had been led to suppose, was seered by sorrow, is contemplating marriage again, in the lightsome mood of eighteen. Poor Temple's devotion, his tragic death, his fatherhood of her six children, all forgotten; not even his memory sacred, for she says she 'never loved before.' What ephemeræ we all are; to be sure, experience leaves no permanent furrow, but, like writing on sand is washed out by every advancing ripple of changing circumstance" (Diary, January 28, 1891).

Charles pruning Carlyle. Between 1883 and 1891 Charles Eliot Norton edited eleven volumes of the letters, reminiscences, and notebooks of Thomas Carlyle (1795–1881); in 1886 his edition of the *Early Letters* had appeared, and in 1887 came the *Correspondence Between Goethe and Carlyle* and Carlyle's own *Reminiscences.* Though much of this material had already been published after Carlyle's death by his friend and disciple James Anthony Froude (1818–1894), the rather harsh light in which Froude's editions had represented Carlyle had aroused considerable controversy: Norton and others accused Froude of misreading the documents and manipulating the evidence, as well as of publishing material (principally love letters to his wife) that Carlyle had explicitly requested him to destroy. In his own editions, therefore, Norton set out to alter Froude's unflattering portrait, both by correcting the latter's errors and by omitting passages he considered "too sacred" for publication (*Early Letters*, II, 368).

sent me a most unpleasant letter from Fanny Meeker*
likening Bob to Father, what a desecration! one must
remember, however, that all she knows of Bob is sound
& if one is not too long within its vibration it is surely very
superior sound. How lucky that his property is in trust, but
it makes his position rather ignoble. I have sent you some
P.M.Gs. to give you an impression of the state here,
it is a plunge back into the middle-ages. I am in a terrible
ferment at moments over it all, desolate at not being
in London, but glad too, because if I had to see my Unionist
friends I should explode from blood-boiling. It is a wonderfull
time to be living in, when things are going at such a pace
& deeply interesting to sit by & watch mankind going
up & down in the earth each with his own little panacea.
Tolstoi with his shoe-making & his non-resistance,
Cunninghame Graham ramming his bare head into a phalanx
of life-guards, & in between the Herberts & Howards tying
their shoes with whip-cord & waiting upon their servants
& "Wilfred" having Lady Anne bludgeoned by the Irish

P.M.Gs. The Pall Mall Gazette. Acerbic comments upon British life as reflected in items from "the shrieking & hysterical
Pall Mall," as she called it (AJ to WJ, December 11, 1887), are
scattered throughout AJ's journal.
Tolstoi with his shoe-making & his non-resistance. Then devoted to a deeply ascetic and pacifist form of Christianity,
the Russian novelist (1828–1910) had recently taken to con-
demning all violence and to celebrating the humility of man-
ual labor by making his own boots.
Cunninghame Graham. Robert Bontine Cunninghame
Graham (1852–1936), traveler, writer, and radical politician,
whose exploits ranged from adventures in remote parts of
Latin America to a career in Parliament.
the Herberts & Howards . . . & "Wilfred." AJ refers here to
several people noted for the radicalism of their political and
social views. Auberon Edward William Molyneux Herbert
(1838–1906) was a radical MP who numbered among his enthusiasms the philosophy of Herbert Spencer, psychic research, bicycling, and vegetarianism. George James Howard,
ninth Earl of Carlisle (1843–1911), and his wife, Rosalind
Frances (1845–1921), shared a commitment to the cause of
temperance, though it was she who was the more intensely
radical of the two. While he was a liberal unionist who devoted himself increasingly to his painting and the friendship of
other artists, she administered the Castle Howard estates, ar-

constables because "the Arabs when they go into a row
always take their wives". *Gladstone will come in with a rush
before long.* * *How fine & noble is the conduct of the Irish
during this waiting time, & that masterly mystery of a Parnell
never breathing an audible breath through it all. I have been
reading lately with great enjoyment Geo. Sand's letters. You,
Alice, must read them if you come across them. The picture
of her latter days among her grand-children is lovely. She
is such a great, healthy, rich, generous, human creature with
such bursts of eloquence. She says somewhere that she has
always been happy because she never did anything wrong,
never had any mauvaises passions! this might be called
carrying the anti-morbid to its extreme limit & perhaps
stretching it a little. Think of poor, dear Fanny Morse whose
excellent mind has been stunted from the cradle by the
burden of uncommitted sin which she clings to as her dearest
possession, perhaps if she fell once it would fascinate her less.
At the risk of stirring Wm.'s evil passions I will state that
Harry's virtues transcend as ever the natural. Has he told you
of his seeing Coquelin who is so enchanted with Harry's
article in Century, & says it is the first time he has been
understood. He is a very brilliant talker. A lady asked*

---

dently supported Irish Home Rule, and worked actively in local movements for political and social reform, later emerging
as a leader in the fight for women's suffrage. Among the
Howards' friends was Sir Wilfred Lawson (1829–1906), also
an active promoter of temperance as well as an advocate of
Irish Home Rule and women's rights: "a fanatic, a faddist, and
an extreme man," in his own words, he sat in the House of
Commons with few interruptions for nearly half a century.
*this waiting time . . . Parnell never breathing an audible
breath.* AJ refers here to Parnell's silence about the incrimi-
nating letter condoning the Phoenix Park murders that he had
purportedly written to the *Times* the previous April. The
"waiting time" would continue; it was not until the following
July that Parliament appointed a commission to investigate
the matter; only in March of 1889 was the letter decisively exposed as a forgery.
Geo. Sand's letters. A three-volume edition of the letters,
translated from the French by Raphaël Ledos de Beaufort, had
been published in England the previous year; the novelist herself had died in 1876.
Coquelin . . . article in Century . . . understood. Constant-

H. *if there* really *was any difference between English
& French conversation. Oh! the conceit of these British! Your
remarks about our inferiority as a race were very crude, I will
put you right some day when I have energy, it is a subject
wh. I have mastered. It strikes me sometimes that I may
seem rather inflated, it comes from perpetually measuring
myself with the lesser, the nurse, the landlady & the decayed
gentlewoman, when I come across the greater, perhaps not
to be found upon this continent, unless you & Alice
immigrate, my proportions will seem less magnificent. But
I shall make you dizzy with too much reading as I am with
too much writing. Love to* every *one Mrs. Gibbens & Margaret
& Elly Temple. How I wish I could see Marg. Mary!*

*Always your loving sister
Alice*

This need not *go to New York*
P.S. *I forgot yesterday my main object in writing
wh. is to say that I am delighted that the furniture
is available. Use everything you can out of the trunks & the
pictures too & the mirror, you will want things for the walls
of the new house wh. I am delighted is so successfull. Do not
have any view to my wanting them, if I ever do it will not
be for yrs. The little gain I have made is simply negative
feeling less tired & having less acute pain, but as usual
it is simply an exchange of sensations as I am much more
nervous than I was. My doctor says that in 18 mths
or 2 yrs. I can try the two remedies that exist for legs like
mine, galvanism & certain douches of Charcot's given on the
Lake of Geneva by some physician. Galvanism now
wd. be fatal to me, this he said without my having told him*

Benôit Coquelin (1841–1909), the renowned French actor, was
perhaps best known for his portrayal of Cyrano de Bergerac.
HJ's tribute to the "admirable talent" and "magnificent execu-
tion" of this "Balzac of actors" had appeared in *The Century
Magazine* for January 1887.

Charcot. Jean Martin Charcot (1825–1893), French physician
and neurologist, founder of the neurological clinic at the Sâl-
petrière, and one of the most influential figures in nineteenth-
century medicine. Charcot's interest in the psychological
causes of hysteria and his studies of hysteria in relation to hypnotism greatly stimulated the later work of his pupil Sigmund
Freud.

LETTERS   139

how nearly it had done for me in Bournemouth. Since Kath.
has again been wrenched away from me & has now
definitively passed from within my horizon for yrs.
I am stranded here until my bones fall asunder, unless some
magic transformation takes place in my state. So do not
consider me in using the things but use them up. There are
some shawls in the trunks wh. Alice wd. find usefull & might
save from the moths. Why don't you use the Wilton rug?
It will wear for yrs.
  It seems sad to think of you with yr. love of kin left alone
in Cambridge with the family melted like snow from about
you, but our dead are among les morts qui sont toujours
vivants. Your wife allies you to the present & your children
to the future, but I live altogether in the past, I have
a momentary & spasmodic consciousness of the present, but
the future beyond the next half hour is a black abyss on the
borders of wh. I stand trembling but into wh. I never allow
myself to glance.
  Be sure & tell me, some one, what the baby's eyes are like.
If she dares not to have Alice's eyes I shall cut her off with
a shilling. What was the use of bringing them into the family
if they are not to descend to future generations & make them
illustrious & lustrous. Forgive me my first pun!
* how sad the lucubrations of the follower are with the touch
of the Master hand left out
* A Conservative Lady asked Lord Hartington if he did not

Galvanism . . . done for me in Bournemouth. For the use of
galvanism (or electrotherapy) in a variety of disorders, see
above, p. 11, n. 22. In alluding to its having nearly "done for"
her in Bournemouth, AJ is probably recalling an incident one
December evening in 1884, when her application of a current to
the base of her neck in order to relieve a headache before going
to bed seemed to trigger a serious attack—later diagnosed by
Dr. Garrod as "an approach to a paralytic stroke." At the time,
Henry reported, Alice thought she was dying (HJ to WJ, January
2, 1885). If this is the galvanic crisis AJ had in mind, however,
she had grown confused about its setting: it was not until several weeks later that she moved to Bournemouth.
les morts qui sont toujours vivants. The dead who are always
alive.
Lord Hartington. Spencer Compton Cavendish, Marquis of
Hartington (1833–1908), was a Liberal MP who had recently
broken with Gladstone over the Irish question; firmly opposed

*wish Gladstone were dead. "God forbid!" was the answer,
"What wd. become of us, he has got to get us out of this
mess."*

to Home Rule, he and his followers came to be known as the
Liberal Unionists. His brother, Lord Frederick Cavendish, had
been one of the victims in the Phoenix Park murders.

. . . .

<to Alice Howe Gibbens James. December 3, 1887>

11, HAMILTON TERRACE,
LEAMINGTON.

Dec 3rd

Dearest Alice

*1000 thanks for your dear letter with the details of Ellen
Gurney's death. I am indeed as you say "triumphant" that her
bruised wings are folded, no more desperate flapping
to prolong that weary flight. In view of what might have been
one cannot murmur at the manner of her end, but with our
imbecile, physical clinging to what we know to be dust
& ashes the thought of that poor wandering body violated
by that hideous iron monster has given a ghastly wrench
to my feeble frame. And that walk for poor Edward Hooper,
was ever man so tried! How noble she seems & what
a desolate void her going makes for you. Beside our silent
& dignified dead, how trivial we living folk seem, do we not!
We are being lopped on every side, may the tender shoots that
have sprung up about you & William over grow all your scars
and make your days fragrant with their innocence.*

God bless you all!

Yr. loving A——

*I wrote a few days since a letter wh. as usual consisted
of things unsaid. Please send us a picture of Margaret Mary
taken with you. This last is essential.*

Ellen Gurney's death. "Still delusional," as WJ had reported
her in mid-October (WJ to HJ, October 16, 1887), Ellen Gurney had wandered out of her sickroom and into the path of a
Cambridge freight train. Her brother Edward suffered a nervous breakdown as a consequence of this last in the series of
terrible shocks his family had recently endured.

. . . .

II, HAMILTON TERRACE,
LEAMINGTON.

March 12th 1888.

My dearest Mary
 William wrote a week or two since of Bob's break-down
& his having gone to Hartford. I have been deeply pained
to have heard of all you have been going through the last year
with him, & have constantly wanted to write & express
my sympathy with you but I knew not how to do so unknown
to Bob & I thought if my letter fell into his hands it might
complicate yr. situation. To write & say nothing seemed
a heartless thing to do. Your courage & devotion are beyond
praise & seem almost incredible. Your reward for standing
by the right at whatever cost will come to you some day
& I hope the affection & respect of your children is rewarding
you even now. I say "right" meaning what seemed to you
to be the right, if leaving him had seemed to you right you
would have been entirely justified. I have been much grieved
to hear how you have been placed with regard to Wm. & his
family. Alice writes of it with great regret & speaks with the
warmest admiration & respect of your heroic conduct. I have
awaked at night out of my sleep with a horrible oppression
upon me & when I have collected my senses have found that
it was only a more than usually vivid impression of the
misery of yr. lot. I hope that you & the children will continue
to live on in Concord it seems such a good place for all of you.
It is such a good influence & atmosphere for the children
to grow up in. I have been so glad to hear that the people are
good to you. Tell me how you like Edward & Mrs. Ed.
Emerson, are they friendly & kind? Also tell me how the
children take their father's eccentricities & also if they
suffered from them personally? Also tell me if you have means
eno' to live comfortably as you are in the Concord house. Also
tell me if the house is comfortable & suitable for a permanent
home for you—did I not hear something of your having

Edward & Mrs. Ed. Emerson. Edward Emerson (1844–1930),
the youngest child and later the editor of Ralph Waldo Emerson, had married Annie Shepard Keyes of Concord in 1874.

*bought it? Write to me and answer all my questions as soon
as you conveniently can. I have written at length but not said
half that is in my heart for you of love sympathy & respect.
The weary journey does not last forever & we do not take our
successes with us only the manner in wh. we have met our
failures, that never crumbles in the dust. May God help
& comfort you is the constant thought & hope of*

*Yr. loving sister
Alice J——*

. . . .

<to Alice Howe Gibbens James and William James.
August 21, 1888>

11, HAMILTON TERRACE,
LEAMINGTON.

Aug 21st '88

*My dearest Alice & William
    I have two delightfull letters to thank you respectively for.
I never rejoiced so much as in hearing that the house
of Dollard has escaped from bondage, but the death of the one
brother I trust will haunt you to yr. grave! I am glad you are
enjoying your place so much & that the young ones are
so hearty. I had meant if I had rented the cottage properly
to give the boys a pony, but tho' the cottage rented the
C. B & Q. has become anaemic so that I am impotent, may
the great-aunt long survive to make up for my deficiencies!
I am doing very well, there is no excitement within doors save
the arrival of a black beetle & his mate upon the premises*

> *the house of Dollard . . . yr. grave.* The Dollard brothers were
> local shoemakers whose services WJ had recently abandoned:
> "By the way 'twill fill you with fiendish joy to hear that I have
> at last had to despair of the Dollards getting my shoe-last
> right. 5 years ago one of them died, and his brother inherited
> both the last and me, & has been tinkering at it ever since. But
> the last shoes are even worse than the first. This winter I got a
> ready made pair, which were better in every respect. And the
> shell of 15 years is broken" (WJ to AJ, June 3, 1888).
> *rented the cottage.* AJ still owned the seaside cottage in Man-
> chester, Massachusetts, in which she and her father had spent
> the summer after her mother's death.
> *the C. B & Q.* The Chicago, Burlington & Quincy railroad, in
> which AJ owned some stock.

*so that my consciousness is filled with his lusty personality
alone. I wish you cd. see the British cachet of the creature,
he having in perfection that look, wh. all the products of their
genius have, of as much stuff as possible having gone to the
making of him. I am getting out more or less & seeing endless
robust & juicefull bits, flowing with milk & honey from every
pore. My outing however has been suspended for the last ten
days by the thunder-bolt, wh. I have long expected, having
fallen at last, i.e., Bowles being drunk. He did not lie down
in a ditch or pitch me out of the chair wh. is their usual way
of diversifying the monotony of their profession, but
he curveted quite eno' to reduce my stomach, always on the
look out for sensational opportunities, to despair.* His
successor, as an object intended to personify Temperance
& to soothe the nerves of a fluttering spinster, wd. convulse
you for all time, he is that rubicund! His fore-fathers have
evidently thro' all the generations of Adam down suckled beer
with the maternal milk, but I shall cling to hope to the last
& meanwhile rejoice that his ten digits are less en deuil pour
le roi de Chine than Bowles's, the human touch wh. mingles
with all my scenic impressions & wh., the four dilutions
to the contrary notwithstanding, I cd. so easily do without.
Imagine my surprise & amusement on having a slip of paper
sent up to me, as I was going to bed the other night, to the
effect that Mrs. Morrell Wyman had been asked to call upon
me by Mr. Denman Ross and to inquire very particularly
about my health!! D.R. is the "4th dilution" isn't he? I never
laid eyes on him. Where & how & why has he fallen in love
with me†? Annie Richards writes this morn. that she has
heard that Charles quelled a mob at Ashfield—was it of hens
& chickens?——H. hears from some Englishman that he has*

en deuil pour le roi de Chine. In mourning for the king of
China.
Mrs. Morrell Wyman. Elizabeth Aspinall (Pulsifer) Wyman
was the wife of Morrill Wyman (1812–1903), a widely respected physician who practiced in Cambridge for more than
half a century.
Mr. Denman Ross. Denman Waldo Ross (1853–1935), a Cambridge acquaintance who later became an influential teacher
and collector of art, especially that of the Orient. He never
married.

met his "charming friend Miss Lodge," can you imagine a less
Virginesque figure!——I was enchanted of course to hear
of Lucy & Charles P.'s marriage. I never saw him except at the
shanty for a few days, but then I felt that beneath his carpet-
slipper & maiden-aunt-like virtue there lurked a subtle charm
that might lead the heart of woman far. There is some
explanation of Mr. Boott's behaviour about H. & the picture,
in the fact that we have since heard that he was "very much
offended" that Harry did not admire it eno' when he was
in Florence. As H. says "one can never imagine the smallness
of the reason for any of his actions."
  I have been much impressed by getting yr. letters & one
from Aunt K. in having none of you mention the elections,
showing how different yr insides must be from mine,
wh. cramp themselves so convulsively over every little public
event here. I seem perfectly grotesque to myself, a wretched,
shriveled alien enclosed between four walls, with such
an extraordinary disproportion between what is felt & what
is heard & seen by her—an emotional volcano within, with
the outward reverberation of a mouse & the physical
significance of a chip of lead-pencil. Henry's genius not
tending to "race-consciousness" or "pivotal beliefs" as A. K.
wd. say prevents his being as much of an outlet as might
otherwise be. But just you see if I don't have a career
somewhere! when perhaps Bismarck & some people who
think a good deal of themselves now may have to take a back
seat—a certain wife & mother & scientifico-philosopher

Lucy & Charles P.'s marriage. The marriage of Lucy Washburn, the daughter of William and Susan Tucker Washburn, to
Charles Putnam, the doctor and philanthropist.
Mr. Boott's behaviour about H. & the picture. The picture was
a sketch of HJ Sr. by Frank Duveneck, of which HJ Jr. was very
fond and which both he and AJ had asked Frank Boott to send
to him after Lizzie's death. Boott, who had already given the
sketch to Constance Fenimore Woolson, reluctantly agreed to
send it to HJ "as a loan"—on the grounds that more people
would see the picture in London than in Miss Woolson's room.
AJ was outraged, especially since "Harry has been like a son to
him" (AJ to CW, July 31, 1888).
the elections. Presumably the forthcoming U.S. presidential
election of 1888 in which the incumbent Democrat, Grover
Cleveland, was challenged and eventually defeated by the Republican, Benjamin Harrison.

whom I cd. mention, e.g. Isn't Bismarck a hideous
spectacle?—like some huge moral cancer eating into the life
of forty-two millions of the human race!
I was afraid that you (Wm.) wd. feel Mr. Gurney's death
as a great loss. But what an interest death lends to the most
commonplace, making them so complete & clear-cut, all the
vague & wobbly lines lost in the revelation of what they were
meant to stand for. Mr. Gurney's death apart from his
psychical value, was not to be greatly lamented on his own
acct. as he seemed to have little hold upon life. I only saw him
twice but he made an impression of weakness upon
me wh. I find is shared by other outsiders. He showed with
me an almost feminine irritability, & talked of his low-
tonedness & of the great effort all work was to him & seemed
to be little in love with existence generally. His marriage was
from all accts. a most singular blunder, but it must
be admitted that however great his faults to her may have
been she is singularly calculated to drive a complicated
& easily exacerbated organization wild, by her tactlessness
& her inconceivable literalness. She is the sweetest

Bismarck a hideous spectacle. Prince Otto von Bismarck
(1815–1898), German statesman and first chancellor of the
German empire. The liberal Frederick III had succeeded Emperor William I in March of 1888, only to die the following
June after a reign of just ninety-nine days. AJ is presumably
referring to Bismarck's jockeying for power with Frederick's
young successor, William II.
Mr. Gurney's death. WJ's friend and fellow-psychologist Edmund Gurney had apparently killed himself by breathing an
overdose of chloroform. "They say that there is little doubt
that Mr. Edmund Gurney committed suicide," AJ later noted
in her journal: "What a pity to hide it, every educated person
who kills himself does something towards lessening the su-
perstition. Its bad that it is so untidy, there is no denying that,
for one bespatters one's friends morally as well as physically,
taking them so much more into one's secret than they want to
be taken. But how heroic to be able to suppress one's vanity to
the extent of confessing that the game is too hard. The most
comic & apparently the chief argument used against it, is that
because you were born without being consulted you wd. be
very sinfull shd. you cut short yr. blissfull career! This had
been said to me a dozen times, & they never can see how they
have turned things topsy-turvey" (August 5, 1889).
His marriage. Gurney had married Kate Sibley in 1877.

*of tempered mortals with a perfectly healthy & absolutely
British simplicity of construction, exactly like her healthy,
blooming, story-less face, labouring under the impression that
she has gone thro' the profoundest subtlest & most tragic
experience & telling! you about it by the hour. The second
time I saw her she revealed indirectly her domestic woes
& told me her life had been spent on the verge of suicide from
the cradle, I believe. Notwithstanding her boring power, one
cannot but be fond of her, owing to her singularly generous
temper & her clearly healthy uninteresting beauty. Clearly,
I am afraid can no longer be applied as I am sorry to hear she
took to painting herself last winter. The story of the marriage
wh. I heard from a man & several women is this. Some half
dozen young men were on the search for beings, one of them
found a being in a lodging-house in Pimlico, a daughter
of a solicitor who had died leaving a large family in poverty.
They flocked to see her & Mr. Fred. Myers who seems
to be more of an idiot even than usual persuaded
Mr. G. to marry her. He wrote to his friends saying he was
going to marry a young woman much beneath him but who
as his wife wd. have a rise in life & larger opportunities,
he wasn't in the least happy but happiness wasn't in the least
in his line, so that didn't matter. To another friend he wrote
making him exclaim "why Gurney writes as if he were
marrying a house maid!" This I know at first hand from the
friends. Mr. Fred. M. joined them in Switz. after a week or two
& began 'training' Mrs. G. in French manners & the musical
glasses, when Mr. G. wanted some pruning done he got
Mr. M. to do it. Apart from the cruelty can you imagine
anything so ludicrous?——She poor soul, as she said had
given her all & got a stone in return! His snubbing of her
in public was proverbial; for him it must be said that she was
very provocative of it for she talks on all subjects human
& divine with supreme infelicity. To have taken the poor,
sweet, inept & blundering creature for "a being" shows
an unexacting standard in the British youth. Mr. G. was*

Mr. Fred. Myers. Frederick Myers (1843–1901), English poet
and essayist, later author of *Human Personality and Its Survival of Bodily Death* (1903), was a friend of WJ and another of
the founders of the Society for Psychical Research.

distinguished *for his fidelity & devotion to his friends & was
high-minded in all ways, but not meant by nature for
a husband. They say he wanted to break off the engagement.
A.K. I suppose will be with you when this comes, give her
my love. I wrote to her to Sharon not long ago. Be sure & give
my love to Mrs. Gibbens & Margaret. With kisses to the
infants*
                                              Always yr. loving sister
                                                      Alice J——
* *Bowles told the people at the Repository when he got back
that the lady was very different from usual*
† *& why does he in this shabby fashion let his passion
percolate thro' the bulky Mrs. Wyman?*
. . . .
<to William James. November 4, 1888>

                    II, HAMILTON TERRACE,
                    LEAMINGTON.

                                                      Nov 4th '88
My dear William
    *It was an awkward moment for you to choose to ask
me whether I was homesick, for I must confess that a certain
portion of your very charming letter of Oct. 14th just 'to hand'
has rather forcibly impressed me with the drawbacks
of a random & good-natured civilization, where rights are not
passionately clung to & where affect. relatives permit
themselves to rattle round the country with the crockery
of their kin. You will not need to know further what portion
of yr. letter I refer to. When I heard last spring that you had
moved the things, left over, to Cam. I was much amazed
& annoyed & wrote to remonstrate, but reflecting that the
milk was already spilled I tore up the letter fearing to seem
unamiable. I made I find a sad mistake! When I asked you
to take all or whatever of the things you might find usefull
I expressly requested that you shd. take nothing whatever
to store, simply, I cannot therefore conceive how you felt free
to transport the remainder to wherever it was most
convenient for you, without a word of consultation with
me. I unfortunately, but very transparently, spoke of the
storage to make the gift seem less to you. I do not remember*

*to have spoken of it a second time or to have intimated that
I felt incompetent to pay for what I considered the proper care
of my things. My having chosen so expensive a lodgment for
the things showed on the face of it that the objects were
precious to me & that I had provided for their safety
in a fire- & thief-proof building, as nearly as possible,
in a place also where they wd. be accessible & above all
concentrated. I made therefore another sad mistake
in supposing that what was so plain to my order of mind
could not be entirely unperceived by yrs.* I have no words
to express my extreme annoyance at yr. having paid the
storage. *You doubtless meant to be kind, but you know that
kindness imposed upon an unwilling recipient,—and that
I was an unwilling recipient you can't have had a* shadow
of doubt—*is likely to go astray & receive small gratitude
in return. I am sorry I have been forced into this ungracefull
attitude wh. a post-card from you asking my wishes wd. have
entirely obviated. If you had not said in yr. letter that the
things were* en route *I shd. have telegraphed to Chocorua
& Cambridge to try & avert the catastrophe.*

    I am delighted to hear that the place *is so satisfactory. Eat
oatmeal & wear homespun if necessary in order to cling
to it on the children's acct. What enrichment of mind
& memory can children have without continuity & if they are
torn up by the roots every little while as we were! Of all
things don't make the mistake wh. brought about our rootless
& accidental childhood. Leave Europe for them until they are
old eno' to have the* Grand Emotion, *undiluted by vague
memories.* A. K. *described an Earthly Paradise, where Nature,
Humanity & Architecture were in friendly rivalry & all the
generations from Grand Mother to infancy displaying new
& unsuspected perfections—especially* Grandmother! *I rather
imagine that ladies who come into the world featured, eyed
& complected like Alice have little difficulty in managing
shirking man, she wd. hardly need to be explained even*

    the place is so satisfactory. The place was Chocorua, as the
Jameses were to call it, an old farmhouse and surrounding land
on the shore of Chocorua Lake in New Hampshire that WJ had
purchased in 1886; the family was to make it a summer residence and retreat for years to come.

*to a Warwickshire peasant. Does Simon Hassett with his
operatic stride still ornament the streets of Cam?
It is gratifying, however late, to have come into 'beauty'
as you & I have done. How has it come about?—as the classic
mould of our features can't have changed it must be that the
popular eye has been educated up to our expression. I have
been told always that* expression, *when once secured,
increased with time so no doubt we shall be more & more
talked about, when our hitherto more fortunate
contemporaries, Gibbenian & other, who have depended
on the bloom of youth for their stock in looks are quite
forgotten. Henry is somewhere on the continent flirting with
Constance. He seems like the "buttony-boy" to have broken
out all over stories. The best for its data is 'The Modern
Warning,' wh. will be considered* unnatural *by the bourgeois.
I feel as if* I *were the heroine. The Sackville affair seems*

Constance. Constance Fenimore Woolson, the novelist.
as if I were the heroine. Agatha Grice, the heroine of "The
Modern Warning" (1888), is an American girl who falls melo-
dramatically victim to one of HJ's international situations.
Having married an English lord despite her brother's strong
opposition, she remains intensely if ambivalently loyal to her
own country; when her husband records his contempt for the
United States in "The Modern Warning," a manuscript intended to alert his countrymen to the dangers of vulgar de-
mocracy, Agatha hysterically opposes its publication—only to
reverse herself when she senses that by her suppression of the
book she has seriously risked the loss of her husband's love.
Rather than face her brother when he arrives in England for a
visit, however, she suddenly and dramatically commits suicide by swallowing an overdose of an unnamed drug.
    AJ's identification with Agatha may have something to do
with the fact that the fictional heroine has "Irish blood . . . in
her veins," and her Irish sympathies, like AJ's own, intensify
her distrust of the English. She resembles AJ too, perhaps, in
the strength of her attachment to her brother. And while HJ's
tale precedes the real event by a year, Agatha's collapse on her
brother's arrival strangely anticipates AJ's own hysteria when
WJ made his sudden appearance in England during the summer of 1889—though in AJ's case, of course, her "going off"
was scarcely to prove fatal.
The Sackville affair. Sir Lionel Sackville-West (1827–1908),
British envoy to Washington for seven years, had just been recalled to London after an indiscreet letter he had written about

*to be very lamentable all round. Politics, politics, what
horrors are done in thy name! The German race must have
some shreds of humanity in its composition, it can't therefore
be denied that the Empress Fred. must be sadly wanting
in tact; as some one said she must be too intelligent,
no Royalty can succeed who has any shadow of mind. Did
you hear that Bismarck said when she was married "That
little washerwoman will spoil the handsomest & healthiest
race in Europe!" if it was wafted on a breeze to her ears it may
acct. for the subsequent tension. The curious thing is that Sir
M. Mac. has no respect in London from the 'profession'.
He was not admitted to the College of Physicians & wd. not
be allowed to perform an operation they say in a London
hospital. He is called Sir Immorell Mackenzie. H. had the*

---

the forthcoming presidential election had received widespread
and damaging publicity in the American press. Sackville-
West's letter was a reply to one ostensibly written by a former
British subject now naturalized and living in California, who
asked whether he should vote for the reelection of Cleveland
in light of the U.S. government's apparently hostile policy toward Canada. The California letter was a political hoax, but
Sackville-West's response—which appeared to favor the incumbent Democrats—was widely distributed by the Republicans; and under the pressure of such headlines as "The British
Lion's Paw Thrust into American Politics," the Cleveland government felt compelled to demand his recall.

the Empress Fred. Victoria ("Vicky"), the oldest daughter
(1840–1901) of Queen Victoria and wife of Frederick III of
Prussia, was known after his death as the "Empress Frederick." Distrusted as an English interloper at the German court,
she was increasingly isolated, not only by Bismarck but by her
own son, the future William II.

Sir Immorell Mackenzie. Morell MacKenzie (1837–1892), a
noted British physician specializing in diseases of the throat,
had been summoned to the German court in May of 1887 to
attend the ailing Frederick III, Queen Victoria's son-in-law.
The German doctors had tentatively diagnosed throat cancer
and recommended an operation, but MacKenzie found no ma-
lignancy and on his advice the operation was vetoed. Mac-
Kenzie was decorated by Frederick and knighted by Queen
Victoria in September; two months later Frederick's cancer
was unmistakable, and the following June he was dead. There
followed an abusive quarrel between MacKenzie and the German medical world. To the German doctors' account of the af-

French ambassador to Spain dining with him one day, who
told some stories, rather amusing. Spain is the most
democratic country imaginable. The ladies of the court
happen to be all very old & ugly & when the poor creatures
go to Court for functions they have to run the gauntlet of the
crowd, who exclaim, 'Look at that one, she is worse than the
last' & so on. One day a mother & daughter were side by side
waiting for the crowd to let the carriage move on and were
both of them incredibly ugly, when a fish wife called out 'Look
at those two they are uglier than all the others put together!'
when the great lady put her head out of the window & said
"Yes, my dear, and they are both very much more sorry for
it than you can be!" some one said imagine an English great
lady chaffing with the crowd on her way to the Drawing-room!
'Our Clara' gave himself away the other day in a delicious
manner. He was speaking somewhere & said that the Tory
party was making great gains as proved by the Municipal
Elections wh. were worked on party-lines (they are supposed
not to be, is the proud boast!) & there had been 7 Tory gains,
the next day when the whole story was known there were
found to be 15 Liberal gains! Clara had to laugh on the other
side of her mouth! The Parnell Commission drones
on & is nothing but 'Parnellism & Crime' read aloud. I had
a cheerfull but touching letter from Mr. Boott, touching from
its breath of old-agedness. It is wonderfull how much one
misses Lizzie from one's consciousness, she didn't furrow the
surface deeply when here but her continuity told more than

---

fair, *Die Krankheit Kaiser Friedrichs III* (1888), MacKenzie
published an intemperate reply, *The Fatal Illness of Frederick
the Noble* (1888), which led in turn to his censure by the Royal
College of Surgeons.

'Our Clara.' A derisive nickname for the elegant and some-
what epicene Arthur James Balfour (1848–1930), then Chief
Secretary for Ireland and an unpopular figure among the
Parnellites.

The Parnell Commission. The commission appointed by Parliament the previous July to investigate the charges against
Parnell arising out of the inflammatory letter about the Phoenix Park murders that had been printed in the *Times* over his
signature. "Parnellism and Crime" was the title of a series of
articles in the *Times* of which Parnell's supposed letter—later
proved a forgery—formed a part.

one suspected. Her having so violently discontinued herself
was a great shock. I hope the beginning of this will not
be entirely indigestible but it is necessary to have
an understanding every now & then. With love to Alice
& Mrs. G. & Marg.

Always yr. loving sister
A.J.

violently discontinued herself. Elizabeth (Boott) Duveneck
had "violently discontinued herself," in AJ's characteristic
words, by dying suddenly of pneumonia the previous March.

. . . .

<to Alice Howe Gibbens James. December 10–11, 1888>

II, HAMILTON TERRACE,
LEAMINGTON.

Dec. 10th–11th

My dear Alice
Thank you a thousand times for your letter & Wms.' P.S.
so full of forgiveness & mansuetude. I can easily imagine
from past experience William's bewilderment & I must have
seemed to him, as of old, like some Fury descending into the
blue of the serene & simple atmosphere wh. surrounds all
his personal relations. I never for an instant imagined that
any other brain had assisted in, or sanctioned the move, it had
in too much perfection our William's cachet! *I read*
somewhere 'that the constructive, without the imaginative,
sometimes leads to the destructive,' with W.'s vast powers
of construction it wd. be too much to ask him to throw
in imagination, as well & so far he hasn't been very
destructive so I grant full forgiveness, especially as there was
such an excessively comic side in the way he put the business,
wh. seems to have escaped him & wh. I have refrained with
the utmost generosity from pointing out, knowing how much
less sharp the arrows of indignation (!) were than the poisoned
ones of ridicule! I wasn't made ill by the affair as you suggest,
but I was *ill after I sent the letter with all the 'mines'*
proclaimed & implied in it & wd. have gladly called it back
& let all the old plates be ground to powder without
remonstrance rather than assert my proprietorship from the
house-top. About the pictures; I heard, or I dreamed that

*I had heard that you had no room for them, I consequently
supposed that they were all boxed & stored in the ware-house.
H. having a great blank wall in his library I thought it a pity
he shd.n't have the Venice the clock & Grandmother Walsh's
picture, as he cherishes so much all associations with the
past. Do not do anything about it until I write, he doesn't use
the room as it is entirely uninhabitable in winter—the whole
flat is draft-trap. The crossing is now so bad too. Its allright for
A.K. to have the portrait, I was however annoyed at having
it assumed, or rather having her assume, that I had no* liking
for it.

*Harry & I were both deeply stricken by the Election
& I devoted a whole night to tears, but as they seemed not
to improve the situation gave them up. I was amused
to receive 3 letters, yours one from A. K. & Theo. Sedg. ones
(written in* such *Nortonese!!) in wh. none of you even mention
the word. I have long thought that patriotism is a centrifugal
emotion intensifying at the outskirts. It all seems so dreadfull
from here, hearing both too much & too little. Is there any
justification for the article in the Nation of Nov. 22nd on the
bribery practised? Let us bury our heads in shame!! My heart
is warmed every now & then by the sight of* Gam. Bradford

the Venice. A painting of Venice.

the Election. In the presidential election of 1888 the incumbent Democrat, Grover Cleveland, received a popular majority
but lost in the electoral college to the Republican, Benjamin
Harrison. The election is notorious for its corruption.

the article in the Nation . . . bribery practised. In an article
headed "The Really Serious Matter," *The Nation* of November
22, 1888, accused the victorious Republicans of spending
money in the recent election "with a profusion never before
known on American soil," and cited testimony that some of
this money had been used in the direct purchase of votes, especially in New York and Indiana.

Gam. Bradford *pegging away at his hobby.* Having earned a
substantial income as a Boston banker, Gamaliel Bradford
(1831–1911) retired before his fortieth birthday and devoted
the second half of his long life to the study of government and
to the fierce advocacy of a number of political reforms; among
his cherished causes were abolitionism, civil service reform,
lower tariffs, and annual Massachusetts elections. He is said to
have written several thousand letters to newspapers and jour-
nals, *The Nation* among them.

*pegging away at his hobby. Mr. Bryce's book is spoken of with
the greatest praise in all the papers, it'll become one's duty
to read it soon. Have you heard that he & Henry have both
been refused, perhaps simultaneously, by the widow historian
Green, H. drowning despair in Italy, Mr. B. in India! A propos
of H. he has got to Paris & will be back in a fortnight,
I suppose. He is, as always, as good as bread & the staff
of my life, of course. I received a letter from Marg. Warner
wh. entirely confirms my impression that her disapprobation
is an affair of features & consequently but skin deep—(a play
of words wh. will not bear close examination) she speaks
of the boys with admiration—'Billy is a dear soul & Harry
very bright & interesting——Mrs. Alice's face very sweet
& handsome & I like to talk to her when we can really have
time to say a great deal, I carry home always something to Joe
when I have called there.'—so, Madam, what more
compliments can you want?——I shall give you none!
   Mrs. Lodge has always given me to suppose that her
affection for the family was based upon Wm.'s Beauty! How
sad to think of her fate, how curious she so satisfied and
unprepared, & here I am all packed up! Perhaps it will seem
to you that I am not as packed up as I imagine, but
if so, I am like other great ones, Geo. Sand e.g., who writes
a long letter to a friend telling him why she is going
to commit suicide & in the end says to be sure & have her
two mattresses corded! Last yr. I read her in her grandmother
period when she is admirable, lately I've been reading her
earlier letters when she seems to have been morally simply
a boy—up to middle life. At the core of all her fine phrases
on love, friendship & humanity there is simply the boyish
ideal of escaping all control, but it is very fine & most
interesting to see her sloughing it gradually off. What
a loathesome pervading of French domesticity there
is, of soiled peignoirs, cheveux parfumés, maux d'estomacs*

Mr. Bryce's book. *The American Commonwealth* (1888) by
James Bryce (1838–1922), British jurist, historian, and politician, later a very successful ambassador to Washington.
Bryce's sympathetic account of American institutions continued to have a high reputation in the United States and was
used as a textbook in this country for more than thirty years.
cheveux parfumés, maux d'estomacs. Perfumed hair, stom-
ach-aches.

& dirty hands—an all-using-of-the-same-towell atmosphere!
I was much amused with Mr. Godkin on French love
of privacy! a propos of the Reverberator. They haven't their
Geo. Flack's, but give me George! he hits in the light of day
& doesn't the moment his nearest & dearest are in the grave
turn a lens of the first magnitude upon their physical & moral
warts & wens for the disgust of coming generations. Geo.
Sand confides to a friend that she is going to separate from her
husband, she having found in rummaging in his secretary the
day before, when he was out, a letter addressed to her upon
wh. was written that it was not to be opened until after his
death, whereupon she calmly opens it & finds there in a list
of his griefs & her shortcomings. She entreats the man to burn
her letter as soon as read, wh. he not only doesn't do, but her
son publishes it! But you will be sick of Geo. & all this may
be ancient history to you. If it is forgive me! but my existence
is somewhat restricted, intellectually confined to Nurse
& Miss Clarke. Nurse told me that Calvinists were a kind
of Jew who were never baptized. Don't you think John must
have heard her & shuddered? 'A kind of Jew,' too, as if there
were possible modifications of the crystallized Hebrew.
I heard an American & an English acct. of the Moshers
in Paris, the former very distastefull & the latter rapturous,
the goodness of the group being dwelt upon. It seems odd that
Mrs. Mosher who with Mr. Breed seem to constitute the demi-
monde of Cambridge shd. now stand for pure virtue,
it shows the difference in the Standard in the two centres
of civilization——Dec. 14th. The only thing that saves you
from another ream is that I have been down with a head.
Another Nation with more appalling accts. of our infamy, one

Mr. Godkin on French love of privacy . . . the Reverberator . . .
Geo. Flack. In HJ's 1888 novel The Reverberator, George
Flack is an American newspaper correspondent in France who
almost wrecks the heroine's marriage into a Frenchified American family by publishing some gossip about them—gossip
that the heroine has learned from her fiancé and in turn passed
on to the vulgar Flack. "It doesn't occur to her to deny innocent complicity with Flack nor to feign sympathy," Godkin
had observed in the October 4 Nation, "and it doesn't occur to
the Proberts to admire her honesty. To the Gallic mind, that
was shameless avowal of shame" (p. 273).
Miss Clarke. AJ's current landlady.

wd. fain pray that the 2 oceans might rise & sweep us & our
shame from the face of the globe! Farewell

Love to all. *especially W.*

Yr. loving sister

A.J.

Another Nation . . . our infamy . . . globe. The columns and
letters of *The Nation* for November 29, 1888, continued to report instances of bribery, "scandal-mongering," and other corruption in the recent elections.

. . . .

<to Catharine Walsh. December 29, 1888.
Dictated to Emily Ann Bradfield>

11 Hamilton Terrace
Leamington
Dec. 29th '88

My dearest Aunt
    Thank you a thousand times for your letter & its roseate
enclosure. I rarely have seen a lovelier shade of pink! I shall
invest it in some luxury, otherwise unattainable. I feel very
rich, of course, at not having to pay the tax, and have
abandoned trying to devise means of reducing Nurse's food,
so as to make two ends meet. I am sorry not to be able
to write myself, but we have *been through a "circus" the last*
week. What do you suppose a young couple, who took the
dining room for a fortnight, sprung upon us as a "Christmas
Box!" An Accouchement*!!! We feared it all Monday*
& Tuesday the battle began & raged until 11.30 p.m.
    My first feeling on Monday was to be immediately carried
over to the Regent Hotel; but after Nurse had towed my heart
back to its moorings by Digitalis & poured a sufficient
amount of Bromide upon my gunpowdery nerves, I returned
to my ordinary passivity, although not serenity. It seems
to have been more silliness than villainy in the people. It was
very curious to lie here, and to hear the Xmas rejoicings
through the gossamer walls on one side, and the groans of the
woman in labour in the room above, where the mystery of Life
& Death was acting itself out. How my heart burned within
me at the cruelty of men! I have been haunted by the thought
of Alice & all the child-bearing women ever since. The little
waxen image held a feeble spark of life which flickered out

at the end of an hour, beneficent Death, rescuing it from
a mother who was "glad" when she heard it would not live,
& who had not prepared a rag to wrap it in.
* Miss Clarke gave the doctor a rag out of which he cut*
a shirt, & fortunately had a yard or two of flannel to wrap
it in. But I must do justice & say that the father has
impersonated woe with great perseverance, but as he has,
when not tramping up & down stairs, devoted his attention
to keeping up his strength with brandy & soda, I think
he makes a neat illustration of William's mechanical theory;
centres of emotion so thoroughly lubricated must exude
somewhere.
* Please thank Ellen Ripley for her charming calendar, & tell*
her she will hear from me before long.
* You might send this to Cambridge, as I shan't be able*
to write them for some time.
* With best wishes for the New Year*
                    Your grateful & loving niece
                              Alice J——
* Alice sends this because of her recent troubles; she has*
improved the "Liege's" letter before she sends it off——At first
I could hardly understand it. I don't want this back. But send
me back the one which Alice sent me.

> Alice sent me. Note in HJ's hand. In observing that Alice "im-
> proved" the letter, he alludes to a number of alterations that
> she made, in her own hand, after dictating to Emily Brad-
> field—changing "told" to "towed" and inserting "by Digi-
> talis," changing "facility" to "passivity"; adding "of life" to
> "spark"; and, perhaps most strikingly, capitalizing "Death" in
> "beneficent Death."

. . . .

<to William James. January 29–31, 1889>

                    II, HAMILTON TERRACE,
                         LEAMINGTON.
                              Jan 29–30th 31st 1889

My dear William
* Your letter enclosing Lilla's—what an excellent letter by the*
way—was of course a great satisfaction to get. H & I had been
anxious so long & Helen Ripley & Lilla had only given
us partial accts. A. K's letters have for several years showed
signs of a loss of memory, but she seemed as vigorous as ever,

until the second *letter she wrote after having got home
from Chocorua, wh. showed the most curious change
& enfeeblement, each successive one more so. I suppose she
did not write to you or you wd. have perceived the change,
it was so very marked. From what they wrote us we had
no idea of how serious & distressing her condition is, but
yours & Lilla's letters brings it all before us. Could anything
be more dreadfull—given Aunt Kate! It is very touching what
you say of her patience & submission, for there is nothing she
has ever dreaded so as to survive her faculties. "The family"
are of course doing what they can for her, but it does not
lessen the grief & regret of this member that she is as usual
lying with folded hands fostering her own aches & pains.
It is to be hoped that the trouble will advance rapidly for then
she will lose the consciousness of her condition.*

*Tell Alice with my love that the photos. are lovely, the baby
charming & Harry like a princeling, to match his manners.
The accts. of Bob & Ellen Emerson are too funny. But what
kind of Episcopacy can flourish in that arid soil?—from
my point of view you may imagine how comic the
combination of Concord & Celebration, Matins, Evensong,
The* Spirit *in the shape of an intoxicating liquid, the Holy
Ghost & the dear knows what! Tell Alice I have read some
of Miss Wilkins' stories & think them Zolaesque in their
rendering of the New England nature, with its raw, formless,
ugliness covering the ever-glowing moral intensity within such
a contrast to the rustics here compact of beef & beer. This
reminds me of the "documents!" What you say of my letters
is quite just, don't fear to be florid or excessive, for like
Dr. Holmes I can never have enough, but I must confess*

Bob & Ellen Emerson . . . the dear knows what. Robertson
James was then living in Concord and seeking solace for his
unhappiness in spiritual enthusiasms as well as in alcohol;
the allusion is apparently to some encounters between him
and Ralph Waldo Emerson's daughter Ellen (1839–1909), in
AJ's eyes a living representative of the old transcendentalist
town.

Miss Wilkins' stories . . . beer. Mary Eleanor Wilkins, later
Mary Wilkins Freeman (1852–1930), novelist and short story
writer best known for the "local color" in her accounts of rural
New England life. Her first collection of tales, *A Humble Romance,* had been published in 1887.

to having rolled over in my bed with laughter at the
suggestion of the collection of "documents humains." *Imagine
the millions of the Empire being labelled & pigeon-holed
by a creature whose field of vision is densely populated
by a landlady, a hosp. nurse & 2 Bath-chairmen, one
perpetually drunk! Its too funny! It is all very well to say
"don't take on so about the Election," but I think if there were
a little more "taking on" things wd.n't be in their present
state. It is a most hideous spectacle from here, when you have
to send the Nation to an English friend, especially. I shall take
on I think until I have drawn my last breath, that is, I hope
so. I am sorry to have to tell you that you have again missed
being released from me. Fate decreed that I shd. begin the
year from the very bottom of my little hill & now Sisyphus-
like I have begun the climb again. Henry was like an angel
& watched beside my couch for a week, but a whirring heart
& panting breath are such child's play compared to what
might be. As the Prince de Ligne says after the death of his
son, an absorbing sorrow shields one from all material woes,
so does a supreme physical misery, nullify the distress of all
other aches. This peacefull & super-virtuous household
we greatly fear, was the scene of a deed of darkness, we have
no certainty, of course, but we know that a little human soul
was left to die, a perfect & beautifull boy who lived for 3 hrs.
& when its mother was asked whether she wanted to see him
exclaimed 'Oh no, take the brat away!' & when told later
that it was dead exclaimed that she was glad & hoped that
the doctor wd. bring her waist into shape, for she had laced
herself as tight as she cd. so as not to show her condition

laughter at the suggestion . . . "documents humains." WJ's
comments have not survived, but HJ too responded to them:
"Your remarks about A's *documentary* position here are excellent & cogent. I wish something might come of it. *I* don't see
her letters—I wish I did" (HJ to WJ, January 19, 1889).
Prince de Ligne . . . aches. The Belgian-born Charles-Joseph,
Prince de Ligne (1735–1814) distinguished himself in the Aus-
trian military and diplomatic service. A cosmopolitan man
whose circles included Voltaire, Mme. de Stael, Goethe, Frederick II, Catherine II, and Marie-Antoinette, he left behind an
extensive correspondence as well as thirty-four volumes of
miscellaneous prose works celebrated for their wit and
charm—the *Mélanges militaires, littéraires, sentimentaires.*

*& "Oh, where is my sealskin jacket!" If in some slum under
a black arch-way a filthy mass of rags creeps in & lays herself
down upon the reeking stones for her hour of agony & then
kills the little diseased object she brings forth & thereby saves
from its hideous fate, penal servitude is meted out to her,
when the possessor of a sealskin jacket & gold bracelets, with
a sodden, sullen creature beside her with his pockets full
of sovereigns, destroys her beautiful child she drives gaily off
in her coach—and this is the 1889th year of Christianity!
I was "under" Dr. Wilmot, as usual—fortunately
he is a perfect skelington—being a fox hunter & the treasurer
of the local Primrose league he cures me by local-colour more
than by his drugs. He is a most perfect type & never had
a theory or made a generalisation in his life, as my symptoms
decline & conversation revives I sicken him more & more
& one day in the course of five minutes he flew back to the
weather three times as a refuge from my "very odd" questions.
One day I said to him, "My mind is simply cramped upon
those people upstairs!" Then that delicious look of cessation
came into his face & I said, "I keep thinking about them all
the time," then the mechanism started up again—"Oh, I see!"
He knew about cramps in the stomach but one in the mind
was without the range of his practice & as H. said "He knew
there was no dose for it at the chemist's". This cessation
is most curious & interesting to watch because it is absolute,
something falls just without the cast-iron limits of their
comprehension & they make no effort to get it inside,
knowing their unexpandable quality they most wisely don't
struggle and the muscles (?) of reflection stop as visibly neatly
& decently as the hands of a clock. This accounts no doubt
for their handsome, firm and consistent features, for how can
the poor Yankee who from the cradle is perpetually stretching
himself out to reach what is beyond him, "for whom," as Mrs.
Parkman said—"there is always an alternative," have any
thing but an accidental profile? But they are delightfull
creatures & one can but love 'em, especially as they titillate
one's vanity by making one feel so exquisitely subtle

the local Primrose league. A conservative political association
formed in 1883 in memory of Benjamin Disraeli, Earl of
Beaconsfield (1804–1881), whose partiality for the flower inspired the group's name.

*&) perceptive!——H. told me some most amusing experiences
of his en voyage and read me such a clever letter from
a French woman, apropos of an article she had written
on English fiction in wh. she said that, it wd. never have any
substance or colour until "Adultery" was made use of! Using
it as a pigment, as Father said of Mrs. Browning's use of the
Deity. I have been "taking in", La Nouvelle Revue lately,
I wd. give all I possess to be inside of Mme. Juliette Adam for
three months—imagine yourself &) Bismarck as the only
known quantities, you having got him by the throat writhing
in yr. grasp—what state could be more glorious?——Isn't
Bismarck a spectacle for gods &) men?—now that he has
reduced him self to an object pour rire the more he does
of it the better for humanity. But forgive my garrulous pen.
Love to all &) thank Alice for her letter with so much
interesting news in it, wh. I will answer when you have had
time to draw breath from this.*

Always
Yr. loving
A. J.——

Mrs. Browning. The poet Elizabeth Barrett Browning (1806–
1861).
La Nouvelle Revue . . . Mme. Juliette Adam . . . Bismarck. A
Frenchwoman of strong republican sympathies, the writer
Juliette Lamber Adam (1836–1936) made her influence felt
both through her salon, which was frequented by a number of
political and literary figures, and through the pages of *La
Nouvelle Revue*, a journal that she founded in 1879 and whose
notes on foreign politics she continued to write for two decades. She was especially relentless in her attacks on Bismarck.

. . . .

<to William James. March 22, 1889>

11, HAMILTON TERRACE,
LEAMINGTON.

March 22nd '89

My dearest William
    *I have been waiting to write until your letters giving
definite details of dear Aunt Kate's end came, indulging
in &) expressing vague conjectures seems so futile. Late*

Aunt Kate's end. Catharine Walsh had died on March 6.

*yesterday came yrs. of the 9th from N.Y. & one to Harry from
Lilla dated the 12th wh. supplemented each other, & we now
feel as if we knew all the outward details; as for the rest our
ignorance, at 3000 miles distance, is no greater than yours
close at hand, we were no more remote from her at the last
moment than those by her bedside. What an inconceivable
relief the rapidity of her illness was, in view of what the early
months promised; the theory wh. Lilla repeats as having been
the doctor's was most highly interesting to hear as the case
seems to have been so different in its advance from that
of usual creeping paralysis. Death at a distance from the scene
is much more shocking & seems to emphasize the almost
brutal aloofness in wh. we are from those to whom we owe
the most, owing to the conditions of life & the unmodifiable
nature of individual temperaments. This experience has given
me a renewed sense of sorrow & regret that you & Harry were
not spectators of the last hours of dear Mother & Father. Poor
Aunt Kate's life on looking back to it with the new
distinctness wh. the completion always gives, must seem
to our point of view such a failure, a person so apparently
meant for independence & a "position" to have been
so unable to have worked her way to them & instead to have
voluntarily relegated herself to the contrary. But the truth was,
as her long life showed, that she had but one motif, the
intense longing to absorb herself in a few individuals, how
she missed this & how much the individuals resisted her, was,
thank Heaven! but faintly suspected by her. My failing her,
after Mother & Father's death, must have seemed to her
a great & ungrateful betrayal; my inability to explain myself
& hers to understand, in any way, the situation made it all
the sadder & more ugly. I am devoutly thankful that Lilla has
been able to fill my place so fully. What an extraordinary gift
for directness & distinctness Lilla has with her pen, giving her
a positive distinction of style. I have no idea of Aunt Kate's
will and am therefore greatly rejoiced to hear that you are
to gain by it. All her silver, Grandmother Walsh's tea set, etc,
wh. she lent to Mother, is in the silver box at the Safety
Vaults, you will have to ask J. B. Warner for it & Alice will
have to divide it as A. K. desires, there is a list of her articles*

Lilla. Aunt Kate had been living in New York with a niece,
Lilla Walsh.

*in the box wh. constitute almost all the silver in the box.
At Cousin Helen's death I asked her if she wanted it & she
said no. The key of the box is in the box in the Vaults where
J. B. W. keeps my papers, it is small, you will have to ask him
to get it for you. The tin box is pretty well worn out, if you
think it best, buy a new box for what remains & charge
it to J. B. W. There are lists I feel pretty sure in the box,
perhaps at the very bottom.*

*I was greatly amused by hearing of my eloquence about
my legs! on a post-card. Pray don't take them so hard
& as if they were new & exciting, they are to me painfully
hum-drum & as if I had never known any others. It seems
a long time since I have written & the "situation" has been
so tremendously exciting, but I can't say anything about
it now, I will write in a few days. I think I wrote last to Alice
about the bad people in the house, who didn't decapitate, but
de-legged me. I'm glad that you are at length blazing upon the
Irish question.*

*Henry is coming the first of the week. Give a heart-full,
or rather divide a heart-full of love between yr. self & Alice.*

*Always
Yr. devoted sister
Alice*

Did Mary Tappan write the little stories Alice sent?

the bad people in the house . . . de-legged me. Presumably the
couple who produced the Christmas baby of the earlier letter
(December 29, 1888).
Mary Tappan. Mary Aspinwall Tappan (b. 1851), daughter of
Caroline Sturgis and William Aspinwall Tappan and first
cousin of Clover Adams. Mary's parents had been good friends
of the elder Jameses.

. . . .

<to William James. March 31, 1889>

II, HAMILTON TERRACE,
LEAMINGTON.

March 31st 1889

My dear William

*Many thanks for your letter telling me the contents of Aunt
Kate's will. As my path is not entirely without its crumpled
rose-leaves I am sure you will allow me my little joke, even
tho' it be at your expense. I was greatly amused by some*

*of your expressions, writing "to put you out of suspense,"
"going on to see about it," "having no right to expect
as much," your ease in yr. position as exceptional nephew,
etc., showed an artless healthy-mindedness suggestive
of primitive man & not attainable by, but very refreshing
to, the more perverted. My amusement, let me hasten to add,
didn't lessen my* extreme satisfaction *at your good-fortune, the
legacies too will give great pleasure—especially poor Carry's.* *
Your post-cards have also come. I had already been
in correspondence with Helen Ripley & Lilla who are* in the
most cousin-like *manner looking after my interests. I had
given instruction to L. about the portrait, but, of course,
if it has gone to Boston you will have to do what she was
going to with it. I am in hopes my letter will get there
in time to save the journey. I have absolutely declined
to stretch out a skinny arm, 3000 miles, & grasp, with
my bird-like claw, some objects out of that little house
in wh. that kind, old man lies dying. Even were he not there
I could never impose such a burden upon poor Lilla or Helen.
There comes to me thro' a legacy to Mother from Cousin
Helen the old blue china (wh. is worth its weight in gold here)
a tray & some spoons & $500. I have asked that the tray
& spoons shd. be sent to you for your use. I don't know what
the tray may be, but, I suppose, the spoons are the pretty old
shape & will be a pleasant reminder for you of the old days.
The china is to be sent here for Harry, he clings so to the old
things that I want him to have some of them, & before long
I shall have sloughed off the old home-set upon you & Alice.†
Harry also wants Grandmother Walsh's portrait & the old
clock, will you therefore have them boxed & sent to the
enclosed address by the agent whose name I send,
as he is Sherlock's agent. The clock will be recognizable from
its peculiar shape, I suppose. Now, dear Alice, I am going
to ask a favour of you. In the cottage at Manchester, there
is a very handsome old mahogany bureau & mirror with brass
knobs, two tables, mahogany & four legs with claw-feet, not
large, also a small fancy sort of stand with drawers & brass
knobs, I want these to be taken from the cottage for your new
house, & new, cheaper articles put in their place, as it seems*

Carry. Caroline Eames (Cary) James, Wilky's widow.

absurd to have the pretty old things knocked about by tenants
& they belong to Quincy St——I forgot also the big press
wh. stood in the hall at No. 20 for linen is there too, if you
could find room for it & use for it, it seems unnecessary where
it is & need not be replaced by anything. If you see any other
old mahogany object wh. I have forgotten abstract
that too. The way will be for you on some possible day
to go to Manchester, where there is always a depot wagon
& drive to F. W. Churchill, carpenter, who has the keys,
& whom you can consult about moving the things for you.
You had better ask Mr. Warner about the keys first. It would
doubtless be easier to do this in the autumn when your house
is ready for the things, the only risk is the miracle happening
of some one taking a lease of the cottage, but as I hear there
is little hope of its renting at all this summer at any price,
there will be little danger of that. I can warn Joseph to say
that some of the furniture will be changed after the first year.
If the ward-robe will be an elephant leave it alone. Take
a candle as the house will probably be pitch dark owing to the
boarded windows. You can make an appointment with
F. W. C. so that he wont be off. Now, I give you these
extraordinarily valuable objects on one condition only, that
you send the bill for the objects wh. you put in their place—
& use your discretion about that if you think the house
is furnished eno' without them all—to me, or rather
partner Joe!

I have a notion that one of the tables is the dining-table
in wh. case the Quincy St. dining table might do as I think
Wm. said you were not using it. If this last is larger for your
new house you could exchange it for the one you have now.
Forgive what may seem an oppressive number of suggestions,
but they are all made in the air for you to scoff at, or to follow,
as may seem to you best. I think I have remembered every
thing & I trust not to have to return any more to the odious
topic of possessions. How ugly is life! I have much to say
besides on "general questions" but refrain as, "I can no more,"
just now, as I am extremely tired these days. I had

Quincy St. From the winter of 1866–1867 until the death of
Mrs. HJ Sr. in 1882, the James family lived at 20 Quincy
Street, Cambridge, where the Harvard Faculty Club now
stands.

a soul reviving day from Harry whose sympathy
& understandingness & brotherly devotion are a treasure
beyond price. I enclose an anti-fat recipe wh. he is trying with
marked success in six weeks time. With much love to all.
                                        Always yrs
                                              A. J.
P.S. *I am so glad not to be the only heiress in the house. The*
slavey has come into a cream-coloured sunshade, "all bugles
at the top & lace at the bottom," thro' the death of a late
mistress. She is, however, of so exalted an intelligence
as to have preferred to have had a "neat black one."
    A certain Miss Blanche Leppington, who writes in the
Contemporary, etc. & who speaks as much like Miss Palfrey
as a Briton possibly can, said to Nurse, one day before my late
illness, "I was so glad to see Miss James looking better
yesterday, there was much less of that going away of her face
in weariness & pain!" Have Wm.'s & Bob's Beauty this
vanishing quality?——The sister Leppington is most
interesting reads Father, etc, & has a pure New England strain
totally different from any one I have seen here—a moral being
in short. It doubtless comes from their Father having been
a Wesleyan minister. She writes charming notes & has a noble
countenance.
    Here are a few names showing the pathetic efforts made
by this amiable race, so constantly, to mitigate the cruel fiat
of Destiny as to their surnames.
    Llewellyn Noott.   Montague Crackanthorpe.
    Wellesley Tompkins.   Percy Bunting.
    Percival Chubb.   Edwin Tubb; ad infinitum
* *"Dim Carry" as H calls her*
† *I don't mean thro' death, that wd. be too long a wait*
to inflict, but when I have more perfectly assimilated the fact
that the lodging-house is my highest attainable abode—
meanwhile the barrels of blue-china are my "humble
romance," their rings clasp not only precious memories, but
my fancy plays about the soup-plates & the gravey boats
as a nucleus of an impossible home. What an extraordinary
luck that I fell ill in the only land where lodging houses exist,
how cd. I have lived else?
    . . . .

11, HAMILTON TERRACE,
LEAMINGTON.

April 7th

My dear William
    A copy of Aunt Kate's will came to me last week,
by wh. I see she has deemed it best to single me out from
amidst all her heirs by simply leaving me a life-interest in the
objects wh. she has bequeathed to me. As, if the silver shd.
come to disaster thro' theft, fire or flood, I shd. be quite
unable, out of my income, to make it good & I shd. be equally
unwilling to burden my estate with the duty of replacing it—
that is my other heirs, Harry & Bob, I have no choice except
to now & forever renounce all claim to it & hand it over
to you, declining further responsibility for it. This decision
is irrevocable, will Alice therefore, kindly put the silver
wh. came to me from Mother & Father* in a box of suitable
size & send it to the vaults in Boston, giving the keys
to Mr. Warner. A life-interest in a shawl, with reversion
to a male heir, is so extraordinary & ludicrous a bequest that
I can hardly think it could have been seriously meant,
my desire wd. of course, naturally be to renounce my passing
claim to that also, as I can hardly conceive of myself under
any conditions, as so abject as to grasp at a life-interest
in a shawl! I, however, refrain from doing so fearing
to be ungracious to you & propose this solving of the
problem—viz., that you, your heirs & assigns should give
me the shawl, renouncing their rights of reversion
in it, & making me its absolute possessor. I may, or I may
not, leave it to you in my will, but if I should, it will
be entirely a voluntary action on my part & in that way you
must look upon it & accept it with any ravages wh. moth
& rust may have brought about. I might make a condition
of doing so, that you shd. drape yr. manly person
in it at my funeral—or, better still, wrap it about you
to protect you from the breezes on the wharf when you
perform that unaesthetic duty, wh. may some day be yrs.,
of passing my skin & bones thro' the Custom House. Owing
to my unbaptized & ecclesiastically detached condition,

I could hardly find burial here—& then what a cruel sell for
the British worm, who must, in the frequency of sudden
death, have such succulent morsels to feast upon!
  Your enclosures from Kate Gourlay & "Katharine" Rodgers
came this A.M. *I can hardly express to you my surprise*
& annoyance that you should, in the presence of Lilla
& Helen Ripley, have mixed Katie up with any of my affairs.
I have been in constant correspondence with the other two
as to what I desired to have done with my things. I had
a most especial reason for no one touching the portrait except
Lilla. Besides the clock & portrait I desire that Harry shd.
have the picture of Venice & he has asked me to send also for
a little picture of Lizzie Boott's, a painting of autumn woods.†
If you will send the bill for packing to J. B. W. he will pay
it for me. I greatly regret that Aunt Kate, didn't leave some
small personal possession to Harry who is always giving
& never receiving.
  When Alice has decided about the Manchester things, will
you please give the store-room keys to Mr. Warner as I think
he will be more central to reach as I am likely to have
a chance of having some things brought to me this summer
when you will be in the country. Have you seen the attack
in the March Universal Review *upon Harry by Buchanan?*
H. says it is base & scurrilous so I have refrained from
reading. The Editor, Quilter, wrote to H. apologising for
it & offering money for an answer, but H. replied very good-
naturedly & declined of course to reply, wh. will disgust
B. more than anything else. The necessity for writing
it, is in itself a compliment to H. Did you write a notice

Kate Gourlay & "Katharine" Rodgers. Kate Gourlay was an
Albany cousin on HJ Sr.'s side; Katharine ("Katie") Rodgers
was a maternal relative.
the attack in the March Universal Review . . . compliment to
H. The attack on HJ in Robert Buchanan's "The Modern
Young Man as Critic" was part of a sweeping assault on the
"young moderns" in France and England. Buchanan classified
James as "the Superfine Young Man": " 'O this superfine
young man! What *does* he mean? What *does* he feel? Why does
he not speak out his mind, and have done with it?' This, however, is not Mr. James's method. His desire is to convince us at
any expense that he sees every side of a question, is familiar
with every *nuance* of a subject; and in the eagerness of this

of a book by Grant Allen recently in the Nation?—
*if so I congratulate you, for never have I seen a book slain
with a surer, lighter, more urbane & gentlemanly touch. You
ask in one of your letters for some thing typical of the Tories.
They simply ring the changes on Lord Salisbury's cue, that the
"authenticity" of the letters not having been proved, does not
prove them to have not been written by Mr. Parnell. Balfour
when asked questions in the House is unable to answer,
because "I have followed the evidence in the Commission
with little interest or attention". A member one night, I have
forgotten who, was making a speech & whenever he referred
to the letters as* forgeries *the Tories shouted out "No, No, No!"
& other forms dissent, the speech over, Mr. Parnell rose
& challenged the gentlemen opposite who had made these
disclaimers, "to, by word of mouth, by any faintest sign,
or motion of dissent," to deny that the letters* hadn't *been
proved to be forgeries & not one of the cowards dared even
to wink, let alone utter an inarticulate sound! Of course the
Tories's position is easily to be understood & they cd., given
what they are, naturally take no other, but the incredible
baseness of the Liberal Unionists is what makes one sick for
our common humanity. They regret the "folly" of the* Times—
"Too bad the poor Times *was so taken in, etc, etc." When you
consider that these men are not the discredited, mushroom
politician of the hour, known to us, but the heirs of centuries
of education, of noble traditions & honourable birth, with
responsibilities, not only to the present & the far-reaching
future, but to the historic past, what an ignoble picture*

---

desire he is paralysed out of all conviction" (*Universal Review,* 3 [1889], 357). Buchanan (1841–1901), himself a poet
and novelist, was well known (and not very well liked) for his
critical polemics.
notice of a book by Grant Allen . . . gentlemanly touch. The
book in question was *Force and Energy: A Theory of Dynam-
ics* (1888) by the English man of letters best known for his
later novel *The Woman Who Did* (1895). Purportedly about
the conservation of energy, Allen's book really belonged, the
anonymous reviewer noted, to a pre-Newtonian world: "It is
not worth while to enter into detailed criticism of a book
every page of which betrays its author's unconsciousness of
the fundamental conditions of research in the department of
which he is writing" (*The Nation,* February 28, 1889, p. 186).

*do they present! Apart from its political bearings the Pigott
episode, or rather tragedy, has been one of the most instructive
revelations of the depravity latent in human nature, the
temptation once given. The spectacle of each of those
dishonest wretches fighting for his own hand, bent only, upon
casting off & driving to his death that poor, abject, scum
of the human race, upon whom they have been living
& growing rich for two yrs., is surely degradation unequaled
in history. But eno' of Pigott & me. With love to all*

                                      Yrs. affectly
                                      Alice——

*   I saw the name of Budd Stubbs, the other day!*
* wh. is all marked.
†I send the addresses again.

> *an ignoble picture do they present.* AJ alludes here to the con-
> tinuing investigations of the Parnell Commission into the in-
> criminating letters the Irish leader had supposedly written to
> the *Times.* Robert Arthur Talbot Gascoyne-Cecil, 3rd Mar-
> quess of Salisbury (1830–1903), was then the Conservative
> prime minister.
> *the Pigott episode.* Richard Pigott (1828?–1889), a disreputa-
> ble journalist (whose "only commendable recreation," in the
> words of the *Dictionary of National Biography,* "seems to
> have been swimming"), proved to be the forger of the Parnell
> letters. On the day after he had been cross-examined by the
> commission, he confessed his guilt to a member of Parliament
> and fled the country; a warrant was issued for his arrest, and
> as the English police entered his Madrid hotel room on March
> 1, 1889, Pigott shot and killed himself.

. . . .

<to Mrs. Francis Rollins Morse. June 9 [1889?]>

II, HAMILTON TERRACE,
LEAMINGTON.

                                      June 9th

My dear Mrs. Morse
*   I am long in answering your pleasant letter wh. you were
so kindly inspired as to write me on your 63rd birthday—
my congratulations however upon that fortunate event are
none the less sincere. Since your letter came I have not been*

Mrs. Francis Rollins Morse. The mother of Fanny Morse.

well. This has not been a happy winter & I am always at the
mercy of what are called the events of life—what
to the active & busy would be an imperceptible breeze
is to me a devastating hurricane—so I am sure you will
forgive my shortcomings. Pray give Fanny a thousand thanks
for all the good letters she has sent to me, for which I shall
shortly punish her by several prosey sheets.

I suppose you are quite settled in Beverly by now having
already had a little summer. How trying such a jump into hot
weather always is. Here it has been what the natives call
intensely 'ot, 78°! a moment upon wh. I seized for getting out
wrapped in a fur coat from my ears to my feet. Never has there
been such a beautiful spring, too green, absurd as it may
sound—stupidly green, as the French say. I have got
a Chairman now who has all the beer of Leamington in his
cheeks and I am sure there can be none left for his legs,
so he wont betray me as the man last summer did. Nurse has
great plans for getting me into some lanes that she knows
of but I'm afraid they are all in Spain. There is a sweet little
bit which I can get to, when I am at my best, where the trees
meet over head & where stands a manor house an over grown
farm house, a delicious little church in its grave-yard—
a microcosm of England in short. It rejoices also in the name
of Lillington. I am very glad to hear that Mary and her doctor
are having a holiday. I am afraid that they will have too many
more interesting objects to contemplate than Warwick Castle
& Me, I bearing the same relation, please observe, to other
creatures as Warwick Castle to the ordinary human
habitation.

Do you remember about a certain clericule, of whom I told
you, who burst, or rather aspired to burst, into my room in the
middle of the night! He has just been taken to London
by a certain Miss Owen and married; to secure permanent
possession of the rare & precious creature she employed five
clergy men & four yards of train, I myself think that this

Mary and her doctor. Mary Morse, Fanny's sister, had married
a Dr. John Elliot. "He is frank and manly and ready to laugh,
that most essential of all things," Alice noted in her diary after
their visit; "think of the multitudes who go thro' life on the
cry!" (June 12, 1889).

*plethora of satin & ecclesiastics was to divert attention from
the exiguity of husband. He is 33 yrs. old & she 48! It was
quite a horrible shock to me for Miss Owen I had seen a good
deal of as she had been very kind in coming to see me & she
is altogether the most amusing and intelligent person
in Leamington being the first English woman I have seen with
a humourous turn. But she has behaved so treacherously that
the poor animalcule seems like an angel beside her. The
desirability of a husband I suppose cannot be grasped
by a Western woman, so we must have charity!*

*What a change Mr. Higginson's death will bring to you, but
after such long good lives isn't it good to have them gain their
rest?——*

*There seems nothing to say about the Pennsylvania floods,
we exhaust our adjectives so upon the trifles that take place
that we have none left for the appalling. How delightful
it is to hear of dear Lucy's happiness, one that seems, to our
limited vision, secure too, may it only be so!*

*There is a young couple who have lately come to the next
house, who are simply bubbling over with youth health
& happiness, giving one infinite satisfaction simply to know
that they exist. They are from 20 to 25 & have a recently
acquired baby whose acquaintance we have made on the
balcony. I hope dear Mrs. Morse that you will have a better
summer than you have had winter. Give my love to Mr. Morse
& Fanny & thank the last for the pretty little photo. she sent
& give my congratulations to the* Aurist *on his charming
daughter. Farewell & believe me*

> *As always*
> *Affectly yrs.*
> *Alice James*

Mr. Higginson's death. An allusion to the death on April 27,
1889, of George Higginson (b. 1804), the father of Henry Lee
Higginson and the founder of Lee, Higginson & Company, the
banking house.
dear Lucy's happiness. An allusion to the recent marriage of
Lucy Washburn and Charles Putnam.
the Aurist. A specialist in ear diseases, possibly Fanny's
brother Henry.

11, HAMILTON TERRACE,
LEAMINGTON.

Nov. 25th 1889

My dear William

I am long in answering your pleasant letter telling of your
happy return & imbedment once more in the soft domestic
bosom, but whilst Katharine was here my tongue babbled
so constantly that my pen was perforce silent with small loss,
surely, to its victims. I look back upon all the incidents of the
summer with great delight & have laid up a store of transatlantic "freshness" which will carry me well through the
winter. K. P. L. was as convenient & stretchable a Yankee
as ever, did all the odd jobs in the house wh. had hopelessly
been waiting for the last two years & explained me to the
native & the native to me by revealing the extraordinary
interpretations they put upon my most commonplace
remarks, so that when she went we all agreed with old Mrs.
Clarke who boomed out with her bassoon-like voice on the
stairs—"I oughtn't to be saying it to yr. face but just as you
are going away there never wasn't nobody like you."
    I had to my surprise a week ago a call from Mrs. Lucian
Carr who was as dropping of eyelid and pallid of face
& manner as ever, she, in truth, made me rather sick
& lessened somewhat that protesting patriotism
wh. is so ardent within me. This wasn't brought about by her
physical anaemia, but her mental, as shown in her talk about
the Mind Cure by wh. hundreds of her friends, she herself
among 'em, have been cured. She cures herself now, altho' her
health is perfect, whenever the necessity occurs having
listened! to a course of 12 lectures by her prophetess each
2½ hrs. long. When I asked her what the attitude of mind
was that she assumed in her wrestle with fate the poor lady
cd. not make an articulate sound notwithstanding her 30 hrs.
of instruction, she finally murmured that it was "to lose one-

your happy return. From a summer in Europe, where he had
attended the International Congress of Physiological Psychology in Paris and twice visited AJ—the first time she had seen
him in five years.

self in the Infinite," wh. process seems to bring one rather
successfully to the surface in the finite as the Curer "says her
power is the same as Christ's only less perfect". You will
be amused at my pouring all this out apparently as news! but
it was new to me & Miss Clarke & Nurse were inadequate
to responding; & it came as a shock as revealing the passion
women have for rushing into any distasteful imbecility
wh. may arise. Why can't they go & be cured by the creature's
"magnetism" or what not, if they can be, without degrading
their minds by assuming that it is an intellectual process.
From a religious point of view its revolting too for losing
oneself in the Infinite is to accept illness or health without
a struggle, surely. But a truce to such "vital" questions. We all
go on here as usual and are all sealed down for the winter,
and the weeks & days fly by like magic. I had an immense
excitement recently, I saw & talked with a man—so good for
the man!

H. is still in Paris but he promises to make his appearance
next week, wh. will be a great pleasure as I haven't seen him
since you & he were here on Aug 14th. He is busy translating
Daudet, a hard job to turn Tartarinese *into English. A propos*
of the Braz. Rev. he writes—'The Orleanists (their Comte d'Eu
etc) seem really to excite the sense of humour of Providence—
wh. shows, I fear, that Providence isn't after all English!'

translating Daudet . . . Tartarinese into English. HJ's transla-
tion of Alphonse Daudet's *Port Tarascon: The Last Adven-*
tures of the Illustrious Tartarin was published by Harper's in
1890—the only novel HJ ever translated. He appears to have
agreed to the task partly out of fondness for his novelist friend
and partly because, as he wrote to Frederick Macmillan, "I was
bribed with gold" (March 24, 1890). Tartarin de Tarascon, the
Provençal hero of this and of three preceding Daudet novels,
became a type of the naive and boastful southern Frenchman,
a comically enthusiastic adventurer and teller of tall tales.
A propos of the Braz. Rev. . . . humour of Providence. An allusion to the "Brazilian Revolution." On November 15—just ten
days earlier—a revolt of the army had forced Dom Pedro II,
emperor of Brazil for more than forty years, to abdicate in favor
of a republic. Dom Pedro's daughter Isabel, the heiress to the
throne, and her husband Gaston, the Comte d'Eu—both unpopular in Brazil—were banished with the rest of the family to
Europe. The count was a descendant of the House of Orléans,
after 1883 the leading claimants to the throne of France.

We are all on a "Merry-go-rond" here, "honest John," Lord
Roseberry etc, etc have plunged in. Since the immortal
Docker's Strike the face of Labour *has been transformed, such*
a shaking up & "awakening" of humanity was never before
seen, all brought about by the most peaceful & absolutely
legitimate means & organization. Did you see that 200 trades
in London had gained 10% increase of wages in consequence,
the masters caving in to keep the men from going on strike.
Lord Roseberry & Sir Chas. Russell taking the Chair at 3. A.M.
at great meetings of the tram & omnibus-men. How ignoble
Godkin would be on the subject were he not so ludicrously
& naively ignorant.

The Parnell Commission has been flickering on Sir Henry
James gesticulating to empty benches. Did you see the neat
shuffle he executed about Pigott? On Saturday it came to its

"honest John." John Morley (1838–1923), later Viscount Morley of Blackburn, statesman, journalist, and man of letters,
was an eloquent orator on behalf of Irish Home Rule and other
liberal causes. "A fine speech by John Morley at the Eighty
Club," AJ noted in her journal for December 1, 1889; "he says
that to him—'A working man who cannot get work is an infinitely more tragic figure than any Hamlet or any Oedipus.'
beautifully & nobly said, *Honest John!*"

Docker's Strike. In the late summer and early fall of 1889,
dock laborers and other workers in the London ports struck,
demanding that they be hired for at least four hours at a time
and be paid a minimum wage of 6d. an hour. The largely successful strike gave a brief but strong impetus to the trade
union movement.

Sir Chas. Russell. Sir Charles Russell (1832–1900), Liberal
MP, former attorney general and later lord chief justice of
England.

Godkin . . . on the subject . . . naively ignorant. Critical of the
strikers and those who supported them, Godkin argued for
"the unfortunate stockholders of the London dock compa-
nies," claiming that the docks were often a "widow and or-
phan" investment: "To the question whether the burden
might not be shared by other classes who were better off, the
answer was no, that the casuals lived round the docks, and
liked the work of unloading ships, and preferred being taken
care of by dock stockholders no matter how poor they were!"
(*The Nation,* September 26, 1889, p. 243).

Sir Henry James . . . neat shuffle . . . Pigott. The Liberal-
unionist MP Sir Henry James (1828–1911), later Lord James of
Hereford, had just completed a notable and long speech argu-

death. There are all sorts of stories to the effect that they have
P.'s diary & it is to be brought out in the House etc, but that
remains to be seen. Meanwhile you are more interested
in seeing the end of this, forgive such a dull scribble of time
worn stuff. Give my love to Alice who is I suppose up to her
ears in business.

Always yr. affect sister
Alice

. . . .

<to Alice Howe Gibbens James. January 9, 1890>

II, HAMILTON TERRACE,
LEAMINGTON.

Jan. 9th 1890

My dear Alice

   Your delightful and charming letter of Dec. 1st would have
been answered immediately had I followed the inward
promptings, but some minute Xmas complications & a sense
of humanity arrested the performance. But pray never feel that
I have to be answered, for that would double my susceptible
quality with an oppressive sense of quantity. You have such
a grace with yr. pen & such sympathetic feminine perceptions
that I am greatly amused to find that you have a Censor—
a male too!—if he ever rears his head again send him about
his business. I would fain not be a creature who has to be kept
under glass—and such very thin glass too as my friends find
to their tribulation—but Fate seems to have decreed
it so & I must submit & the friends endure, I suppose; theirs
is the hardest share, for I have the measure of my quiverings,
whilst their imagination roams at large. I was deeply sorry
to hear of poor Mary's loss. The wrench of the maternal
bowels is the one experience that cannot be entered into from
the outside, but there is surely hope that another may come,
not to take this one's place, but to fill her empty heart

---

ing the case of the London *Times* before the Parnell Commission. Though he barely alluded to Pigott's forgery, on the
grounds that the case was still pending, he reminded his lis-
teners that even Parnell's counsel admitted the newspaper
probably did not know the letter to be a forgery when it was
published.

Mary. AHJ's sister, Mary Sherwin (Gibbens) Salter.

& arms. *Pray give her my deepest love & sympathy when you
write to her.*
    *I have many things to say, but I must begin with the
furniture. Don't try to spare it with a view to my wanting
it. Should I be strong eno' in five or six years to go home,
I never could stay there, as lodgings are not possible & I never
could afford to keep house; this is the place for me (I mean
Europe) during Harry's life, at any rate. So use the things just
as you need them carpets & all—they are all left to you
in my Will. What a marvel that green carpet, it descends from
the Thies days! Thank you for the offer of Father's portrait.
I should be sorry to have it knocked about with the journey
& as I live it wd. be so much of an incumbrance as to greatly
lessen the pleasure. In many lodgings you can't put anything
on the walls & have to mind your ps & qs at every turn,
or you are turned out at a week's warning. Invalids & Nurses
are greatly objected to so I feel as if this was a haven of refuge.
I am rejoiced to hear that the house is so comfortable
& delightful but can easily picture the strain upon your
domestic sinews & consequent sinking of yr. heart at its size.
You will get used to that. Tell Wm. not to complain of his
Irish servants, whatever their vices they are creatures with
whom it isn't a degradation to live, not polishing machines
with the spiritual substance of a dead life wh. crumples
to dust at the first human contact. Also remember that on the
score of wages things are pretty well made up, for Mr & Mrs.
Smith would have to be multiplied by 3, at least, to do the
work of your house & family, they wd. have to have five meals
a day & beer ad libitum. Towards the end of my stay I had
to suspend intercourse with Mrs. S. she affected me morally*

the Thies days. The house at 20 Quincy Street, Cambridge—
in which the Jameses lived from the winter of 1866–1867 until the death of the mother in 1882—had been rented from a
Mr. Louis Thies, who had retired from his position as curator
of the Gray Collection of Engravings at Harvard and returned
with his family to his native Germany.
the house. The William Jameses had recently moved into the
large and comfortable three-story house at 95 Irving Street in
Cambridge that was to be their home for the remainder of WJ's
life.
Towards the end of my stay. In the autumn of 1889 AJ had
stayed in HJ's London flat while he was in Europe.

*just as a black-beetle does bodily, she has, by the-way, just
the furtive manners & scuttling motion of that interesting
native. Had you heard her rushing along the corridor in a fury
of rage at Nurse who had picked up, or laid down a book,
it being Smith's function to perform said ceremony, you
wd. have thanked Heaven that your lot was not cast with
"Upper Servants," or any Servants. Their function is abject
& they must be abject.* Never lisp a word to Harry.
*Since I began this a letter of a pleasing nature has come
from Wm. I am sorry you are down with the influenza—five
out of seven in this household have had it. As it is supposed
to attack chiefly the "general strength," I, having no more
of that useful quantity than wet blotting-paper, present
an invulnerable front to the enemy. I hope it will go lightly
with you all & not lead to suicide, wh. the papers say is the
American form.*

*The photos. of the house are charming, many thanks for
'em & for the burial suggestion, it is a good idea to preserve
me beauty for coming generations instead of surrendering
it to the envious flame to lap up. In view of the congruous
& picturesque what a pity Sarah Bernhardt wasn't burnt
at the stake! Chance lost in this wasteful world. One grieves
for the Lodge! how incongruous that that flow of human
health & jollity shd. have been arrested by that peculiarly
morbid, unholy disease. I am thankful that she suffered
no pain at the last. I heard something of Mrs. Bell that I liked
not much, the other day. I sent the* Speaker *& shall continue
to do so unless you tell me to stop. It promises to be solid
& good & it is a great relief to have a decent Liberal paper
at last, after five years of the* Standard *& shrieking Rad.
sheets. We are over our heads in scandals. No hope for Parnell*

Sarah Bernhardt wasn't burnt at the stake. On January 3, 1890, the legendary French actress Sarah Bernhardt (1844–1923) appeared as the martyred national heroine in the opening performance of Jules Barbier's *Jeanne d'Arc*. To AJ, Bernhardt was "a moral abscess, festering with vanity" (Diary, March 9, 1890).
the Speaker . . . a decent Liberal paper . . . the Standard. A newly founded weekly devoted to literature and liberal politics, *The Speaker* was edited by Thomas Wemyss Reid, former editor of the *Leeds Mercury*. *The Standard* had a long history of political conservatism.

this time I believe but Irish Home Rule, like Emancipation, is one of the immutable moralities sure of triumph in spite of all set backs. The whole thing brings back the old ups & downs of the War days. If you can remember tell me sometime if any tree or planted thing has ever grown & come to anything at the cemetery. I fear I shall strike a very jangling note when I say that I am not sorry to be out of range of Bob's exaltation. His luminosity & enthusiasm on the subject of humanity always strikes me as having as little body as "a dancing ray of sunlight reflected from a mirror," as was said once of the eloquence of another. The chance of his being likened to Father makes me shiver, which I am doubtless making you do at the present moment, but the protest will have its way. You must have heard me shouting over your acct. of Grace Norton's dissolute pruderies. A being writing about the nieces of Mazarin whose chaste lips cannot emit the word 'mistress,' the sticky Montaigne & the condition of poor Mabel Quincy's fingers as she turns the glued leaves, wh. I do her the justice of thinking she immediately applied to the spout of the tea-kettle—is the ludicrous carried to the sublime & a rare treat to hear of! Oh Lord, how thankful I am I didn't take to refined spinsterhood, to be able, if only once in one's life, to call a spade a spade is more productive of labial & mental health & decency than all the prunes & prisms & prudish evasions of a life time. But, my dear Alice, how can you steam yr. clear vision to make out the blurred outlines thro' Grace's polysyllabic fog?—isn't her clumsy handling of creatures whose raison d'être was the graceful & the light & sure

the nieces of Mazarin. The numerous nieces of the French cardinal and statesman Jules Mazarin (1602–1661) were married by their powerful uncle into some of the greatest houses of Italy and France. The principal architect of French diplomacy after the death of Richelieu and the chief advisor of Queen Anne during the minority of Louis XIV, Mazarin was widely hated for his avarice and nepotism.

the sticky Montaigne . . . Mabel Quincy's fingers. "Grace gave Mabel Quincy as a wedding present a copy of Montaigne with the 'naughty' pages gummed together," Alice noted in her journal; "could there be anything more deliciously droll!" (December 14, 1889). Grace Norton later produced several books on the French philosopher.

of touch, most irritating!——But I must hold up. Give my
love to all & the young ones especially & tell them I hope
they will have fun with their skates. Tell Marg. I hope she
hasn't any more Professors to put to bed & give a warm
bath to.

Always
Yr. loving sister
A. J.

Tell Wm. that I am much pleased to hear such good accts.
of the children, but that I hope Marg. Mary will not attain
"sister Alice's elevation" thro' so much prostration
. . . .

<to Alice Howe Gibbens James. February 5, 1890>

11, HAMILTON TERRACE,
LEAMINGTON.

Feb. 5th 1890

My dear Alice

You will fear that the mantel of 'communication,' which has
been wrenched so cruelly away from poor, tragic Cousin
Henry Wyckoff, has descended upon my shoulders, but I only
have a word to say. Spinster-like I am driven to re-enforce
your maternal wisdom with advice about the babes. Bend all
your energies to instil in them the most conservative habits
with regard to their family letters, their own, *as well as the*
rest, they will have priceless value in time. This has been
brought home to me by the arrival of the dear old Davenport
about a fortnight ago, in it were father's & mother's old
letters, I fell upon them and wallowed for two days in the
strangest & most vivid experience. I had to tear myself away
for pathologic causes & I do not dare return yet, but they are
perpetually soliciting me ; like living things sucking me back
into the succulent past out of this anomalous death in life—
an existence as juicy as that of a dried cod-fish! They both
exist *so in their letters! The rich robustness of Father's texture*
is simply overpowering when you have been divorced from
it for a little & I hadn't looked into the Lit. Rem. for a good
while. What "fun" it must have been to roll out his adjectives.

the Lit. Rem. The Literary Remains of the Late Henry James,
edited by William James (1884).

And the curious thing is that notwithstanding the broad swing
and sweeping volume of the current, his style never mastered
him & degenerated into "manner," but in the least little note
springs as from a living fountain, as unconscious as a singing
bird.
   How inestimable this too from the blessed Mother, written
to me in '66 when I was spending the winter at Dr. Taylor's
in N.Y. at my life-long occupation of "improving", —
"I am so sorry to hear that round waists are coming in, they
are so unbecoming to my figure and Miss Marchington has
just made my new rep with very long points!"—giving
instantly, that wh. the wisdom of the sages is inadequate for,
body to her ghost! for doesn't yr. feminine soul immediately
picture to itself your 'new rep' coming home, at this long-
drawn-out, pancake moment, with a huge Bustle? Such are the
real tragedies of life! Tell Wm. that I find from one of the
letters that I am neck & neck with him in the race for Beauty.
Remind him of his "having dropped teeth into the
consciousness of a Mrs. Smith" in days gone by, it turns out
that at some unknown moment, that I too dropped a feature—
nose, probably or beetling brow—into the consciousness
of Prof. Lovering of all people in the world! Does his half-
baked family, by the-way, of the boarding house pie
complexion, still indigest & remain indigestible?
   A p.c. from Wm. just arrived. I shall send regularly the
Speaker. Did you discover Henry in Westminster Abbey?
Wemys Reid, the editor, told him he had had many letters
about it, "the last from Wm. Minto, Prof. at Aberdeen
declaring that it must have been written by Geo. Meredith,
or the Devil." I thought it quite beautiful. I am very sorry

Dr. Taylor's in N.Y. Charles Fayette Taylor (1827–1899), author of The Theory and Practice of the Movement Cure (1861),
who treated nervous invalids with a set of exercises known as
the "Swedish movements."
rep. A textile fabric (wool, silk, or cotton) having a corded surface; here, presumably, a dress made of such a fabric.
Henry in Westminster Abbey. The allusion is to "Browning in
Westminster Abbey," HJ's unsigned obituary tribute to the
poet (The Speaker, January 4, 1890); Robert Browning, who
had died in December 1889, was buried in the Abbey.
Wm. Minto. The Scottish critic and professor William Minto
(1845–1893).

to hear that Billy is ill but hope 'tis o'er by now. A good letter
has come from Mary Tappan, what a curious product of that
fantastic pair, embodying as she does the unexcessive—altho'
of course from here, enthusiasm over lectures upon Kant
seems sadly morbid. If the Miss Ashburners die I suppose
Theo. & Charles will permanently intertwine and have done
with "loungun 'roun 'en suffer'n" from wet feet! how
dangerous for a man of his age. How old it makes one feel that
there should be only three of the old men left at Harvard.
I have received a most remarkable letter from Wilkie's Alice,
as if it were written by a woman of 30.

Did Kath. tell you of the old maid here whose bosom was
fluttering over the hope that I was an irregular growth! what
Sarah Bernhardt calls "un petit accident," not however, a fleur
du mal in any way, but only an efflorescence of dislocated
virtue, from that land whence all things are possible and
acceptable. Can't you see Father's expression at this view
of his cherished daughter!———It comes over me sometimes
as I lie here among this baser sort with the breath of scandal
in the air, that I may be "broadening" too much and that
to your New Eng. snowdrop souls I may seem to be developing
a Rabelaisian strain. I haven't read the Master, but get
the chaste Grace to send me over a gummed copy. What
a talent for expurgation the family have, when you think
of Charles's Froude. Have you seen Father's wonderful letter
to Mr. Emerson about Hawthorne & Charles's "spectral
smiles." Mary was inspired enough to send me a copy. Think
of all that substance *hidden away from the world, as packed*
with meat as a nut. But as H. says it all belongs to us, *wh.*
is best. Loads of love & apologies for my length.

Yr. affect.
A. J———

a woman of 30. GWJ's daughter Alice was then fourteen.
Father's wonderful letter . . . "spectral smiles." The letter—
written to Emerson early in 1861—contains HJ Sr.'s famous
description of Hawthorne at dinner looking like "a rogue who
suddenly finds himself in a company of detectives." AJ had the
letter copied in its entirety into her journal.

. . . .

                    II, HAMILTON TERRACE,
                        LEAMINGTON.
Dear Mr. Godkin

*Should it seem the duty of a true patriot to print the
enclosed in the* Nation, *please do so, if, on the contrary, 'tis
too frivolous for that valuable weekly, please tear it up!—:
confident, in either case, of the unalterable friendship of*
                            Yours very sincerely,
                                Alice James
                                July 4th '90
                True Considerateness.
To the Editor of The Nation:
*Sir: For several years past I have lived in provincial
England. Although so far from home, every now and then
a transatlantic blast, pure and undefiled, fans to a white heat
the fervor of my patriotism.*

*This morning, most appropriately to the day, a lady from
one of our Eastern cities applied to my landlady for
apartments. In the process of telling her that she had no rooms
to let, the landlady said that there was an invalid in the
house, whereupon the lady exclaimed: "In that case perhaps
it is just as well that you cannot take us in, for my little girl,
who is thirteen, likes to have plenty of liberty and to scream
through the house."*
                            Yours very truly,
                                Invalid.
England, July 4, 1890.

        to print the enclosed in the Nation. AJ's letter appeared in *The
        Nation* of July 17, 1890 (p. 51); the Houghton ms. of her note to
        Godkin is accompanied by a clipping rather than the original
        of "Invalid's" letter, and it is thus the printed version that is
        reproduced here, the heading "True Considerateness" proba-
        bly having been added by the editors of the journal.

. . . .

South Kensington Hotel
Queen's Gate Terrace
London S.W.
Nov. 26th

Dear Alice

I am going to ask of you a sisterly favour, that you should tell us of any favourable *notices there may be of William's book, as we are quite out of the way of getting any here. Our absorbing interest just now is of course Harry's dramatic debut at the end of next month, which I suppose you have heard of by now. In case you have not, I will say that it is "The American" dramatized, to be brought out by the Compton's at Stockport, which is the Brighton of Liverpool, and their best provincial audience. It is* commercially most important *that this should not be spoken of before its production.*

I have been on tenterhooks about it for a year & a half now. If it succeeds at all, it will be a very brilliant success, and a very interesting illustration of the law that you can't hasten the moment, in any development.

In first reading the play, the impression of the perfection of its stage mechanism is quite overwhelming, and astonishing as a first effort, every word seems to act itself. The movement is very rapid and direct, the dialogue very "bright," and emanating from the whole a subtle human

William's book. WJ had just concluded twelve years' work by publishing his *Principles of Psychology* (1890).

"The American" dramatized . . . the Compton's at Stockport. HJ's dramatization of his 1877 novel about an American millionaire in Europe first opened in Southport (not Stockport as the dictated letter has it); after a tour of the provinces the Comptons' troupe brought the play to London, where it ran for some seventy nights. Edward Compton (1854–1918), the English actor-manager, played the hero Christopher Newman; in the provincial performances, Virginia (Bateman) Compton (1853–1940) appeared as the Frenchwoman Newman loves and loses.

It is commercially . . . production. This sentence, tightly squeezed into the letter and marked with an asterisk (not reproduced here), was apparently an afterthought.

*beauty. The public density is of course an immeasureable
quantity so we must not let our hopes run too high.
How Harry, Katharine & I are to live through the first night
I have no idea. There is little change in my state, the only
variety in the day being the varying degrees of discomfort,
& I find much entertainment therein. I am working
away as hard as I can to get dead as soon as possible,
so as to release Katharine; but this play of Harry's makes
a sad complication, as I don't want to immerse him
in a deathbed scene on his "first night," too much
of an aesthetic incongruity! The trouble seems to be there isn't
anything to die of, but there are a good many jokes left still,
and that's the main thing after all.*

Love to all,
Your affectionate sister
A. J.
(E. A. B.)

....

<to William James. July 30, 1891.
Dictated to Katharine Loring>

41, ARGYLL ROAD
KENSINGTON, W.

July 30

My dearest William,
   *A thousand thanks for your beautiful & fraternal letter,
which came, I know not when, owing to Katharine's iron
despotism. Of course I could have wanted nothing else, and*

have wanted nothing else. William's moving letter of July 6,
1891, read in part: "Of course if the tumor should turn out to
be cancerous, that means, as all men know, a finite length of
days; and then good bye to neurasthenia and neuralgia and
headache, and weariness and palpitation and disgust all at one
stroke——I should think you would be reconciled to the pros-
pect with all its plusses and minuses! I know you've never
cared for life, and to me now at the age of nearly fifty life and
death seem singularly close together in all of us—and life a
mere farce of frustration in all, so far as the realization of the
innermost ideals go to which we are made respectively capable
of feeling an affinity and responding. Your frustrations are only
rather more flagrant than the rule; and you've been saved
many forms of self-dissatisfaction and misery which appertain
to such a multiplication of responsible relations to different

*should have felt, notwithstanding my "unsentimentality" very
much wounded & incomprise, had you walked round & not
up to my demise.*

*It is the most supremely interesting moment in life, the only
one in fact, when living seems life, and I count it as the
greatest good fortune to have these few months so full
of interest & instruction in the knowledge of my approaching
death. It is as simple in one's own person as any fact
of nature, the fall of a leaf or the blooming of a rose, & I have
a delicious consciousness, ever present, of wide spaces close
at hand, & whisperings of release in the air.*

*Your philosophy of the transition is entirely mine & at this
remoteness I will venture upon the impertinence
of congratulating you upon having arrived "at nearly fifty"
at the point at which I started at fifteen!——'Twas always
thus of old, but in time, you usually, as now, caught up.*

But you must believe that you greatly exaggerate the tragic

people as I, for instance, have got into. Your fortitude, good
spirits and unsentimentality have been simply unexampled in
the midst of your physical woes; and when you're relieved
from your post, just *that* bright note will remain behind, together with the inscrutable and mysterious character of the
doom of nervous weakness which has chained you down for
all these years. These inhibitions, these split-up selves, all
these new facts that are gradually coming to light about our
organization, these enlargements of the self in trance etc., are
bringing me to turn for light in the direction of all sorts of de-
spised spiritualistic and unscientific ideas. Father would find
in me to day a much more receptive listener—all that philosophy has got to be brought in. And what a queer contradiction
comes to the ordinary scientific argument against immortality
(based on body being mind's condition and mind going *out*
when body is gone) when one must believe (as now, in these
neurotic cases) that some infernality in the body *prevents*
really existing parts of the mind from coming to their effective
rights at all, suppresses them and blots them out from par-
ticipation in this world's experiences, although they are *there*
all the time. When that which is *you* passes out of the body, I
am sure that there will be an explosion of liberated force and
life, till then eclipsed and kept down. I can hardly imagine
your transition without a great oscillation of both "worlds," as
they regain their equilibrium after the change! Everyone will
feel the shock, but you yourself will be more surprised than
any body else."

element in my commonplace little journey; & so far from ever
having thought that "my frustrations were more flagrant
than the rule", I have always simmered complacently
in my complete immunity therefrom. As from early days the
elusive nature of concrete hopes shone forth, I always rejoiced
that my temperament had set for my task the attainment
of the simplest rudimentary ideal, which I could carry about
in my pocket & work away upon equally in shower
as in sunshine, in complete security from the grotesque
obstructions supposed to be life, which have indeed, only
strengthened the sinews to whatever imperfect
accomplishment I may have attained.

You must also remember that a woman, by nature, needs
much less to feed upon than a man, a few emotions & she
is satisfied: so when I am gone, pray don't think of me simply
as a creature who might have been something else had
neurotic science been born; notwithstanding the poverty
of my outside experience I have always had a significance for
myself, & every chance to stumble along my straight
& narrow little path, & to worship at the feet of my Deity,
& what more can a human soul ask for?

This year has been one of the happiest I have ever known,
surrounded by such affection & devotion, but I won't enter
into details, as I see the blush mantle the elderly cheek
of my scribe, already——We are smothered in flowers from
kind friends: Annie Richards has been perfect in her constant
& considerate friendship, that you must remember in the
years to come, her atrophied cousin of Basset is incroyable!
You can't imagine the inspiring effect of Baldwin, from amid
your surroundings.

atrophied cousin of Basset. Sara Sedgwick Darwin.
Baldwin. William Wilberforce Baldwin (1850–1910), an American physician who practiced for many years in Florence and a
good friend of HJ. Baldwin confirmed that AJ's tumor was cancerous, though he judged it "not immediately fatal." "He is
very 'live,'" HJ observed to WJ, "clever, intelligent & inge-
nious—remarkable in his way; &, as a good friend of mine,
has taken an added interest in her, besides having evidently
been most careful & attentive. He appears to have been almost
the only doctor that she has ever *liked* to see . . ." (July 31,
1891).

*Ansonia, Conn., pur sang! emitting a theory about you from
every pore, grasping you as a whole, instead of as a stomach
or a dislocated elbow, after the fashion of the comatose
creature sicklied o'er with bed-side manner, manufactured
by the wholesale here. The soothing nature of his imaginative
manipulations after the succession of bruises administered
by the anchylosed joints to which I have been exposed of late
years, has been most restorative.*

*Give much love to Alice & to all the household, great
& small.*

*Be sure, please, to give my love to Henrietta Child
& to thank her for her sweet & pretty letter, & my love
to Mrs. Child, too.*

*Your always loving & grateful sister
Alice James*

P.S. *I have many excellent & kind letters, but the universal
tendency "to be reconciled" to my passing to the summer
land, might cause confusion in the mind of the uninitiated!*

pur sang. Pure-blooded.
Henrietta Child. The daughter of Francis James and Elizabeth
(Sedgwick) Child, Henrietta was the beneficiary of $1,000 in
AJ's will—one of the very few nonrelatives, apart from Katharine Loring, whom Alice thus singled out.
the summer land. "The summer land" was the term for the
afterworld current among the members of the Society for Psychical Research.

. . . .

<to Frances Rollins Morse. August 5, 1891.
Dictated to Katharine Loring>

41, ARGYLL ROAD,
KENSINGTON, W.

Aug 5

My dearest Fanny,

*I have been trying for the last weeks to be able to write
to you with my own goose-quill, but I have now left such
hopes behind: you will, however, be able to hear through the
hand of Katharine the quavering chirp of Alice. I send
a thousand thanks for your lovely letters, all your expressions
of affection deeply touched my heart although I felt that they*

*reflected the generous subject much more than they were
deserved by the unworthy object. But we are both of us sure
that all that is best in our long & happy friendship will never
perish.*

*I feel selfish in rejoicing over my easier lot, leaving all you
good people to struggle under the dreary burdens & illusive
pleasures. Thank you very much for the kind thought
of sending me Mary's sketch, I think there is great delicacy
& refinement in the expression & it gives me great pleasure
to have it.*

*I want you to know, directly from us, just what
my condition is: Sir Andrew Clark, when he examined
me, beside the trouble in my heart, said that a lump, that
we had felt in my breast, since February, was a tumor, about
which he could then give no decided opinion. A little while
ago, Dr. Baldwin of Florence, told us that it is unmistakeably
a cancer, which explains very satisfactorily to us, my long,
slow decline, and, at times, extreme distress—for which,
however, he has given us many alleviations, in true Yankee
fashion, & has changed our outlook for the next few months.*

*We have not spoken about it before, because one dreads
imposing the details of one's degenerate state on such
sympathetic hearts; I now inflict it only on you & two or three
others, one shrinks so from parsimonious gossip, but I hated
the thought that you might hear it accidentally, for you must
know that it sounds so much worse than it is. I have every
alleviation, blessing & consolation.*

Tell your mother that we are enjoying the garden

dreary burdens & illusive pleasures. Correction and addition
in AJ's own hand. The dictated original had simply "illusive
burdens."

Sir Andrew Clark. The distinguished physician and surgeon
Sir Andrew Clark (1847–1913) was head of the cancer department at Middlesex Hospital and later honorary surgeon to Edward VII. "Sir Andrew is doubtless good & kind at bottom," AJ
observed in her diary, "but they are all terrible, with that
globular manner, talking by the hour without *saying* anything, while the longing pallid victim stretches out a sickly
tendril, hoping for some excrescence a human wart, to catch
on to, but it vainly slips off the polished surface, as comforting
& nourishing as that of a billiard ball" (January 4, 1892).

*immensely, & it does Katharine the greatest credit; for she
has worked it all herself, having had a man, only to cut the
grass; our poppies are exquisite.*

*Give a great deal of love to Lucy when you write, & tell her
I am so glad of her happy future, but abnormal as it will seem
to her, I think I have the better lot: the Spouse is, of course
included in this message.*

*With loads of love to your mother & thanks for her letters
& to the sweet Mary & her husband, believe me, as always,
your loving*

                                                Alice James

. . . .

<to William James. December 2, 1891.
Dictated to Emily Ann Bradfield>

                        41, ARGYLL ROAD,
                        KENSINGTON, W.

                                                Dec. 2nd

Dear William

*Supposing that your being is vibrating with more or less
curiosity about the great hypnotic experiment on Campden
Hill, I report progress. As far as pain goes the result is nil, save
on four occasions the violent resuscitation of a dormant
toothache, a wretched dying nerve which demands an agony
of its own, impatient of waiting for, or too vain to lose itself
in the grand mortuary moment so near at hand. What
I do experience, is a calming of my nerves & a quiescent
passive state, during which I fall asleep, without the
sensations of terror which have accompanied that process for
so many years, & I sleep for five or six hours, uninterruptedly.*

the great hypnotic experiment on Campden Hill. WJ had recommended that AJ try hypnotism to relieve her pain and to
help her sleep; he had also recommended that she send for a
Dr. Charles Lloyd Tuckey, the author of *Psycho-Therapeutics:
or Treatment by Hypnotism and Suggestion*—"the hypnotic
Tuckey, the mild radiance of whose moon-beam personality
has penetrated with a little hope, the black mists that envel-
oped us" (Diary, December 4, 1891). Campden Hill in Kensington was the location of the furnished house at 41 Argyll
Road that AJ and Katharine had taken the previous spring;
the house was ten minutes away from HJ's flat in De Vere
Gardens.

But then, I slept like a dormouse all last year before taking
morphia. *Katharine has very much better results than
"Tuckums",* that is as long as she remains silent & operates
only by the gesture; but when she with solemn majesty
addresses herself to the digestive Boreas & with persuasive
accents suggest calmness & serenity of demeanour,
cachinnation is the sole resource.*
 We were fortunate in our ignorance, to have fallen upon
an experienced doctor as well as hypnotist. *He seems
to be much penetrated with my abnormal susceptibility
& says that to put me actually asleep would be a very risky
experiment. He seems to look upon the reckless use
of it as absolutely criminal. He is only coming once this week
& then he will die, of course, a natural death. My pains are
too much a part of my substance to have any modifications
before the spirit & the flesh fall asunder. But I feel as if I had
gained something in the way of a nerve pacifier & one of the
most intense intellectual experiences of my life. Too tired for
another word——Love to all*

Alice——

P.S. *Tuckey is a white soul & sheds a gentle social radiance
which has made grateful the various occasions.*
* *meaning Lloyd Tuckey her hypnotizer. W. J. [in W.J.'s hand]*
. . . .

<to Frances Rollins Morse. December 5 [1891?].
Dictated to Emily Ann Bradfield>

41, ARGYLL ROAD,
KENSINGTON, W.

Dec. 5th

My dearest Fanny
 I sent Mary a little while ago, a line apropos of the son,
whom you so kindly told me had just taken upon himself the
burden of existence—how interesting to compare with him
the point of view, & how little should we wish for an exchange
of generations! But you have been in my mind as the person
chiefly concerned, for doesn't the Aunt bear the heat & brunt
of the battle & where is the Aunt-essence so perfectly
embodied as in thee, my beloved spinster?
 I send thanks from my heart for all the loving words
& memories which you have addressed to my unworthiness,

*& I should return them multiplied a hundredfold, were I not
a paralysed dictator. Don't let the "sound" of us reverberate
within your imagination. The echo of our ills as it is tossed
from billow to billow on its long journey must fall with the
most exaggerated magnitude upon your too sympathetic ear.
It is all so natural & simple & nothing comes to which we are
not adequate, save when morphia, destroying pain tilts
us from the philosophic attitude all too suddenly; but under
the hypnotic suggestion, or rather pawings of an amiable
necromancer I have regained all my native dignity. You will
be glad to hear that Katharine grows fat under all her
harassments, & keeps us constantly jovial by her relations
with the outside world, which however, are sadly curtailed
by my unbridled demands upon her. Best love to your mother,
Mary & Harry and all the good.*

    *How I should like a look at you, although I am sure that
this even could not add to the sense of unity & understanding,
an understanding to grow even more perfect as the mists
vanish before the glories so close about us, my long & always
to be loved friend,*

Farewell & God bless you
Alice

Harry. Henry Morse, Fanny's brother.
Farewell & God bless you. Valediction and signature in AJ's
hand.

. . . .

<to William James. March 5, 1892. CABLE>

London 5

Tenderest love to all farewell am going soon.

Alice

Cable. This cable was sent by Henry, Alice having whispered
its message to him. She died the following afternoon.

A NOTE ON THE TEXT

The letters of Alice James reproduced in this book were chosen both for their inherent appeal and for their representativeness, to help the reader sense the range of her concerns and the shape of her "mortal career." They constitute about a third of her letters known to have survived. The vast majority of these are in the collection of the James family papers in the Houghton Library, Harvard University. Alice James's correspondence with her friend Annie Ashburner, later Annie Richards, is in the National Library of Scotland in Edinburgh. A small number of Alice's letters to her relatives are among the papers belonging to Mr. and Mrs. Henry James Vaux of Berkeley, California. Several other letters can be found in the Schlesinger Library, Radcliffe College, the Pierpont Morgan Library in New York, and the Colby College Library in Waterville, Maine.

The text of Alice's letters has been edited as lightly as possible—the general aim being to reproduce the informal style of the letters as she wrote them, even at the risk of a certain irregularity of syntax, spelling, and punctuation. To this end, ampersands and abbreviations (both of which Alice used liberally) have been retained; most of her abbreviations are quite familiar ones ("thro'" for "through," "wd." for "would," "wh." for "which," "yr." for "your," and the like); occasional obscurities are clarified in the notes. The spelling is Alice's, save where correcting it seemed preferable to confusing or distracting the reader. Such corrections as have been made are indicated in Alterations in the Manuscript by page and line number. The word as it is spelled in the text is followed by the word as Alice actually wrote it, for example, "there is": "their is." Punctuation is also Alice's, except that the editor has taken the liberty of supplying missing periods when both syntax and subsequent capitalization clearly call for them, and of slightly regularizing Alice's erratic use of single and double quotation marks, to the extent of concluding a quoted phrase or passage with the same sort of mark with which it began, even when these differed in the manuscript. No attempt has otherwise been made, however, to systematize her method of indicating quotations. When Alice omitted all final punctuation before the signature of a letter, as she frequently did, her practice has been followed here. In a very small number of cases where Alice's punctuation seemed likely to produce serious confusion, editorial changes have been made and noted in Alterations in the Manuscript by the same system used for corrections of spelling.

Alice had a habit of running two clearly separate words together as she wrote; "I" and "am," for example, are frequently written as one word; these have been divided. Occasional doubling of a minor word—usually a preposition or conjunction, written at the bottom of one page and inadvertently repeated at the top of the next—has also been corrected.

Like most writers, Alice often acted casually as her own editor—striking over some words as she caught an error or simply changed her mind, canceling some passages and inserting new material as she wrote. Her cancellations have, for the most part, been respected and followed; where these have seemed significant, they have been indicated in the Alterations list as: " 'pleasure' *follows canceled* 'trouble.' " In one or two cases, where a passage seemed quite obscure without the canceled material or where the canceled material seemed of exceptional interest, the cancellations have been restored and the fact also noted. To preserve the appearance of the printed page, all words that Alice inserted above the line have been included as if they appeared on the line to which they were added. One rather unusual editorial practice of Alice's should be noted: on occasion, she apparently inverted her intended word order, and rather than canceling and beginning again, simply added numerical subscripts indicating the order in which the words should actually be read—"the genial Lodge" to whom she refers in her letter of November 20 [1887?], for example, appears in the manuscript as "the Lodge$_2$ genial.$_1$" When she thus signaled a change in word order, her wishes have been followed and the words reproduced in the sequence finally intended.

Dictating her letters—especially when the amanuensis was her nurse Emily Bradfield—appears often to have prompted Alice to act as editor in a more formal way, rereading the dictated manuscript and correcting it in her own hand after it was completed. Her changes have, of course, been followed; when these are of unusual interest, they have been recorded in the notes. Since she does not seem to have reread such dictated letters consistently, however, obvious errors in spelling and punctuation have been corrected on the assumption that they are not necessarily Alice's own. The fact that a letter has been dictated, along with the name of the scribe, has been recorded in brackets at the letter's head. Except when Emily Bradfield appended her own initials after Alice's, the signature of the dictated letters is always Alice's own.

When, as sometimes happened, another hand added a note or otherwise emended Alice's text and left no signature, the anonymous commentator is identified in the notes.

The shift from manuscript to printed page has necessitated some stylizing in the appearance of the original texts. All new paragraphs are thus indented, though Alice often marks these simply by ending a line in the middle of a page and beginning again at the margin. While she occasionally begins the body of a letter directly after the salutation, separating the two only by a period, all letters begin here with an indented paragraph, though the period has been preserved in those cases in which Alice used it. So too when Alice squeezes some final observations into the margins of a page—sometimes of several pages—rather than take up a new sheet of paper, these have been reproduced as if they simply continued in the body of the text; in such cases the placement and lineation of Alice's closing phrases and signature have been stylized, since the crammed margins make it difficult to tell what line divisions she originally intended. Marginal comments that appear after the signature do so here as well. Marginalia clearly intended as footnotes and indicated by an asterisk are reproduced as such, the asterisk at the end of the letter supplied by the editor when Alice herself seems to have forgotten it. In order to avoid confusion when two such notes appear to a single letter, the editor has changed the asterisks of the second note to daggers (†). All marks of emphasis—Alice occasionally underlined a word three or four times—are typographically distinguished from the italics in which the letters are set. The lines which Alice sometimes drew under dates and place-names in the heading of the letters have, however, simply been omitted.

Each letter is preceded by a regularized heading giving the name of Alice's correspondent and the editor's best judgment as to the letter's date, whether or not the full date is actually recorded in the letter itself. Doubtful dates are bracketed and followed by a question mark. The date and salutation as Alice wrote them are then reproduced below; their placement has, however, been normalized to follow Alice's most common practice.

Alterations in the Manuscript

p. 1 : l. 21 *My aspirations : may aspirations*

7 : 15 *Perkins was : Perkins, was*

7 : 18 *write to : write, to*

8 : 12 *to thee : to the* [WJ's hand]

8 : 20 *à la seule : a la seule* [WJ's hand]

16 : 5-6 *that when : than when* [HJ Sr.'s hand]

20 : 34 *hypochondriacal : hypondriacal* [HJ Sr.'s hand]

25 : 24 *cripples : criples*

25 : 29 *there is : their is*

26 : 10 *physically : phisically*

26 : 24 *irresistible : irresistable*

27 : 3 *toppling over : toppled over*

31 : 12-13 *Imagine hearing that some man . . . here in Leamington whom I had never seen had said that I was "very charitable"!* canceled

35 : 26 *'means' follows canceled 'ends'*

35 : 31 *'abortive' follows canceled 'wobbling'*

37 : 5 *life (the : life, (the* [WJ's hand]

41 : 17 *an uncontrovertible : & uncontrovertible*

42 : 34 *(Annie), : (Annie,)* [HJ's hand]

56 : 23 *There we : Their we*

p. 61 : l. 21 *woman's : women's*

64 : 22 *drawn : down*

67 : 22 *'pleasure' follows canceled 'trouble'*

69 : 4 *boarding house : boarding a house*

74 : 30 *Perkins was : Perkins, was*

97 : 5 *an old : & old*

105 : 6 *and severity : an severity*

105 : 13 *lose : loose*

111 : 22 *breathe : breath*

112 : 15 *conversation : conservation*

114 : 8 *'about her of all people' follows canceled 'for other people'*

116 : 13 *wear : where*

120 : 2 *parlour rug : parlour, rug*

133 : 10 *and arbitrary : an arbitrary*

134 : 19 *unburthen : unburthened*

134 : 21 *more : 'more' inadvertently canceled*

135 : 11 *charming verses : charming, verses*

135 : 13 *hear : here*

138 : 6 *'rather inflated' follows canceled 'over-satisfied with myself'*

145 : 32 *hide it, every : hide it every*

151 : 3 *imaginable : immaginable*

p. 151 : l. 13 *an English: & English*
    169 : 12 *"No, No, No!" : "No,"*
      No," No"!"
    175 : 14 *gesticulating:*
      geticulating

p. 177 : l. 30 *affected: effected*
    177 : 30 *'morally'* follows can-
      celed *'materially'*
    178 : 13 *blotting-paper: bloat-*
      ing-paper

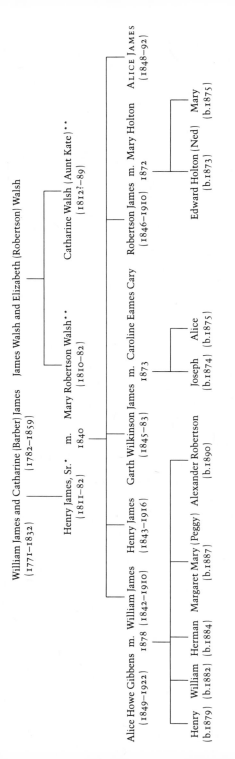

JAMES FAMILY GENEALOGY

(showing principal figures only)

William James and Catharine (Barber) James
(1771–1832)   (1782–1859)

James Walsh and Elizabeth (Robertson) Walsh

Henry James, Sr.*   m.   Mary Robertson Walsh**
(1811–82)   1840   (1810–82)

Catharine Walsh (Aunt Kate)**
(1812?–89)

Alice Howe Gibbens   m.   William James   Henry James   Garth Wilkinson James   m.   Caroline Eames Cary   Robertson James   m.   Mary Holton   ALICE JAMES
(1849–1922)   1878   (1842–1910)   (1843–1916)   (1845–83)   1873   (1846–1910)   1872   (1848–92)

Henry   William   Herman   Margaret Mary (Peggy)   Alexander Robertson
(b.1879)   (b.1882)   (b.1884)   (b.1887)   (b.1890)

Joseph   Alice
(b.1874)   (b.1875)

Edward Holton (Ned)   Mary
(b.1873)   (b.1875)

* One of eleven surviving children.

** One of five children.

JAMES FAMILY CHRONOLOGY

ALICE	WILLIAM	HENRY	OTHER FAMILY MEMBERS (PARENTS; GWJ AND RJ; AUNT KATE)
1848–55 Born August 7, 1848 in New York City; childhood in New York	1848–55 Childhood in New York	1848–55 Childhood in New York	1848–55 In New York
1855–58 Travels with family in Europe	1855–58 Travels with family and attends school in Europe	1855–58 Travels with family and attends school in Europe	1855–58 Travel in Europe
1858–59 In Newport; attends school	1858–59 In Newport; attends school	1858–59 In Newport; attends school	1858–59 In Newport
1859–60 Travels with family in Europe and is privately tutored	1859–60 In Europe with family; attends school in Geneva	1859–60 In Europe with family; attends school in Geneva	1859–60 Travel in Europe; GWJ and RJ at school in Geneva
1860s Attends school in Newport	1860–61 Studies painting with William Hunt in Newport		1860 Family in Newport; GWJ and RJ at school in Concord
	1861 Attends Lawrence Scientific School at Harvard	1861 Suffers "obscure hurt" while fighting fire	
		1862–63 Briefly attends Harvard Law School	1862–63 GWJ and RJ enlist in Union army; in 1863 GWJ seriously wounded
	1864 Attends Harvard Medical School	1864 First story published anonymously	1864 Family moves to Boston
	1865–66 With Agassiz in Brazil	1865 First signed short story published	1866 Family settles in Cambridge

Alice	William	Henry	Other Family Members (Parents; GWJ and RJ; Aunt Kate)
1866–68 First major breakdown ("violent turns of hysteria"); spends winter 1866–67 in New York undergoing "Motorpathy" with Dr. Taylor	1867–68 Nervous illness and thoughts of suicide; travels in Europe for study and health		1866–69 GWJ and RJ experiment with Florida plantation; in 1868 RJ goes West to work for railroad; GWJ later follows
	1869 Awarded M.D., Harvard	1869 First adult travels in Europe	
	1869–70 Probable date of near-breakdown ("panic fear"); in spring 1870 records belief in free will and rejects suicide	1870 Publishes first novel, Watch and Ward	
			1872 RJ marries Mary Holton
1872 Summer travels in Europe with HJ and Aunt Kate		1872–74 Travels in Europe	
1873 Meets Katharine Loring	1873 First teaching appointment at Harvard		1873 GWJ marries Caroline Cary; birth of RJ's first child, a son
	1873–74 Travels in Europe for health		1874 Birth of GWJ's son
1875 Joins Society to Encourage Studies at Home as teacher of history		1875 Publishes Roderick Hudson; sails for Europe and settles first in Paris	1875 Birth of RJ's daughter; birth of GWJ's daughter
	1876 Assistant professor of physiology at Harvard	1876–77 Establishes residence in London; in 1877 publishes The American	
1878 Major breakdown; thoughts of suicide	1878 Marries Alice Howe Gibbens; signs contract for Principles of Psychology	1878 International success of "Daisy Miller"	

1879 Birth of first son

1881 Publishes Portrait of a Lady; visits United States
1882 Returns to United States on father's death

1882 Mother dies in January; father dies in December
1883 GWJ dies

1884 WJ publishes father's Literary Remains

1882–83 Birth of second son in 1882; travels in Europe in 1882–83

1884 Birth of third son

1885 Professor of philosophy at Harvard; death of third son
1886 Buys summer home in Chocorua, New Hampshire
1887 Birth of daughter
1889 Builds house at 95 Irving Street, Cambridge
1890 Publishes Principles of Psychology; birth of fourth son

1886 Publishes The Bostonians and The Princess Casamassima

1889 Aunt Kate dies

1890 Publishes The Tragic Muse

1891 The American dramatized

1881 Summer in Europe with Katharine Loring
1882 Cares for father after mother's death
1883 Summer in Adams Nervine Asylum
1884 Galvanic treatments in New York in the spring; sails for England with Katharine Loring in late autumn

1889 Begins diary

1890 Publishes letter to Nation; begins dictating diary
1891 Breast cancer diagnosed; experiments with treatment by hypnosis
1892 Dies on March 6

INDEX